ASIAN GRILLS

ASIAN GRILLS:

*250 Recipes
for Exotic Barbecues,
Their Accompaniments,
and Desserts*

ALEXANDRA GREELEY

DOUBLEDAY

New York London Toronto
Sydney Auckland

PUBLISHED BY DOUBLEDAY
a division of Bantam Doubleday Dell Publishing Group, Inc.
666 Fifth Avenue, New York, New York 10103

DOUBLEDAY and the portrayal of an anchor with a dolphin
are registered trademarks of Doubleday, a division of Bantam
Doubleday Dell Publishing Group, Inc.

Library of Congress Cataloging-in-Publication Data
Greeley, Alexandra.
Asian grills : 250 recipes for exotic barbecues, their
accompaniments, and desserts / Alexandra Greeley.—1st ed.
p. cm.
1. Barbecue cookery—Asia. 2. Cookery, Oriental. I. Title.
TX840.B3G743 1993
641.5′784′095—dc20   92-16417
CIP

ISBN 0-385-42212-1

BOOK DESIGN AND ORNAMENTATION BY
SIGNET M DESIGN, INC.

Illustrations Copyright © 1993 by Hugh Harrison

Copyright © 1993 by Alexandra Greeley

To Michael, Susan, and Christopher—
with love and gratitude
for your patience
and gastronomic curiosity

Acknowledgments

MY GRATITUDE TO EVERYONE WHO HELPED WITH THIS PROJECT. There have been so many people that they fall into several categories. For basic day-to-day encouragement, information, advice, commentary, and assistance, special thanks to Michael, Susan, and Christopher Greeley, particularly for clerical input; Mary Hager and Jane Roberts, particularly for all their hours in the kitchen; and Bob Alcorn of Globe Travel, Washington, D.C., particularly for his passport to all of Asia. I also thank Katherine Gauld and B. J. Fletcher for traveling along to Asia.

For their recipes, their time, and their knowledge, I thank all the chefs, cooks, and the others: particularly William Mark; J. Inder Singh (Jiggs) Kalra, Chef Madan Lal Jaiswal and Chef Manjit S. Gill, Bukhara Restaurant, Maurya Sheraton Hotel & Towers, New Delhi, India; Ranjit Rai, *Tandoor—The Great Indian Bar-Be-Cue;* Bounsou Sananikone; Chef Joyce Piotrowski, Epicurean Events, Chantilly, Virginia; Chef Mok Tai Heng, Palm Beach Hotel, Penang, Malaysia; Chef Jimmy Lim Lam Boo, Hyatt Regency Singapore; Mrs. Abdul Jabar; David Quang; Yvonne and U Khin; Mary Lord; Chefs Hubert Lorenz and Nenjah Sujartha, Bali Hyatt, Bali, Indonesia; and Diana and Peter Semon, Minka Japanese Country Inn, Roslyn, New York; as well as Zainul Abdein, Karim's Hotel, New Delhi, India; Kenji Akiho, Cafe Japone, Washington, D.C.; Chef Paul Amado, The Manila Restaurant, Washington, D.C.; Lenor Basto; Janky Bhandoola; Joey Bogambal; Brigade of Ghurkas, Hong Kong; Chef Alan Chan, The Foreign Correspondents' Club, Hong Kong; Khampain Chanthavisant; Sivong Chea; Mrs. Chen Yu-ping; Chef Cheung Hoi Cheung, Kowloon Shangri-La, Hong Kong; Bora Chu; Alan Davidson; Yamuna Devi; Kitty Dugal; Chef Carlos Elespura, Unkai Restaurant, Washington, D.C.; Prabeen Garewal; Muttika Setatayak Gladson, Thai Luang Restaurant, Herndon, Virginia; Chef Detlef Greiert, Jakarta Hilton International, Jakarta, Indonesia; Bounheng Inversin; Chef Tokuji Iwai, Mikado Restaurant, Washington, D.C.; Chef Sareth Kim, The Cambodian Restaurant, Arlington, Virginia; Darunee Kunchai; Chef Kyung Yul Kim, Yokohama Restaurant, Wheaton, Maryland; Aminah Lanif; Visith Laohapant, Bangkok Garden Restaurant, Bethesda, Maryland; Douglas Lauw; June Lee; Anna Leow; Chef Leung Kit, Lee Gardens Hotel, Hong Kong; Lucy Lo; Macau Tourist Information Board; Mandarin Oriental Hotel,

Macau; Nittaya Maphungphong; Saree Maphungphong; Katie McDonald; Mahani Mohamad; Rachmi and Rasuna Musa; Suku Nair and Chef Sohan Singh, Aditi Restaurant, Washington, D.C.; Chef Hiroyuki Ohashi; Ildefonsa Pabros; Tri Pham, Lan's Vietnamese Restaurant, Falls Church, Virginia; Somboon Phulek, Saw Ying Thai Restaurant, Bangkok, Thailand; Harry Rolnick; Shirley Janairo Roth; The Royal Orchid Sheraton Hotel & Towers, Bangkok, Thailand; Rungnapa Routh; Sahid Jaya Hotel & Tower, Jakarta, Indonesia; Vasouthep Sananikone; Chef Khun Satit, Dusit Inn, Chiang Mai, Thailand; Chef Noorhayati Shafie, Shangri-La Hotel, Kuala Lumpur, Malaysia; Surinder Singh and Coco Vaish; Mrs. Narain Sinha; Mrs. Soetjepto, Sabang Restaurant, Wheaton, Maryland; Teng Kim Souen, Angkor Wat Restaurant, McLean, Virginia; Princess Moun Souvanna-Phouma; Tanh Sykhammountry; Master Tang Hin Wa, Yung Kee Restaurant, Hong Kong; Thai Cooking School, The Oriental Bangkok Hotel, Bangkok, Thailand; Vicky Varma; Nom Viponsanarath; Chef Tò-Ly, Viet Royale Restaurant, Falls Church, Virginia; Judy Watanabe; Chef Akira Watanabe, Tako Grill, Bethesda, Maryland; Mrs. Tatie Wawo-Runtu, Tandjung Sari Hotel, Bali, Indonesia; Mr. Charles Wilding-White; Young Ja Yun [Jamie Faeh]; and Duangrudee Zier, Bangkok West Restaurant, Reston, Virginia.

For their valuable help, I thank Kathryn Burns, ITT Sheraton Corporation, Boston, Massachusetts; Magdalene Leong, Shangri-La International Hotels and Resorts, Hong Kong; Tracey Buswell, Hyatt Regency Washington, Washington, D.C.; Karisa Lui, Hong Kong Tourist Association, Hong Kong; Evelyn Koe, Globe Travel, Washington, D.C.; Robert Dirmeyer; Heddy Reid; Martha Beshers; Maura Kennedy; Jemima Morse; Debra Jayesuria, Rasa Sayang Hotel, Penang, Malaysia; Mr. Abdul Jabar, Embassy of Malaysia, Washington, D.C.; Mr. Jamaluddan Ramli, Embassy of Malaysia, Washington, D.C.; Ms. Niniek Naryatie, Embassy of the Republic of Indonesia, Washington, D.C.; Mrs. Tien Kumoro; Mr. Hannief Djohan, Embassy of the Republic of Indonesia, Washington, D.C.; Mrs. Eleanor Law-Yone; Pheng Chu, Apsara Gourmet Oriental Food Market, Herndon, Virginia; Violet Oon; Robert Halliday; Yann Ker; Edwin Gauld, Jr.; Shirley Ping, Lee Gardens Hotel, Hong Kong; and Li Jian, Embassy of the People's Republic of China, Washington, D.C.

For recipe-testing, in particular I thank Mary Sherwood; Josephine Mensch; Mr. and Mrs. Peter Sparber; Ruth Gutheridge; Mary Hager, Jr.; and Jenifer Newton; as well as Anne Hager; Leah Shimer; and Jan Shaw.

And, of course, a special thanks to my agents, Muriel Nellis and Jane Roberts, and to my editor, Judith Kern.

Contents

Foreword
x

Preface
xi

Introduction
xv

Chapter 1   INDIAN PASSAGES
3

Chapter 2   THAI FIRES
49

Chapter 3   SAILING THE STRAITS
81

Malaysia
84

Singapore
106

Chapter 4   TREASURE ISLANDS
121

Chapter 5   WESTERN OUTPOSTS
155

Hong Kong
157

The Philippines
190

Macau
204

Chapter 6 ANCIENT KINGDOMS
209

Burma
211

Cambodia
220

Vietnam
232

Laos
244

Chapter 7 NORTHERN NEIGHBORS
261

Korea
263

Japan
281

Glossary
305

Bibliography
318

Index
323

Foreword

OVER TEN YEARS AGO, I HELPED INTRODUCE ALEXANDRA GREELEY TO the glorious flavours and distinctive ingredients of Asian kitchens when she served her apprenticeship as the food writer for the *South China Morning Post* here in Hong Kong. Since that time, I have watched her early interest blossom into a true appreciation for the richness of flavours, textures, and traditions embodied in Asian cooking, including that of my own native Cantonese.

Asian Grills captures the natural blending of the Western zest for barbecues and the West's fascination with Asian foods of all kinds. By going to the sources—the native cooks and chefs who have perfected their own versions of these dishes—Alexandra successfully has bridged the gap between Asian and Western kitchens. The recipes are authentic, many of them passed from generation to generation. They are presented here with familiar measurements—if not always with familiar ingredients—and with clear instructions and descriptions that can be followed easily by the adventurous cook.

Ms. Greeley has not adjusted the fiery flavours nor modified recipes to suit Western palates, for she discovered—as true Asian chefs know—that the ingredients, textures, aromas, flavours, and the unexpected nuances are there for a reason. They are to be savoured.

The diverse array of subtle (and the not so subtle) flavors unique to Asian cooking now transcend national and regional boundaries. While many of our recipes remain where they originated—in the family kitchen—*Asian Grills* provides a wonderful introduction to Asia's grilled dishes and accompaniments and a treasure trove of recipes where East delectably meets West.

WILLIAM MARK
HONG KONG, 1992

Preface

THREE RECENT EVENTS HAVE LEFT ME SHAKEN. THE FIRST OCCURRED when I was cooking for a small business party. One of the young servers, an all-American teen who knows her hamburgers and fries, nibbled on a piece of mint-leaf garnish and said to me, "Yuck, I can't believe I ate a *leaf!*"

Months later, while at my local supermarket, a gentle Southern lady and I stood together in the produce department over the green beans. She picked up several, and turning to me, drawled, "How do I cook these things?"

And a distressing article in a recent *New York Times* caught my attention. According to writer Trish Hall, America has a new "lost generation"—its young adults, whom she calls "kitchen illiterates." Fed for a decade on packaged or take-out foods, they do not know their way around the kitchen. Worse yet, they do not even know such basic kitchen skills as thickening a gravy.

For someone writing a cookbook, this is pretty disheartening, let alone challenging. How to make Americans feel comfortable with buying lime leaves, tamarind paste, and suckling pigs? How to encourage them to start a dish from scratch, even if that means some extra time in the kitchen? How to convince Americans to pick up their skillets and light their grills, so they can sample some of the best of Asian foods, and some of the finest meals in the world?

■　■　■

More than a decade has passed since my family and I returned from living in Hong Kong for four years. Our lives had changed permanently in many ways—and for me, one of the most obvious changes was this: I craved Asian flavors and ingredients. I had spent my time there trying out every sort of dish from every Asian country. And during the last year there, I was the food writer for the *South China Morning Post.* I had as my mentor and friend Hong Kong's—and possibly Southeast Asia's—foremost food authority and gourmet, William Mark, a Hong Kong businessman and food writer for the Chinese press.

From him, I learned about sensing and savoring multiple and complex flavors. I

learned about using only the freshest ingredients. For Chinese—all Asians, in fact—that's no hackneyed phrase aired out by food writers. In Hong Kong, for example, Chinese housewives and amahs shop daily at the local food markets, a collection of stalls selling everything from freshly slaughtered chickens and pigs to blocks of tofu and neatly wrapped bundles of spring onions. The shoppers poke. They sniff. They inspect. They haggle with the hawker. In the end, they buy the best they find and head home to cook it. Food, often scarce, is taken seriously. It is respected, treasured, and revered. Thus, I learned in Hong Kong from William Mark the truism that eating is one of life's greatest pleasures.

I started this project as my way of paying tribute to the glories and astounding diversity of Asian cooking. I never imagined that this book would finally take on a life of its own and become something of a pilgrimage, a food lover's real-life adventure. First, I discovered how little I really knew about Asian food, and I felt humbled, wanting to learn everything I could. Next, my recipe search led me through colorful escapades, down crowded alleys in Old Delhi where I brushed past wandering cows and tethered goats, and into countless Asian kitchens where cooks wrapped foods in banana leaves, ground fresh chilies with their stone mortars and pestles, and discussed the merits of fresh coconut milk.

Finally, I was amazed to find out how vast the Asians' repertoire of grilled foods is— far beyond the juicy *satays* sold in colorful stalls in Singapore or the grilled suckling pigs served at some hotels on Bali beaches. Far beyond the ingredients sizzled on mirror-bright grills in a Japanese *teppanyaki* room or the famed Peking duck which was—and still is— in traditional Chinese kitchens in Hong Kong and elsewhere, roasted in a Chinese charcoal oven.

Grilling is a way of kitchen life in most parts of Asia, even in its sophisticated cities where home cooks can flick on a microwave oven or an electric stove. The wife of one Malaysian official in Washington, D.C., in her all-electric modern kitchen, pointed proudly to her native charcoal brazier. She then showed me a decades-old cookbook from Malaysia written for girls in high school who wanted to learn about domestic arts. Besides discussing such interesting tidbits as how to prepare fresh bamboo shoots for cooking, and how to make *santan* (fresh coconut milk), the author tells how to care for and clean charcoal stoves.

And grilled foods are always visible somewhere. Consider the crowded streets of Thailand's capital city, Bangkok. Street vendors with their charcoal cookers—grilling

racks, charcoal stoves, or concrete barbecue pots—hawk their freshly cooked food, everything from bananas and corn on a skewer to coconut-milk-and-rice flour pastries, and flattened, slightly scorched, and skewered squid. Pedestrians shop for a snack, housewives for some portion of the day's lunch or dinner. Standing at dusk on the edges of the Chao Phraya river that dissects the city into a crazy-quilt pattern, one can sniff the humid evening air, heavy with the aroma of smoldering coals.

A stroll through parts of Kuala Lumpur, Malaysia's capital city, and through its congested city markets turn up more grilled foods: quartered chickens brushed with a yellow-tinted marinade, whole fish, and cubes of seasoned meat threaded on long bamboo skewers. The hungry crowds who spend an evening at the hawker stalls at the Malaysian beach resort of Penang indulge in a batch of grilled chicken *satay* with their bowl of *laksa* (noodle soup).

In neighboring city-state Singapore—a twenty-first century steel-and-glass marvel standing on Asia's toes—outdoor food marts, such as the Newton Circus, feature hawkers selling their *satays* and shiny crustaceans still squirming from their capture in the local seas. And what a glorious four-star grilled seafood dinner you can enjoy there: ten-inch long tiger prawns, glistening green on their bed of shaved ice, threaded onto bamboo skewers, slathered with a piquant baste, grilled over red-hot coals, and accompanied by an oyster omelet and chili crabs.

Across the South China Sea, Indonesians grill many things, say two big-hotel chefs —Detlef Skrobanek and Detlef Greiert of the Jakarta Hilton International. And on the Indonesian island of Bali, tourists should not be totally distracted by the island's brilliant batiks, languid air, exotic dances, and frantic tour guides. They should also seek out the island's grilled suckling pig, the cavity stuffed with lemongrass, chilies, and a handful of exotic seasonings. Or the local dessert, *lak-lak,* a pancakelike confection grilled in a metal mold. And if tourists look closely, they'll see Balinese grilling along city squares, at public markets, even at desolate roadside stands, such as the one near the bat cave at Goa Lawah on the eastern side of the island. There, in the blazing noonday beach sun, an ancient woman grilled a curious sort of food, almost blackened by hours of smoke, while she waited for a sale.

For many, no food is too exalted or even too humble to grill: in northern Thailand— ants and snakes; in Laos—frogs, eels, and river fish; in Hong Kong—geese, ducks, and suckling pigs. Everywhere, Asian cooks repeated, "All food tastes much better when

grilled." Or, "We love the smell of the smoke on the food." In her 1975 Indian cookbook *Shahi Tukre,* Savitri Bhatia wrote, "There is a certain barbaric splendour about a good barbecue which rises above any other form of cooking." But perhaps Heihachi Tanaka, a head chef for Japan Airlines, said it best when he once wrote in *The Pleasures of Japanese Cooking,* ". . . it should be pointed out that broiling food over charcoal imparts a unique flavor that cannot otherwise be duplicated."

Would that I had the time and energy to walk down every dusty path to every remote village in every Asian country. There are hundreds—even thousands—of other grilled foods, turning dark and juicy over glowing coals, just waiting to be eaten with a scoop of vinegared hot chilies and a bowl of steamy rice.

As I am, I hope you will be captivated by the flavors and aromas of Asian grills.

Introduction

ON GRILLING

WHENEVER I NEED GASTRONOMIC INSPIRATION, I TURN TO THE PAGES of J. Anthelme Brillat-Savarin's volume about food, *The Physiology of Taste* (M.F.K. Fisher's translation). Despite his archaic phrasing and dubious science, Brillat-Savarin offers wit and wisdom for anyone who loves to eat. He describes how early cooks discovered the technique of skewering meats before cooking them and then moved on to experiment with other ways of grilling. And about grilling, he observes, "Meat thus treated was found to taste much better. . . ." He adds that grilling "gives the flesh an aroma which has never ceased to tempt us." That about sums it up.

By now, everyone must know that grilling or barbecuing food is man's oldest way to cook. Many barbecue cookbooks include a note on barbecue history, discussing the etymology of the word "barbecue" and describing primitive man laboring over his cooking fires with a fresh kill. Some discuss the distinctions between "grilling" and "barbecuing" and others may use these terms interchangeably. Some cookbook authors, in fact, mean grilling or barbecuing (cooking under, over, or with live fire) when they use the terms "broiling" and "roasting." Certainly foods did barbecue, as we think of it, in primitive ovens heated with burning wood or coals. (Of course, one can grill, broil, barbecue, and roast with electric or gas heat, too.) "Grilling" also applies to the Japanese technique of broiling foods on a griddle set over direct heat—that is, *teppanyaki* (see recipe, page 294).

Sometimes even the experts can't quite nail down the definitions. For example, the editors of the textbook *The New Professional Chef* put out by the Culinary Institute of America note that "barbecuing" can mean different things to different people—either a food grilled and basted with a barbecue sauce or a type of food simmered in a barbecue sauce. To avoid confusion, the cook should simply go with the Institute's definition of grilling: "Grilled foods are cooked by radiant heat from a source located below the food. . . . Broiling, barbecuing, and pan-broiling are all forms of grilling." Their text further describes how that wonderful smoky taste of grilled foods results from the juices seeping out as the food cooks. The editors also describe the indirect-heat cooking method of

roasting by radiant heat in an enclosed space. This includes such standard barbecuing techniques as spit-roasting and smoke-roasting.

Barbecue writers elaborate on fire-building techniques, tell how to select meat cuts for certain methods, and suggest marinating and cooking times. Many describe the types of equipment to use and accessories to buy, others, the best ways to skewer, smoke, and spit-roast. But essentially, most authors would agree with Brillat-Savarin: Grilled foods taste wonderful.

ON ASIAN GRILLS

Research on the history of grilling in Asia is scanty: It seems that only a handful of food writers have traced any part of its course through the centuries. For example, Reay Tannahill in her book *Food History* describes a Chinese ceremonial dish—a suckling pig stuffed with dates and wrapped with clay and roasted until done—that was served during the Han Dynasty (206 B.C. to A.D. 220). In fact, this is not unlike several present-day Chinese recipes, such as the one for Beggar's Chicken (see recipe, page 160).

Kenneth H. C. Lo's book *Peking Cooking* tells how seventeenth-century Mongolian princes introduced their distinctive barbecuing techniques to Peking during the Ming Dynasty. Mongolians—inveterate outdoorsmen and nomads—apparently favored grilling their meats over open fires, a mobile cooking technique that precluded dragging bulky pots around. Lo says Mongols used beef or lamb splattered with water before cooking. (In the past, neither meat had found much favor with the Chinese: few could afford to eat plow animals; lamb was too pungent.) May Wong Trent in *Oriental Barbecues* says the Mongols' meats of choice also included venison and goat. Author E. N. Anderson points out in *The Food of China* that today the Mongolian Barbecue (see recipe, page 172)—still calling for lamb and beef, but now including chicken, pork, and a host of other meats—is a "ritual," and a favorite way of eating in Peking and parts of northern China. This special way of cooking is also popular with Westerners abroad: One can find restaurants offering Mongolian barbecue as far away from urban China as suburban America.

Indian food writer and gastronome J. Inder Singh (Jiggs) Kalra hypothesizes that there may be such a thing as a "skewer crescent"—that is, a curve of countries starting from Morocco or Spain and stretching across the globe through Thailand, down to the

most remote Indonesian island, up again through Japan and Korea, and out across the Pacific, where ancient cooks invented their own versions of cubed, skewered, and grilled meats. Today we eat these as shish kebabs and *satays*.

Another Indian source, Ranjit Rai—a cookbook author and businessman from New Delhi—talked to me about a far earlier chapter in the history of Asian grills. Describing his access to ancient archaeological and Vedic texts, he told of the very ancient history of the *tandoor* (or tandour) oven, a clay vessel lined with live coals on the bottom and used above- or belowground for grilling meats, breads, and other foods. (Muslim *tandoors* are made of iron and are used primarily for breads.) Then he generously shared information from his forthcoming book, *Tandoor—The Great Indian Bar-Be-Cue* (then in the final editing stages) that describes how ancient cooks used the antecedent of today's *tandoor* before 7,000 B.C. Mr. Rai disagrees with others who say that the Moghul princes introduced *tandoori* cooking to India—these princes, he says, were only great patrons of the art of *tandoor* cooking, not its originators. As proof of its proud Indian origins, he points out that the word *tandoor* is derived from the ancient Indian word *kandoori*.

In other countries, the *tandoor* was a "counter-sunk pit" used for baking breads. Indians used both the pit *tandoor* (for baking breads) and one that was shaped like an "inverted crucible" and used aboveground for baking breads and meats. Mr. Rai continues in his praise of the *tandoor*. It is "the most scientific and versatile of all cooking apparatus" because it works on the principle of "wrap around dry heat" that evenly and quickly cooks food. Because the *tandoor*'s heat is so intense—about 600° Fahrenheit— say both Mr. Kalra and Mr. Rai, the meat's surface is instantly sealed shut, trapping in all its juices and making it succulent.

Still used routinely for grilling foods in Northern India—and in most Indian restaurants everywhere—*tandoori* ovens are not a consumer item in Western hardware stores— yet. But, even without the authentic item on hand, Westerners can approximate a *tandoori* meal with their own backyard equipment, since much of the appeal of *tandoori* foods comes from the flavors of the exquisite marinades that also tenderize the meat, making it almost butter soft. In fact, cookbook author Savitri Bhatia assures her Indian readers that they, too, can barbecue successfully "with a brazier or a bucket broiler."

In fact, Northern Indians, like many other Asians, continue to cook with what works best for them: hot coals and a container to hold them. Shapes of grilling containers may vary from country to country: concrete or sturdy clay pots with vent holes; long metal

stands with metal grilling racks; squat cast-iron boxes; stone-lined pits dug into the ground; freestanding, fancy, tiled woodburning ovens. The names even change—braziers, *hibachis, kamodos, tandoors,* smokers, Genghis Khan grills, and *thaos.* Some people even have different words for the different ways to grill. Bounsou Sananikone—who has worked hard for her people in her Laotian homeland and in America—talked at length about the various Lao ways to grill: *yang* (food is suspended in a latticework grill over the fire); *mok* (wrapped food is set to the side of the fire); *khang* (one side of the food is put facing the charcoal or fire); *ping* (food is skewered and held over the fire; it is turned as with a rotisserie or held stationary); *nung* (food is steamed over the fire); and *tom* (food is boiled by fire in a coal-burning container). *Phao* and *chi* are similar techniques—for the former, the foods are put directly in the fire, and for the latter, the foods are put on the fire. One old cookbook refers to a Lao way to wrap a fish in banana-leaf bark and "bury the parcel thus obtained in red-hot ashes, under the fire." There is also the Lao way of grilling foods that have been stuffed and sealed into animals' intestines or into hollowed sections of bamboo that are then set on the fire.

Not only do grilling containers and methods differ, but so do the types of fuel—special woods, hard and soft coals, leaves, charcoals, sawdust, or even cow dung in Indian villages. While the final results may be much the same—that is, the food gets cooked—there are differences in cooking flavors and times. Dr. Sambhu Banik, an Indian clinical psychologist working in Washington, D.C., and an amateur chef, explained that every fuel type has a different rate of heat transmission and gives a distinctive taste to the food. For example, he notes, "The fragrances that come with leaves intermingle with the food. Leaves give a natural flavor, and the food almost needs no garnishing." Fuel selection, then, is important for several reasons. The choice of *tandoori* genius Chef Madan Lal Jaiswal at the Bukhara Restaurant, Maurya Sheraton Hotel in New Delhi, is charcoal from the tamarind tree. It retains a consistent heat for long periods of time because there is "wood within the wood." (Chef Lal, by the way, tests the correct temperature of the fire not by using a thermometer, but by sticking his arm into the bowels of the *tandoor* oven!) Master Tang Hin Wa, the chef at the Yung Kee Restaurant in Hong Kong, famous for its goose (see recipe, page 170), orders his favorite hardwood coal from Singapore, because, he says, it cooks best.

Everything else about grilling may have individual or national variations. But one fact remains universally true: Unless a meat is inherently fork tender, meat toughens when

seared by the intense heat of direct fires. Before being cooked, therefore, less tender cuts of meat need an application of moisture. That's where marinating comes in. For example, Indian marinades usually do double duty. Not only do they tenderize the meats—for example, both cream and yogurt are tenderizers—but the marinades also infuse or coat meats with flavor.

Even with twentieth-century electric and gas ranges and fancy microwave ovens, many Asians still yearn for the grilled-food taste. And if some big-city apartments forbid that type of smoky cooking, its residents may head out to the local hawker for a quick grilled snack. They do that in Malaysia, said one Malaysian woman, who noted that hawkers' food centers are conveniently scattered throughout the capital city of Kuala Lumpur. And American journalist Mary Lord, a former resident of Tokyo, talked about watching businessmen walking home from the late-night train and stopping along the way at a street vendor's cart to pick up a bedtime snack of *yakitori* (grilled skewered chicken), or about listening to the persistent cries from vendors in winter as they hawked their grilled sweet potatoes on city streets. In fact, she says, grilled foods are everywhere in Japan—even in Tokyo, where grilling may now be relegated mostly to professional restaurants or the small "red lantern" grill shops. She described her lasting memories of Japan as a composite of aromas: the sulfur smell from open gutters; the fresh "vegetable" scent from greengrocers and noodle shops; and the smoky-salty fragrance of grilling foods blowing across sidewalks.

For most of my life, I have believed that Americans were the definitive barbecue chefs. We had James Beard, the early *Sunset* magazine barbecue book, and others years ago who popularized this outdoor sport. And if I thought about other peoples charcoal-grilling foods, it was a passing thought, nothing more. Americans certainly have devoted plenty of time and attention to constructing barbecue equipment, writing barbecue cookbooks, and creating lively barbecue sauces. But American grill cooks and their Asian counterparts are separated by more than several oceans. The difference is simple: Many Westerners consider the complex art of barbecuing a backyard, hot-weather, casual pastime. Asians, on the other hand, treat grilling with respect. For many, cooking over a charcoal or wood fire is still a daily necessity. For others, it has become an art form and a science. A professional *tandoor* chef, for example, trains many years before taking up his position behind the fire. Should he be skilled, he can achieve a certain celebrity status.

Take Chef Madan Lal Jaiswal, for example. While interviewing him at the Bukhara

Restaurant in New Delhi—where he is its premier *tandoor* chef and has made this possibly the world's most successful Indian restaurant—I gaped as colleagues and underlings came to greet him, touching their forehead to his foot as a sign of reverence. "What you just witnessed," said Jiggs Kalra, "is one of the senior chefs coming to touch his foot. That man is older than he is, yet he touched his foot. Every single day when Madan Lal Jaiswal's colleagues come to work, that's the first thing they do." Such is this chef's prestige and power, Mr. Kalra continued, that if he told a colleague to cut himself and put a spot of blood on his forehead, the colleague would do so immediately. Perhaps because he was born in a kitchen, he may literally have been born to cook. But Madan Lal Jaiswal has paid his culinary dues: He has been learning the secrets of *tandoor* cooking and spice combining from other gurus since he was twelve years old, working as an apprentice for ten of those years. His genius lies in his ability to master the fire and to work creatively with flavors. In fact, he personally dries and grinds hundreds of pounds of fresh seasonings and spices with a giant stone contraption each day. He is, indeed, a revered figure, a master of his craft. Mr. Kalra describes him as "the most creative barbecue chef in the world."

Centuries down the road, culinary history books may discourse on grilling by noting that Americans specialized in charcoaled steaks and wrinkly hot dogs for summer eating. But it would be safe to say that historians would at least partially define North Indian food by its *tandoori* meats and breads, Malaysian and Indonesian cuisines by their *satays* (*sates,* in Indonesia), and Japanese cooking by its *yakitoris.*

ON ASIAN FOODS

Exotic travels, an influx of Asian refugees, and the foresight of several cookbook writers —such as Craig Claiborne and Madhur Jaffrey—some years ago, have introduced many Americans to the commonplace Szechuan orange beef and the not-so-commonplace lamb *korma.* If you wonder about the impact of Asian cooking in metro or suburban America, just flip through the Yellow Pages of your phone directory and count how many restaurants and groceries offer Asian foods.

What Americans have found among this Asian influx of culinary exotica are sharp, sparkling flavors and a diversity of foods that are often less caloric than American fare.

Without any comparative calorie counts, it's safe to bet that a bowl of Hanoi-style beef soup *(phở),* a rich stock with noodles, meat, and vegetable trimmings, is less fattening than a plate of crispy fried chicken with mashed potatoes and a side of buttery corn muffins. Of course, those wary of fatty foods won't find total freedom at an Asian meal— not every Asian food is low-cal. For example, Indians liberally use heavy cream, whole-milk yogurt, and clarified butter *(ghee)* in their cooking. Malaysians, Indonesians, Singaporeans, South Indians, and Thais turn to fatty coconut milk—an ingredient that seemingly takes the place of Western butters and heavy and soured creams—to enrich, moisten, and gently sweeten their dishes. *Rendang,* a popular dish in several Asian countries, is a good example. It calls for slow-cooking chunks of meat, usually beef, in cups and cups of thick coconut milk, which, when finally reduced to a paste, clings to the meat like a thick butter cream frosting. The cook who taught me her West Sumatran version of this dish (see recipe, page 146) talked about how her American doctor warned of coconut milk and clogged arteries. But when I asked about the consumption of coconut milk in her native Indonesia, she agreed that generations of healthy Indonesians have considered it a kitchen staple. Grilled foods—because they are not swimming in cream or wringing wet with butter—are singularly appealing to the health conscious, provided, of course, that they scrape away the marinades and enriched seasonings that brighten many Asian grilled foods.

Asian food is also valued for its freshness. As one Asian cook remarked, "We think frozen food is dead food." And indeed, in many parts of Asia, frozen and packaged foods, even if available, do not usually replace what's fresh from the local food stalls. This means, of course, that housewives or their servants make frequent trips, at least once a day, to the open markets. But modern life is slowly making insidious inroads into that custom. For example, many more women now work outside the home and many fewer have household help. As a result, harried housewives may reach for a foil packet of powdered spices to season their *nasi goreng* (Indonesian fried rice) rather than grinding the fresh spices from scratch. Certainly in the West, many Asian women make no bones about using convenience foods. The same West Sumatran who taught me her *rendang* recipe—something that needs hours of cooking time—opened cans of coconut milk, commenting as she did so that making fresh milk is very time-consuming and that she rarely makes it, even though it is superior to the canned. Of course, Asian cooks in the West must often resort to canned or frozen ingredients, since many staples are simply not available otherwise.

Take, for example, frozen ant eggs from Thailand, an ingredient both the Thais and Lao use as a snack or as a salad ingredient. Without doubt, no Western purveyor offers these fresh. Or take the banana leaf, a kitchen item used in numerous Asian recipes for wrapping and flavoring foods. If you live in Florida, you may be able to pick your own leaves. If not, frozen leaves may be your only choice. And they may not be very satisfactory—frozen leaves are often brittle, and I find that making them pliable is sometimes difficult.

As to speed and Asian foods, Americans became hooked on wok cooking some years back. They wanted to produce delicious, healthful meals quickly, and they discovered that stir-fries might take only a few minutes to cook. Yet, no one seems to focus on the earlier preparation steps required: the cutting, slicing, chopping, grinding, and mincing; or the sautéing of spices; or the lengthy marinating of ingredients. There is no getting around it: Many Asian dishes are very labor intensive and suited to households where many hands make light work or where at least one pair of hands working a good part of the afternoon gets the work done. I remember watching a group of men and women in an artists' compound in Bali, working communally to grind enough chilies and other spices to cook a ceremonial meal several days later. This, said our guide, is typical. And in the Indian cities of New Delhi and Jaipur, several women admitted that they (or a servant) spend most of the day cooking and grinding fresh *masalas* (seasoning mixtures).

Spending that amount of time in a kitchen would not be possible for overworked Americans who do not even have time to read a newspaper. But perhaps it's a question of priorities. Making time for occasionally cooking the old-fashioned way can have many bonuses, not the least of which is a superlative meal. If you are pressed for time, take advantage of having a well-stocked kitchen: Use frozen or packaged ingredients, such as coconut milk, whenever possible, and use your short-cut appliances for grinding spices and combining seasoning pastes and marinades. Even if the results are not the same— Asian cooks say these appliances make the texture too fine—a food processor or blender (someone also suggested a coffee grinder) whisks in seconds what muscle power would take many minutes to do. That eliminates some drudgery. But keep one thing in mind: the quality factor. Mr. Kalra explains why using a blender to grind freshly dry-roasted spices (dry-roasting enhances spice flavors) for an Indian *garam masala* can be dangerous: "If you don't allow the heat to dissipate, the spices are broiling a second time and are getting burnt. It is better to pound spices so the heat leaves right away." If you do use a blender, he adds, you must grind spices in short bursts, taking the cover off often so the spices can

cool. I used both a blender and a food processor when grinding spices for these recipes, although there were times when neither appliance did an adequate job, and I wished for a stone mortar and pestle. Finally, I broke down and bought a set—they are not cheap— and appreciate how much better hand-ground seasonings taste and look.

Speed, flavor, freshness, health benefits, and exotica aside, Asian food has one particular and compelling appeal: Eating it is a sensual experience. An Asian meal dances with colors and flavors and fragrances and contrasting textures. And for those many traditional Asians who still eat with one hand, touching and feeling the food is pure pleasure, particularly when delicious aromas cling to the fingers hours later.

ON MAJOR INGREDIENTS

Asian cooks rely on numerous assorted and complex seasonings and ingredients for their daily cooking. But I would wager that most Asians would consider three items completely indispensable: rice, chilies, and coconut milk. Of these, rice is unquestionably the queen of the kitchen.

Rice: Fried, steamed, baked, grilled; plain, sweetened, soyed, salted, or spiced, rice is a vital staple for Asians and for many, a day without eating rice is unthinkable. To understand how important rice is to the Chinese, for example, consider that to the Chinese, plagued historically with famine, the fear of famine means that there will not be "enough rice to go around." But most Asians depend on this complex starch to fill their daily bowls, and even the wealthiest consider wasting a single rice grain sinful.

Asians have plenty of rice varieties from which to choose, but probably the most commonly enjoyed is the long-grain, soft-cooking rice of the Chinese, the Malaysians, and the Thais. Indians often choose a long-grain dry-cooking—and wonderfully fragrant— basmati rice. The Lao eat a long-grain chalky-white glutinous (also known as "sweet" or "sticky") rice that clumps together when cooked and warm. The Japanese also prefer a glutinous rice, but theirs is plump and short. Indonesians, particularly the Balinese, save a black rice for festive dishes but eat long-grain white rice with almost every meal. And the Filipinos grow several dozen fragrant varieties of rice that range in color from violet to black.

According to the *Hong Kong & China Gas Chinese Cookbook,* the Chinese have about

"one hundred methods for boiling rice." So, it is not too surprising to find that if you put two dozen Asian cooks together, you may get at least two dozen different recipes. Some rinse rice and some do not. Some swear by the "add-water-to-the-knuckle" theory. Chef Joyce Piotrowski explains this: Into the saucepan pour enough rice to fill the pan up to your first knuckle. Then pour in enough cold water to cover the rice up to your second knuckle. Turn the heat on and let the rice boil. When the "dragon's eyes" appear—that is, when the level of the rice and the level of the water are equal, and little steam holes blowing starchy bubbles (the dragon's eyes) appear on the rice's surface—lower the heat and put a lid on the saucepan.

For this straightforward method, some cooks give the water-to-rice ratio as two to one. Others want drier rice and say the ratio is really one water to one rice. Still others say the true ratio is one and a half water to one rice, and I have found that this produces the rice I like best—firm but moist. Others swear that the amount of water you use really depends on the age of the rice. Of course, many modern Asians measure rice and water into an electric cooker and forget about "dragon's eyes" and all other formulae altogether.

Unlike other Asians, the Lao do not cook their glutinous rice in water, but steam it in a traditional woven-bamboo cone suspended above furiously boiling water (see recipe, page 254). Some recipes, however, do call for boiling this type of rice. To do so, you must first soak the glutinous rice for several hours, then cook it with an equal amount of water. Japanese boil their shorter-grained sticky rice in heavy-bottomed pots—the traditional rice pot is called *kama* and was once set directly on the charcoal-heated *hibachi* for cooking. More often today they cook the rice in electric rice cookers.

Westerners—who may eat only a few pounds of rice per person each year—would benefit by exploring the Asian rice shelf. They will quickly appreciate the differences in rice tastes and textures—particularly with such delights as the wonderfully textured, nutty black rice. They will discard forever any ideas that rice is difficult or time-consuming to prepare—a meal's worth of long-grain rice cooks up in about twenty minutes. They will also toss away their instant, parboiled, plastic-bagged rice as being unworthy.

Chilies: Any serious discussion of chilies should start with this Lao folk remedy: According to Bounsou Sananikone, "When red pepper jumps into the eye during pounding, drop a little salt on the tongue—and put water in the eye." Indeed, the Lao acknowledge the sting of chilies, but Mrs. Sananikone looked at me as if I were completely mad when I asked if Lao cooks, when handling chilies, wore rubber gloves. Few Asians are

scared off by the volatile oils that make chilies so piercingly, deliciously hot. Apparently, few Asians bother to wear gloves.

But that should not deter Westerners from protecting their hands. The cautious, conservative, and probably sensible, approach to working with chilies is to handle them with care: Wear rubber gloves if your skin is sensitive. Never rub your face or eyes with unwashed fingers during or after handling chilies; and, wash your hands, knife, and counter area thoroughly with warm, soapy water after cutting chilies, rinsing everything down well. If your skin starts to burn from chili oils, milk, yogurt, or buttermilk will help ease the burn.

There are several varieties of long, short, thin, and fat chilies in reds, greens, oranges, and yellows. And, say Asian cooks, each has its own particular taste and heat. For most of these recipes, I used the generic short red or green chilies that my Cambodian grocer Pheng Chu called ''Thai hot'' and the long, green chilies he called ''finger hot.'' Both are readily available at most Asian markets, but you may encounter other varieties as well—I have some in the freezer that are about the size of a large drop of water. Two Indian food writers—Mr. Jiggs Kalra and Ms. Yamuna Devi—suggested using the very familiar jalapeños for all the recipes: They are only medium-hot and have a mild taste that won't compete with other flavors. I chose not to, simply because to me jalapeños and Mexican food are synonymous. You can play around with chili varieties, tastes, and heat and determine what you like. But jalapeños are certainly an option if you find other chilies too fierce. Unless the cook said to, I did not remove the seeds.

You should know some ground rules first: The rule of thumb is that the smaller the chili, the hotter it is. The heat of the chili comes from the inner membranes, not the seeds, write chili experts Dave DeWitt and Nancy Gerlach. To tone down the heat, they recommend removing the membrane, and the seeds too, for good measure. All recipes in this book are authentically hot. To be on the safe side, start with fewer chilies than the listed amount—unless you have an asbestos palate. You can always add more, but you cannot subtract. Several recipes call for dried chilies, which may seem hotter than the fresh, so use them keeping that in mind. If you want to stock up on chilies, or if you have several left over, you can refrigerate them in a plastic bag for about a week. Fresh chilies also freeze well in plastic bags, but they do not usually retain their shape or texture when thawed. A mushy thawed chili is suitable for grinding into a sauce or marinade.

Coconut milk: This rich product is the last in the trio of Asian necessities. Most

commonly used in India and Southeast Asia—the tropical countries where coconuts grow abundantly—coconut milk is a miraculous ingredient that suits equally well moderate soups, blazing curries, pungent marinades, sweet puddings, and sticky cakes. Coconut milk is a broad term that really refers to the thick cream from the first pressing of the coconut meat and to the thinner liquid, or milk, from the second pressing. Unless you have time to make your own coconut milk—and it really does taste better fresh than canned or frozen—you can readily substitute a commercially made product and get satisfactory results. This is not a product endorsement, but most cooks recommend the Thai Chaokoh brand of coconut milk, and that is what I used throughout. Some brands are very oily; others are too watery. If you want to shop for another brand, shake the can before buying it: If you hear a splashing sound, there is not enough thick cream in the can and the milk is not rich enough to use. A good quality product has a thick cream layer on top—to homogenize your milk, set the can in a pan of hot water to liquefy the top layer and shake the can before opening it. If a recipe calls for using the thick cream, omit this step and scoop out the cream from the top of the can.

If you wish to make your own coconut milk and cream, you should start with several fresh coconuts and cut out and scrape their flesh for use. Failing that, you can make a reasonable facsimile by soaking two cups of dried grated coconut in two cups of boiling water. Let the coconut steep for twenty minutes, then puree it in a food processor or blender and drain off the liquid; or squeeze off the liquid by wrapping the coconut in several layers of cheesecloth and wringing it dry. Fresh coconut milk and opened cans of coconut milk are perishable and last only two days or so in the refrigerator.

ON OTHER COMMON INGREDIENTS

A handful of other ingredients really also rate as essentials, for few Asian meals come together without them: ginger, garlic, soy sauce, coriander, shallots, spring onions (scallions), and tofu (also known as bean curd). Fresh gingerroot is such a commonplace ingredient that it really needs no introduction. It appears grated, minced, pureed, as juice, slivered, diced, and grated, and its wonderful cool-hot flavor enhances anything it

touches. Many Asian cooks measure ginger by the inch—very roughly speaking, a one-inch slice of ginger equals about one tablespoon of grated fresh ginger. When selecting ginger at market, buy pieces that are firm and a pale buff color and avoid any that look wrinkled and dried out. Wrap fresh ginger in paper towels and then in a plastic bag and store it in the refrigerator. It should keep crisp and fresh for at least a week. Discard the ginger when it starts to wrinkle and soften.

Garlic is as ubiquitous as ginger. Keep plenty of fresh garlic on hand. You will use large quantities if you cook Asian food seriously. You can use a garlic press if you wish, but a small-holed metal grater is easier and faster for grating or "pressing" garlic.

Soy sauce turns up in many Asian dishes other than Chinese. Thais often call for a so-called "white" soy sauce, which is really only a lighter-colored soy sauce that is used to prevent darkening a dish's color. Indonesians use a soy sauce called *kecap manis,* an indispensable seasoner that is heavier and sweeter than plain soy sauce. Both the light soy sauce (not the Western "light" or "lite" soy sauce with its reduced salt content) and the Indonesian soy sauce are readily available at Asian markets.

The parsleylike coriander is so ubiquitous in Asian cooking—except in China—that it's hard to imagine many meals going by without it. Cooks use both leaves and stems, and the musky aroma that coriander imparts is quite unmistakable. Coriander, also known as cilantro or Chinese parsley, is widely available at most supermarkets.

The little red onions known as shallots are used throughout Asia and have a milder flavor than the standard yellow or white onions. They are sold everywhere.

The Chinese spring onions and scallions are the same.

Like garlic, tofu needs no introduction except to note that the freshest tofu is often sold in tubs at Asian markets. You fish out of the tub the amount you need.

Because of its possible health implications, MSG is one of the most controversial Asian ingredients, but one that many Asian cooks use without fail for enhancing flavors. Where a recipe calls for it, I have made it optional. I never used it except in the recipe for Macau's African chicken. It is also known as *vi-tsin* and *aji no moto.*

ON EQUIPMENT

Taking up Asian cooking could mean dedicating some of your kitchen space to new utensils and equipment. Besides a Chinese wok, you may want to purchase a tiered steamer, bamboo steamer baskets, a small hand grater, an electric rice cooker, and a mortar and pestle. You must have a good quality knife or cleaver that keeps its edge.

ON GRILLING TIPS

For someone who used to grill outdoors maybe five times a year, and knew almost nothing about setting a fire or keeping it hot, I have come to appreciate the skill involved in barbecuing. There are several tips: Start with clean equipment—empty out the ashes so the heat can distribute itself more evenly throughout the barbecue and cook the food more uniformly.

Scrape food particles from the grill rack. This may seem like extra work, but if you don't, you run the risk of having the cooking food cling to the cooked food and this can create a mess.

Use ample coal. If you are skimpy with fuel, your fire will not get hot enough nor last long enough to cook the meal. A general rule of thumb: Make a double layer of coals wide enough in circumference to extend two inches beyond the area the food will cover on the rack. For example, I have a twenty-two-and-a-half-inch round grill, and the manufacturer's directions recommend using fifty pieces of charcoal for this size barbecue. I often end up using more than that, because I do not want a fire that does not throw off enough radiant heat.

Pile the coals in a mound and ignite them. When the coals are ready for cooking, spread them out. Preheat your fire adequately—that means, let the coals burn to the red-glow, white-ash stage, which can take up to forty-five minutes after you have set and lit the fire. Cooking your food too soon over a too-hot fire only scorches the food and ruins the flavor. You can test fire readiness by holding your hand a few inches above the hot coals: If you can count only to two before the heat is too intense to leave your hand there, the coals are too hot. If you can count to four in some comfort before pulling your hand away, the coals are at the right stage.

Gas and Electric Grill Cooking

Grilling on gas- and electricity-heated barbecues is a popular and convenient way to cook. Both work on the same principle: heating a permanent heat source, such as lava rocks or metal bars. This heat source is easy to control, and the cook can maintain the same "fire" temperature throughout the cooking process, a major asset. These grills are also very easy to keep clean, another plus. The major drawback is that neither type of grill, apparently, imparts a smoked aroma or flavor to the food. That can be overcome to a degree by adding water-soaked hardwood chips to the unit during cooking. Before purchasing a gas or electric grill, shop around for the type of unit that will best suit your grilling needs.

The Indirect Cooking Method

I used a covered, kettle-type barbecue for testing all the grill recipes, but you can cook most of these recipes with an uncovered, regular barbecue grill. The major benefit of the kettle barbecue is that it allows the cook to regulate the intensity of the fire and it also provides for uniform heat distribution. I wasted both time and money and ruined several meals by not reading the manufacturer's booklet first. For one, it explains how and when to use indirect and direct fires. An indirect fire is required for large cuts or large quantities of meat. For this method, set a drip pan in the middle of the lower section of the barbecue and place an equal number of hot coals on both sides of the drip pan. You will probably have to add more coals as you cook if your meat needs more than one hour. Always cook with the lid on and the bottom vents open—control the heat by opening and closing the top vents only. If your barbecue does not have a lid, you can fashion one by making a tent of aluminum foil that will fit over the food you are cooking, or over the entire rack surface.

The Direct Cooking Method

Use a direct fire for smaller cuts of meat and spread the ash-covered coals into a single layer before putting your food on the grill. For very small pieces of meat that cook quickly, such as skewered meats for *satays,* you can choose to cook directly over an open fire without a lid or covering over the food. Cooking directly over an open fire can involve flare-ups so you must watch the meat at all times and be prepared to take it off the grill quickly. Let the fire cool down before putting the meat back on the grill to finish cooking. By comparison, modern kettle barbecues help you control and moderate the heat.

As for fuel, use commercial briquettes from the supermarket, if you wish. But do not

skimp on quality. If you do, chances are excellent that you will need twice the number of coals to get the heat you need. And even then, the coals may burn away to ash before you finish cooking. I learned this from bitter experience. Using quality wood and charcoal makes all the difference in having a good cooking fire.

Cooking times are only approximate—the type and amount of fuel you use, the heat of the fire, the type of grill, and the outdoor temperature all affect how quickly food cooks. Covered grills with top vents that open or close offer cooks the chance to regulate temperatures, at least to some extent. Trial and experiment help you find the correct cooking times for your barbecue. Recipe directions tell when to use a medium, medium-hot, or hot fire and whether to cook by the direct or indirect method. You can decide whether you want to cook skewered foods over an open or closed fire.

Beyond the basic equipment—the grill, the coals, a pair of long tongs, a roasting rack to set on top of the barbecue rack to hold large cuts, and insulated mitts—you can outfit yourself with an array of sophisticated extras, such as thermometers, timers, and fish racks. That is up to you. But if you plan to grill Asian foods often, you should consider buying a fish basket and a small metal or enamel-coated metal "mesh" rack that fits on top of the regular rack. A properly oiled fish basket cooks fish beautifully and keeps it from sticking to the regular rack. The "mesh" rack with its smaller openings is ideal for use under small cuts of meat or skewered meats that would otherwise be trapped by the metal rods of the regular rack.

ABOUT THE RECIPES IN THIS BOOK

Keep in mind that Asians usually do not sit down to a one-course, one-plate meal the way Westerners do. Rather, they prefer several small courses with balanced textures, colors, and flavors. Some serve the entire meal at once; others bring on one course at a time, but typically, an Asian meal has many components.

Many Asian cooks do not refer to cookbooks either, since printed recipes are a relatively recent innovation. In fact, many cooks told me that they still prepare meals as their mothers and grandmothers did—by eye measurements and by tasting as they go along. This may result in some interesting inconsistencies of flavor, however. For example, in an Indian kitchen, once a guru was gone, so were his recipes, and his disciples were

often hard pressed to reproduce many dishes. Even though their best recipes would go to the grave with them, these older master chefs routinely refused to part with their special seasoning secrets—a habit known as "in the pocket," meaning that a chef would turn his back away from onlookers and reach into his pocket for a pinch of his secret spice mixture before seasoning his food. Motivated by fear of losing a rich tradition, Indian food expert Jiggs Kalra set about codifying Indian cooking, resulting in his volume *Prashad: Cooking with Indian Masters,* a compilation of many classic dishes that he urged and browbeat chefs to share, and the recipes for which both Chef Madan Lal Jaiswal and Chef Manjit S. Gill of the Bukhara Restaurant helped him perfect. (Some of the grill dishes in this book appear in his book too.) But for daily home food, in India as elsewhere, cooks still rely largely on a pinch of this, a grind of that. And measurements are often inexact since they depend on the cook's whimsy or palate or on ingredient availability.

All recipes in this book have been tested with the measurements given by the cook—except where I have adapted a recipe for American tastes and pantries. I have included all ingredients suggested except in some cases when I have omitted an obscure ingredient altogether, or substituted something much more familiar or available. The Glossary describes unusual ingredients that are called for more than once throughout the book. Notes at the bottom of the recipes describe an unfamiliar ingredient that is called for only once. I give instructions to use a food processor or blender to puree ingredients to make marinades and seasoning pastes. But unless otherwise noted, the ingredients are not really liquefied into a smooth paste so much as blended together into a textured paste. If you wish to use a mortar and pestle when making the marinades and seasoning mixtures, you will most certainly achieve more authentic textures.

Feel free to adapt ingredient quantities to suit your particular taste. This is particularly true when it comes to using chilies. The cooks gave their recipes with authentic doses of chilies, and several recipes call for chili quantities that most Americans would find intolerable. Take the Indonesian *ayam rica-rica* (Spicy Grilled Chicken) from the Sahid Jaya Hotel and Tower in Jakarta, for example. It calls for using a total of thirty chilies (250 grams, or about half a pound), which are then combined with other ingredients, ground, and sautéed in oil. While testing this, I turned my kitchen into a blur of chili fumes, even though I had already cut down on the numbers of chilies I was prepared to use. My family and I gasped for fresh air and evacuated the kitchen. The chicken itself was too hot to swallow, and the chili-oil residue clinging to my well-scrubbed skillet

seeped into a subsequent dish. With chilies, you alone must judge what you can tolerate. (See discussion on chilies, page xxiv).

Unless one is native-born, he or she may never really understand all the subtleties of a particular cuisine, or know which dish goes properly with which. Because I am a foreigner and have no native-born knowledge to guide me, I have broken the rules and assembled recipes in an eclectic way, more for their pleasing flavors than for an authentic combination of regional, seasonal, or home-style dishes. In doing this, I may horrify the purists, and I apologize. But the Western cook can assemble a dazzling meal by selecting a grilled entrée and accompaniments from that particular chapter. Unless otherwise noted, all recipes serve four to six people.

ASIAN
GRILLS

*Chapter
1*

INDIAN

PASSAGES

IN THE MID-1980S, AMERICA WAS SWEPT AWAY BY A PASSION FOR
India, sparked by the Festival of India, the cultural exchange arranged by the late Prime
Minister Indira Gandhi and former President Reagan. Epic movies, such as *Gandhi* and
A Passage to India, and the television series "The Jewel in the Crown," brought Americans face to face with a gigantic technicolor land as mysterious, complex, and bewitching
as the Indian tales spun years ago by Rudyard Kipling. Everywhere, we heard Indian
music, saw Indian art, watched Indian dance. We also ate Indian food. And that's where
my real enchantment with India begins.

   When I first touched down in New Delhi, I expected to find a Gandhian paradise of
brilliant orange flowers, peaceful ashrams, and breathtaking landscapes, all set up as a
backdrop to a parade of endlessly intriguing creamy curries, rose- and cardamom-scented
sweets, fragrant grilled meats and seafoods, and hot, textured breads. While much of
Indian reality does not fit a Hollywood image, its food in their infinite complexities do,
and they capture the soul. Recipes read like a Keats' poem: Saffron and ginger. Cinnamon
and *ajwain. Paneer* and basmati rice. Fenugreek and poppy seeds. Hypnotizing, sensuous
words that seduce the senses. The food—much of it exotic and totally unfamiliar to
foreigners—catches the eye or tempts the palate everywhere: sidewalk vendors, *dhabas*
(curbside eateries), open-air markets, and restaurants, some of which offer such culinary
triumphs as *tandoor* grilled meats and vegetables, or stews of the *Dum* tradition in which
the food is slow-steamed in a sealed, charcoal-covered pot.

   Traveling by *tuk-tuk* (motorized rickshaw), my Indian friend, Vicky Varma, and I
spent a day eating some of Delhi's food, seeing a fraction of the local face of Delhi
gastronomy. We stopped first at a *chaat,* or snack shop, to cool off from the morning
swelter. Crouched on his perch in a low window opening, the vendor offered passersby
puffs of fried dough filled with a mixture of potatoes and icy chick-peas stirred with a
spicy sauce. He served these to patrons on a folded, toss-away leaf. Walking around the
corner to a popular sweet shop, we eyed the proprietor's glass case filled with a rainbow

of offerings. Some were silvered with *varaq* (edible silverleaf), others plain—stacked according to color, variety, and shape. And we walked to the rear of the shop, where cooks in separate cubicles grilled South Indian *dosai* (rice pancakes), steamed *iddli* (rice cakes), and stirred batches of thickening, sweetened cream. Later in Old Delhi, we watched bakers flipping *paratha* (plain or potato-stuffed breads); ate a deep-fried *jalebi* (a pretzel-shaped dough dipped in a sticky syrup after cooking); and stopped for lunch at the Karim's Hotel, a Muslim eatery famed for its grilled foods, particularly goat, and its dark, savory stews. A late-afternoon tea at the Hotel Imperial—which reminds one still of lingering ties to India's colonial past—ended the day.

And on several different nights, Delhi food writer J. Inder Singh (Jiggs) Kalra ushered me through some of the city's finest *tandoori* kitchens and restaurants, including the Bukhara, Chor Bizarre, Oberoi, and The Meridien. There we ate grilled venison and quail, lamb and cauliflower, prawns and pork, the latter an uncommon non-Muslim offering.

People argue that the real food of India is cooked in the home. Without a home invitation, a foreign visitor will rarely taste anything authentic. Not everyone would agree to that as a blanket truth, however. Jiggs Kalra points out that those few restaurant chefs who are true artists have at their fingertips a wealth of ingredients and equipment that home cooks do not have.

But everyone would agree that India's cooking tradition is ancient, influenced by its many invaders and immigrants over thousands of years. India has been home, sometimes temporarily, to Mongol and Hun, Portuguese and Jew, Hindu and Muslim, Greek and Turk, Saracen, Persian, and Tartar, prince and pauper, to name just a few. As it would be impossible for a Westerner to define what being Indian means, it would be equally impossible for anyone to capture in a few sentences the heart and soul of Indian cooking. The cuisine varies not only from region to region, but from state to state, town to town, community to community, and possibly even from household to household. Add that into the number of cooking styles—the *Handi, Kadhai,* and *Tawa,* for example—each with a welter of interpretations.

Other complexities enrich the melange. For example, the ancient Indian Ayurvedic medical concept links food to health. This provides the fundamental philosophy of Indian cooking and spicing. And differing religious practices make some foods—such as all meat for some, but just pork for others—absolutely taboo. Then climate and geography are factors that determine who eats what where.

And finally, explains Jiggs Kalra, Indians define three aspects to the human personality: the spiritual, the royal, and the mundane. And those three aspects extend to all foods—the spiritual, encompassing all fruits, nuts, and vegetables; the royal, encompassing subtle blendings of flavors and textures; and the mundane, encompassing all the excesses of richness, flavor, and quantity. Thus, it seems that individual personalities may actually help influence food choices. What you have is a dizzying kaleidoscope of flavors and aromas, colors and textures that make eating Indian food a profound experience and that should dispel any Western idea of Indian food as simply a complement of yellowed curries.

There are some very general truths to tell, however, and these do help define the cuisine. Indians have a great respect for ingredients and the finished product. To a Westerner who shakes salt and pepper on a cut of meat and calls it seasoned, the Indian preoccupation with subtle and complex flavors seems bewildering. And the time and care spent preparing ingredients would be unheard of to many Western cooks, as would be the idea that some household members do not have the "right" hands for handling food—that is, someone might not have the right spirit, or touch, or vibes, as I understand it—and would ruin or spoil it.

Indian food is eaten in courses—for example, a simple Northern meal would start with a grill, followed by a curry, and finished with a *dal* dish, all accompanied by breads, yogurt, and vegetables.

In general, North Indians are the meat eaters of the Subcontinent—except those who are northern vegetarian Hindus. Because they live in the frontier regions, which were invaded by the meat-eating Moghuls centuries ago, North Indians are also considered the masters of the grill, and *tandoori* cooking predominates. In fact, except for certain instances, grilling does not extend very much farther south than the central city of Hyderabad. Northern seasonings are gentler and subtler; the sauces creamier and silkier. Basically, it is North Indian cooking that Westerners know best. In sharp contrast to the drier, meat-laden Northern diet, South Indian cooking is generally more fiery, replete with dazzling curries, and is primarily a vegetarian cuisine.

And one other generality: The single common culinary thread that binds India's diverse cooking styles is the ingenious use of seasoning blends, or *masalas*. The backbone of Indian cooking, the *masala* has as many versions and variations, it seems, as cooks. *Masalas* can transform humble portions of chicken, goat, or lamb into dishes fit for

maharajahs. Cooks formulate *masalas* to suit their palate, their style, and the particular dish. Some *masalas* are blends of dry spices, the most familiar being the *garam masala* ("hot spices"), whereas other *masalas* are pastes of dried spices, moistened possibly with lemon juice, yogurt, or coconut milk.

Even after a lifetime spent sampling countless Indian dishes, no one could run out of descriptive superlatives, I'd wager. But maybe this no-frills sentence by Punjabi housewife and cookbook author Mrs. Balbir Singh in her 1961 edition of *Indian Cooking* sums it up best, "Indian food has an uncanny charm and those who once taste Indian food find that all other food is insipid and tasteless in comparison."

OK

THE GRILLS

Sikandari Raan

One 4½ pound leg of lamb, bone in
Vegetable oil for basting
Sweet butter, for brushing
Rum for brushing, optional

Seasoning Rub
1 tablespoon red chili powder
2½ tablespoons salt
2 tablespoons ginger paste
4 teaspoons garlic paste
1 teaspoon grated fresh papaya,
   mixed with the garlic paste

Seasoning Mixture
¼ cup malt vinegar
4 green cardamoms
3 cloves
2 black cardamoms
2 bay leaves
One 1-inch stick cinnamon

Devised by Chef Madan Lal Jaiswal of the Bukhara Restaurant at the Maurya Sheraton Hotel in New Delhi, the Sikandari Raan, or Alexander Lamb, is the single most exquisite dish I have ever eaten anywhere. "Did you eat the lamb at the Bukhara Restaurant?" people asked when they heard I had been in Delhi. Such is this lamb's superlative flavor that it is one of the few dishes I know that is synonymous with a single restaurant and a single chef. The lamb is served on a bronze platter and its juices slowly seep to the surface as it reaches the table. It's a pull-apart entrée that should be eaten along with tandoori *breads and a creamy* dal. *As carefully as you follow the recipe, what you eat may only be an approximation of the original—Western lamb tastes different, the spices may not be as fresh, and none of us is, after all, Chef Madan Lal Jaiswal. But even so, a facsimile of the original is as close to gastronomic heaven as one can get. (Recipe: Chef Madan Lal Jaiswal/Jiggs Kalra/Chef Manjit S. Gill, Bukhara Restaurant)*

1

Remove the blade bone from the lamb. With a sharp paring knife, carefully loosen the meat from around the central bone without actually pulling it off the bone. One at a time and in order listed, rub forcefully, or massage, each ingredient of the seasoning rub inside the lamb (where you have loosened the meat from the bone) and on the surface. Do not combine the ingredients for a general coating. Put the lamb in a baking dish, cover with foil or plastic wrap, refrigerate for 4 hours.

2

Preheat the oven to 350°. Place the leg in a small roasting pan or heatproof baking dish just large enough to accommodate it. Combine the seasoning mixture ingre-

dients, and add to the roasting pan. Pour in enough water to cover the lamb. Cover the roasting pan with a lid or with several layers of foil, but do not seal it tightly —the steam should be allowed to escape. Braise the lamb for 1 hour. Lower the oven temperature to 275° and continue braising until the lamb is tender and the meat leaves the bone end—this may take another 2 hours, but check after 1 hour. Turn off the oven and allow the lamb to cool in the oven. Remove the lamb from the liquid and gently pull the meat off the bone. Reserve the bone.

4

Grill the lamb by the indirect method (page xxix) over medium-hot coals for 7 to 8 minutes. Remove and baste with oil. Grill again by the indirect method for 2 to 3 more minutes. Remove from the fire. Brush with melted sweet butter. Before serving, you may reassemble the meat on the bone, and flame the lamb with rum, if you wish. Serve immediately. Ambrosia.

Tandoori Prawns

16 jumbo prawns
Melted butter for basting
First Marinade
7 tablespoons lemon juice
2½ teaspoons garlic paste
2½ teaspoons ginger paste
½ teaspoon red chili powder
Salt to taste
Second Marinade
½ cup plain yogurt
¼ cup heavy cream
1¾ teaspoons crushed garlic
1¾ teaspoons crushed fresh ginger
4 teaspoons lemon juice
2 teaspoons ajwain
¼ teaspoon ground turmeric
½ teaspoon red chili powder
⅔ teaspoon garam masala
  (page 27)
⅓ teaspoon white pepper

If the Sikandari Raan comes first as the most dazzling tandoori dish, these prawns must come second. Jumbo prawns—that is, shrimp that come 6 to 10 per pound—are ideal for this grill, but they are costly. For the best results, select the largest, most succulent fresh (never frozen) shrimp or prawns you can find and can afford. If you end up using large shrimp, not jumbo prawns, you may need to buy extra to make large enough servings. (Recipe: Jiggs Kalra/Chef Manjit S. Gill)

1
Shell and devein the prawns but do not remove the tails. Put the prawns into a shallow baking dish. Combine the ingredients for the first marinade and pour them over the prawns, stirring to cover completely. Set aside for 15 minutes. Afterwards, squeeze the prawns gently between your palms to remove excess moisture. Put the prawns back into the baking dish.

2
Combine the ingredients for the second marinade and pour them over the prawns, stirring to cover completely. Cover the prawns with foil or plastic wrap and set aside for 1 hour.

3
Thread the prawns on a metal skewer leaving an inch between each one and allowing 4 prawns per person. Grill the prawns by the direct method (page xxix) over medium-hot coals for 3 to 4 minutes, turning once. Remove and allow the excess moisture to drip off for about 2 minutes. Brush the prawns with butter and grill for another 2 minutes, turning once. Remove from the fire. Remove the prawns from the skewers and serve immediately.

Tandoori Fish Tukra

1 pound fish cut into 2-inch cubes
3 tablespoons gram flour
Vegetable oil or ghee for basting
First Marinade
3 tablespoons garlic paste
3 tablespoons lemon juice
3 tablespoons ginger paste
Second Marinade
2 tablespoons lemon juice
⅓ cup chopped onions
2 cloves
Seeds from 3 small green cardamom
   pods
½ teaspoon ajwain
One 1-inch stick cinnamon
½ teaspoon freshly ground black
   pepper
1 tablespoon salt
½ cup plain yogurt

Be sure to use the best quality and freshest of fish—a strong-flavored fish such as swordfish, monkfish, red snapper, or halibut is fine. Never use fish that has been frozen. (Recipe: Ranjit Rai, Tandoor—The Great Indian Bar-Be-Cue)

1

Rinse the fish cubes and put them in a shallow baking dish. Combine the ingredients for the first marinade and smear it on the fish. Set the fish aside for 5 minutes. Rinse off the marinade and sprinkle the fish with the flour. Set aside for 30 minutes.

2

Meanwhile, put the ingredients for the second marinade in the container of a food processor or blender and puree. Rinse the flour off the fish and put the fish back into the baking dish. Add the second marinade and set aside for 30 minutes.

3

Thread the fish on skewers and grill by the direct method (page xxix) over medium-hot coals for 10 to 15 minutes, basting the fish with oil or *ghee* every 5 minutes. Remove from the fire. Serve immediately.

Chicken Breasts with Paneer Filling

8 chicken breast halves, wing bones
   still attached
3 cups vegetable oil or more for
   frying

Stuffing Mixture
8 green chilies, finely chopped
4 tablespoons fresh coriander stems,
   minced
32 raisins
20 cashews, crushed
1 teaspoon garlic-ginger paste
Salt to taste
½ pound, or 1 cup, paneer (see
   page 36), made from 1½ quarts
   whole milk and 3 tablespoons
   lemon juice

Coating Mixture
1 teaspoon all-purpose flour
4 tablespoons cornstarch
4 large eggs
Salt and freshly ground black
   pepper to taste
4 teaspoons ginger paste
2 teaspoons garlic paste

The Nair brothers, owners and managers of Aditi Restaurant in Washington, D.C., told me that their chef, Sohan Singh (originally from the Taj Mahal Hotel in New Delhi) has a specialty dish of chicken breasts stuffed with a spiced cheese. The recipe he gave me calls for kismir, *or dried grapes, and I wondered if this would be too exotic to find here. A clerk at an Indian grocery looked at me strangely and handed me some raisins. You must use whole breast halves with the wing bone attached—the bone helps the cutlet retain its folded shape during cooking. (Recipe: Chef Sohan Singh, Aditi Restaurant)*

1

Carefully cut away the breast bone from the chicken halves and remove the tip and second joint sections from each wing, leaving the shoulder joint attached to the breast. Remove the skin from the breast and wing and discard it. Starting from the thick edge of the breast and using a very sharp knife, carefully slice each breast piece in half lengthwise but do not slice all the way through it. You must be able to open up the two halves you have just created like the pages of a book. Flatten each opened breast with a rolling pin and spread each breast section out flat on a baking sheet. Set aside.

2

Combine the stuffing mixture in a large mixing bowl and shape it into 8 individual balls. Place a spoonful of mixture into the center of one half of the breast and fold the top over to cover it. This wraps the mixture within the breast. Repeat this process until all breasts are stuffed.

3

Heat the vegetable oil in a saucepan to deep-fry the meat. Combine the ingredients for the coating mixture. Dip each stuffed breast into the mixture. When the oil is

hot, carefully put in the breast pieces and fry them until they are brown on both sides, about 4 minutes per side. Remove from the pan and set aside.

4

Thread the breasts on skewers or put them on the rack of a covered barbecue. Grill the breasts by the direct method (page xxix) over hot coals for about 3 minutes. When evenly browned, remove from the fire. Serve immediately.

Grilled Leg of Goat

One 4½-pound leg of goat
Salt for sprinkling
⅓ cup fresh lime juice
Vegetable oil for brushing
Lemon juice for sprinkling

Marinade
8 whole cloves
2 sticks cinnamon
2 teaspoons cuminseed
Pinch freshly ground nutmeg
Pinch ground mace
16 peppercorns
2 tablespoons gram flour, roasted
4 tablespoons water
1 tablespoon vegetable oil

Mutton in India means goat meat, not lamb meat. In America, goat has an undeservedly poor reputation, since many people think it tastes gamey and has a shoe-leather texture. To the contrary, properly prepared goat can be very tender and flavorful. Goat, however, is not commonly available unless you live in farm country, have a specialty butcher to order it, or can find a Middle Eastern or Indian market with its own halal butcher. As an Indian friend explained, in keeping with Islamic practices, a halal butcher blesses an animal before slaughtering it. Then he lets all the blood drain out before cutting the animal up. If you cannot find goat, substitute lamb. (Recipe: Karim's Hotel)

1
Prick the leg all over with the tip of a sharp knife or with the tines of a fork. Combine the salt and lime juice and coat the surface with the mixture. Place the leg in a large baking dish. Cover with foil or plastic wrap and set aside for 1 hour at room temperature.

2
Place the leg in a large kettle or soup pot and fill it with water to cover. Bring to a boil, then lower the heat and simmer for 1 hour. Combine the marinade ingredients.

3
Remove the leg from the hot water, drain, and cool slightly. Smear the marinade over the surface of the leg, being sure to get it into the holes made with the knife. Return the leg to the large baking dish. Cover with foil or plastic wrap and set aside for 3 to 4 hours.

4
Grill the meat by the indirect method (page xxix) over medium-hot coals for 30 to 40 minutes, brushing the meat with oil as it cooks. Remove from the fire and put on a serving platter. Sprinkle with lemon juice and serve.

Tandoori Chicken

2 *whole frying chickens, 2 to 2½ pounds each, skin removed*
Melted butter for basting
Freshly ground black pepper to taste
First Marinade
Salt to taste
1 teaspoon red chili powder
¼ cup fresh lemon juice
Second Marinade
6 tablespoons plain yogurt
7 tablespoons heavy cream
2½ teaspoons ginger paste
2½ teaspoons garlic paste
1 teaspoon ground cumin
½ teaspoon garam masala (see page 27)
Several threads saffron

Known as Tandoori Murgh, this dish is probably the best-known tandoori offering in the world. Use the smallest chickens you can find—the original recipe calls for 1½-pound chickens. (Recipe: Chef Madan Lal Jaiswal/Jiggs Kalra, Bukhara Restaurant)

1
Make 3 deep slashes on each chicken breast and thigh, and 2 slashes on each leg. Combine the salt, chili powder, and lemon juice for the first marinade and rub the mixture over the surface of the chicken, making sure to work it into the slashes. Place the chicken on a baking sheet and set aside.

2
Place the yogurt for the second marinade into a large bowl and whisk in the remaining marinade ingredients, mixing well. Rub the chickens with this mixture. Put the chickens in a large baking dish, cover with foil or plastic wrap, and refrigerate for 4 hours.

3
At cooking time, if you plan to barbecue the chickens on a rotisserie, skewer both chickens from tail to neck ends on one long metal skewer, leaving a gap of at least 2 inches between the birds, and grill over hot coals (on an uncovered fire) for 25 to 30 minutes. Alternatively, you can grill the chickens by the indirect method (page xxix) over hot coals for 20 to 25 minutes, turning 2 or 3 times during the cooking. Remove the birds from the fire and allow them to drip off excess moisture for about 5 minutes. Baste them with the melted butter and return them to the fire for another 10 minutes of grilling.

4
Remove from the fire and put the chickens onto a large serving platter. Cut them into halves or quarters, sprinkle with fresh black pepper, and serve immediately.

Pasanda Lamb Barbecue

One 5-pound leg of lamb, trimmed of excess fat
3 cups plain yogurt, well drained
1 large onion, peeled and quartered
10 cloves garlic, peeled
½ cup olive oil
½ cup fresh mint leaves, chopped
One 1-inch piece grated fresh ginger
1½ tablespoons salt
2 tablespoons black peppercorns
1 stick cinnamon, 1 tablespoon whole cloves, and 4 cardamoms: Dry-roast the spices before grinding and measuring them to get 1 teaspoon each

Garnish
2 whole lemons, thinly sliced
1 whole onion, peeled and thinly sliced

Devyani Singh Hinshaw, an Indian friend from Hong Kong days, gave me this recipe many years ago. She always oven-roasted it, but said that it could just as easily be barbecued. I have adapted the recipe slightly and have often barbecued it, with wonderful results. You can drain yogurt by lining a colander with a kitchen towel or several layers of cheesecloth and pouring in the yogurt; the more liquid that drains out, the thicker the yogurt. (Surinder Singh)

1
Make 1-inch-deep slits all over the entire leg of lamb, being sure to cut through the fat into the meat.

2
Combine the yogurt, onion, garlic, oil, mint, ginger, salt, and pepper in the container of a food processor, and process until smooth. Stir the ground spices into the yogurt mixture.

3
Place the lamb in a roasting pan and pour the yogurt marinade over the meat, making sure the marinade gets into the slits. Cover the meat with foil or plastic wrap and marinate it for up to several hours, preferably up to 2 days, in the refrigerator.

4
One hour before cooking time, remove the lamb from the refrigerator so that it can come to room temperature. Pour the marinade into a saucepan and reserve. Remove the lamb from the baking pan and set it on a large sheet of foil. Place the lemon and onion slices over the surface of the lamb. Wrap the lamb in the foil and grill it over low to medium heat by the indirect method (page xxix) for about 4 hours. You will have to add extra coals during cooking. You must cook the meat until it is so

tender it falls off the bone. If that has not happened, rewrap the lamb and continue cooking.

5

Unwrap the upper part of the lamb when it is thoroughly cooked, leaving the leg in the foil "tray" that contains the meat juices. Return to the fire and grill another 15 minutes or so to make the surface slightly crisp. Remove from the fire and put on a serving platter. Heat the reserved marinade and pour it over the roast, leaving the onion and lemon slices in place. Serve immediately.

Kastoori Kebab

Seasoning Rub
6¾ teaspoons ginger paste
6¾ teaspoons garlic paste
3 tablespoons fresh lemon juice
Salt to taste
1 teaspoon ground white pepper

12 chicken breast halves, skinned
  and deboned
4 tablespoons butter
2 teaspoons vegetable oil
⅔ cup gram flour
¾ cup bread crumbs
2 tablespoons minced fresh ginger
⅓ cup fresh coriander

Batter
3 large egg yolks (reserve the whites
  for another use)
½ teaspoon black cuminseed
¼ teaspoon saffron threads,
  crumbled and dissolved in 1
  tablespoon of warmed milk

⅓ teaspoon green cardamom
  powder

This unusual dish calls for coating chicken breasts in a saffron-tinted egg batter for surprising and delectable results. (Recipe: Chef Madan Lal Jaiswal/Jiggs Kalra, Bukhara Restaurant)

1
Combine the ginger and garlic pastes with the lemon juice, then add the salt and pepper. Rub the chicken pieces with this mixture. Place the chicken in a shallow baking pan. Cover the pan with aluminum foil or plastic wrap, and set aside for 1 hour.

2
Meanwhile, heat the butter and oil in a heavy skillet. Add the flour and sauté over medium heat until the flour turns golden brown. Remove 1¼ tablespoons of this mixture and set aside. To the remaining flour, add the bread crumbs, ginger, and coriander and stir well to combine. Add the marinated chicken and sauté for 3 to 4 minutes.

3
Combine the egg yolks with the cumin, saffron, and reserved flour. Whisk together well.

4
Thread 6 chicken pieces on to one skewer, closely touching one to another. Repeat with the remaining pieces on the second skewer.

5
Grill the chicken by the indirect method (page xxix) over medium-hot coals for about 6 or 7 minutes, turning at regular intervals. Remove, quickly coat the chicken evenly with the egg mixture, and grill again for a minute. Remove from the fire and sprinkle with cardamom powder. Serve immediately.

Murgh Malai

12 chicken breast halves, skinned
 and deboned
5½ teaspoons ginger paste
5¼ teaspoons garlic paste
Salt to taste
1 teaspoon ground white pepper
Melted butter for basting
Marinade
1 large egg
⅔ cup finely grated Cheddar cheese
4 fresh green chilies, stemmed,
 seeded, and finely minced
⅓ cup rinsed and chopped fresh
 coriander leaves
⅔ cup heavy cream
½ teaspoon each ground nutmeg
 and mace
3 tablespoons cornstarch

The addition of grated Cheddar cheese has slightly Western overtones. The toasted cheese clinging to the meat gives the chicken an unexpected flavor and texture. (Recipe: Chef Madan Lal Jaiswal/Jiggs Kalra, Bukhara Restaurant)

1
Put the chicken breasts in a large shallow baking dish. Combine the ginger and garlic pastes with the salt and pepper. Rub the chicken well with this mixture. Set aside for 15 minutes.

2
Break the egg into a mixing bowl. Combine the cheese, chilies, and coriander leaves. Mix these and the cream, nutmeg, mace, and cornstarch with the egg and whisk until well blended. Rub the chicken with this mixture. Cover the baking dish with foil or plastic wrap and set aside for 3 hours.

3
Thread the chicken breasts onto skewers. Grill by the direct method (page xxix) over medium-hot coals for about 5 minutes. Remove the skewers from the fire and hang them upside down for about 5 minutes to let excess moisture drip off. (You can prop or stand the skewers in a sink or large container too.) Brush the chicken with melted butter and grill again for another 3 minutes. Remove from the fire and serve immediately.

Subz Seekh Kebab

2 medium potatoes
¼ cup peanut oil
1 tablespoon cuminseed
1¾ teaspoons ginger paste (optional)
1¾ teaspoons garlic paste (optional)
2 large bananas, not overripe, mashed
1 cup finely shredded cabbage
1 cup finely chopped cauliflower flowerettes
¾ cup shredded carrots
½ cup green beans, trimmed and cut into small pieces
½ cup fresh or frozen peas
¾ cup bread crumbs
½ teaspoon ground turmeric
Salt the taste
2 teaspoons chaat masala (see Note)
½ teaspoon garam masala (see page 27)
2½ tablespoons chopped fresh coriander leaves

This is a vegetarian's delight, providing many of the tantalizing flavors of tandoori meat kebabs, but without the meat. Yet these make a savory accompaniment to meat as well. There are several tricks to making this dish successfully. Use slightly unripe bananas, preferably the creamier small Latin or Asian bananas. Be sure the potatoes cool completely before peeling them, and mash them with your hands, not by machine. Mix ingredients together well, and fry them only lightly. When you mold the vegetables on the skewers, make sure you press the mixture on evenly. And put them on a greased "mesh" frame to keep them from falling through the widely spaced metal rods of the grill rack. Despite these precautions, this is a very simple recipe to prepare. (Recipe: Chef Madan Lal Jaiswal/Jiggs Kalra/Chef Manjit S. Gill, Bukhara Restaurant)

1
Put enough water in a saucepan to cover the potatoes and cook them until tender. Drain off the water and cool the potatoes completely before peeling or mashing.

2
Heat the oil in a skillet. Add the cumin and stir over medium heat until the seeds begin to crackle. Add the ginger and garlic pastes, if using them, and sauté until golden. Add the bananas, all the vegetables, including the mashed potatoes, and the bread crumbs. Sauté and stir until all the liquid has evaporated. Add the turmeric, salt, and *chaat masala* and sauté until the oil leaves the sides of the skillet.

3
Remove the mixture from the skillet. Sprinkle with *garam masala* and coriander, stirring until well mixed. Divide the mixture into 12 equal portions. Using a wet hand, spread the balls on the skewers by pressing them

along the length of the skewers 2 inches apart. Make
kebabs 4 inches long.

4

Grill by the indirect method (page xxix) over medium-
hot coals until golden, about 6 to 7 minutes. Remove
from the fire and serve immediately.

Note:

Chaat masala is a blend of various seasonings usually
used sparingly on fruits and vegetables. Well-stocked
Indian groceries sell it commercially packaged.

Reshmi Purdeh Mein

2¼ pounds ground chicken breast
  meat
1 large egg, well beaten
1 tablespoon ground cumin
1 teaspoon ground white pepper
Salt to taste
1¼ tablespoons peanut oil
⅓ cup crushed cashews
3 tablespoons minced fresh ginger
2 tablespoons minced onion
⅓ cup rinsed and chopped fresh
  coriander leaves
1 teaspoon garam masala (see
  page 27)
Melted butter for basting

A specialty of the restaurant Chor Bizarre—a play on the name of the local shopping area in Old Delhi, Chor Bazaar—these kebabs are served there with a fine net casing of spun sugar—hence the name, which translates to "behind a curtain of silk." That step is omitted in this recipe. Do not use supermarket-ground chicken unless it is marked 95 percent fat-free. A high-fat content makes the meat too slippery and runny, causing it to drip off the skewer. Either grind the chicken breast meat at home or ask a specialty butcher to grind it for you. (Recipe: Chor Bizarre/Jiggs Kalra)

1

Put the ground chicken into a large mixing bowl.

2

Add the beaten egg, cumin, white pepper, salt, and oil to the ground meat and stir well. Set aside for 15 minutes.

3

Add the cashews, ginger, onion, chopped coriander, and *garam masala*. Divide the meat into 8 equal portions and shape into balls.

4

Thread the balls on skewers by using a wet hand to press the meat uniformly along the length of the skewer. Make the kebabs about 5 inches long and space them about 2 inches apart. Grill the meat by the direct method (page xxix) over medium-hot coals for about 6 minutes, basting once with butter, until the meat is light golden. Remove from the fire. Serve immediately.

Tandoori Pomfret

4 whole pomfret, about 1 pound
   each, rinsed, cleaned, and scaled,
   heads and tails left intact
Butter for basting
Marinade
¼ cup plain yogurt
2 large egg yolks (reserve the whites
   for another use)
3 tablespoons heavy cream
3½ teaspoons ginger paste
3½ teaspoons garlic paste
4 teaspoons ajwain
½ teaspoon ground white pepper
Salt to taste
1 teaspoon red chili powder
2 tablespoons fresh lemon juice
½ teaspoon ground turmeric
2 teaspoons ground cumin

Coated and cooked properly, the pomfret—a flat fish with a delicate flavor that is popular in India and the rest of Asia—emerge from the grill with an orange hue —a pretty and delicious seafood dish. Check a local Oriental seafood market for pomfret. If unavailable, substitute pompano or red sea bream. Flounder is also a reasonable substitute for pomfret, one chef told me. (Recipe: Chef Madan Lal Jaiswal/Jiggs Kalra, Bukhara Restaurant)

1

Use a sharp knife to make 3 deep slashes on both sides of each fish. Put the yogurt into several layers of cheesecloth and hang it for 15 minutes to let the excess liquid drip off.

2

Combine the marinade ingredients in a large mixing bowl, and whisk them together until well blended. Rub this mixture onto the fish. Place the fish in a shallow baking dish, cover with foil or plastic wrap, and refrigerate for 30 minutes.

3

At cooking time, thread each fish from mouth to tail on a metal skewer. If you put more than one fish on a skewer, space them about 2 inches apart. Grill the fish by the direct method (page xxix) over medium-hot coals for about 8 minutes, turning once. Make sure you oil the grill rack liberally so the fish do not stick. (If you have a metal basket for grilling fish, you may use that instead.) Remove the fish from the fire, let the excess moisture drip off for about 3 minutes, brush with butter, and grill again for another 3 minutes. Remove from the fire. Place the fish on a serving platter and serve immediately.

Tandoori Aloo

8 medium baking potatoes
3 cups peanut oil
2 small raw onions, unpeeled or
  peeled

Filling Mixture
1 tablespoon cashews
1 tablespoon raisins
2½ teaspoons minced fresh ginger
4 fresh green chilies
3½ tablespoons chopped fresh
  coriander
Salt to taste
1¼ teaspoons chaat masala (see
  Note)
1 teaspoon garam masala (see
  page 27)

Grilled whole potatoes stuffed with a sweet-savory mixture studded with nuts and raisins make an unusual vegetarian entrée or a flavorful accompaniment to grilled meat. Hollowing out raw potatoes is simple if you use a melon baller or a grapefruit knife. Take care not to slice through the shell, otherwise the juice from the filling will seep out during cooking. (Recipe: Chef Madan Lal Jaiswal/Jiggs Kalra, Bukhara Restaurant)

1

Use a sharp paring knife to peel the skin from the potatoes and to cut around the outside in 5 or 6 lengthwise strips, so that each potato has 5 or 6 "sides" and resembles a barrel. Slice off both ends. Starting at one end, scoop out the potato flesh with a melon baller or a grapefruit knife leaving ¼-inch thick walls all around and at the bottom. Do not cut through the opposite end—it must be closed so that the stuffing does not fall out. Dry off any excess moisture on the potato surface. Reserve the flesh and discard the peels.

2

Heat the oil in a deep saucepan or wok and, when bubbly, carefully put the potatoes in the oil, one at a time. Do not crowd the pan; cook 2 or 3 at a time. Remove from the oil when the shells become light golden in 5 to 7 minutes. Drain on paper towels and set aside. Deep-fry the reserved potato flesh until light golden. Cool and mash and set aside in a bowl.

3

Soak the cashews and raisins in lukewarm water to cover for about 10 minutes. Drain and set aside.

4

Meanwhile, put the ginger in a mixing bowl. Remove the stems of the chilies and wash, seed, and finely chop them. Combine chilies and coriander with the ginger.

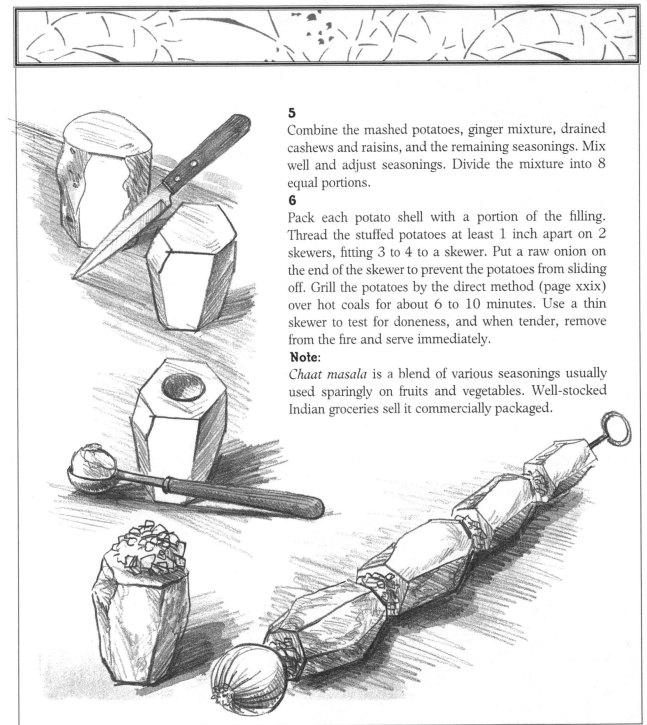

5

Combine the mashed potatoes, ginger mixture, drained cashews and raisins, and the remaining seasonings. Mix well and adjust seasonings. Divide the mixture into 8 equal portions.

6

Pack each potato shell with a portion of the filling. Thread the stuffed potatoes at least 1 inch apart on 2 skewers, fitting 3 to 4 to a skewer. Put a raw onion on the end of the skewer to prevent the potatoes from sliding off. Grill the potatoes by the direct method (page xxix) over hot coals for about 6 to 10 minutes. Use a thin skewer to test for doneness, and when tender, remove from the fire and serve immediately.

Note:

Chaat masala is a blend of various seasonings usually used sparingly on fruits and vegetables. Well-stocked Indian groceries sell it commercially packaged.

Paneer Ka Tikka

1¾ pounds paneer (see page 36)
1 teaspoon black cuminseed
2 teaspoons ajwain
2 teaspoons garam masala (see page 27)
½ teaspoon ground white pepper
½ teaspoon turmeric
Salt to taste
2 small raw onions
1½ teaspoons fenugreek
Batter
1 large egg, well beaten
3 tablespoons gram flour
½ cup heavy cream
Salt to taste

Made with fresh Indian cottage cheese that has been compressed into a solid chunk, these kebabs are ideal for vegetarians who want a zesty and flavorful grilled dish. See the Glossary for information about paneer. *You will need to use about 2½ gallons whole milk to obtain enough* paneer *for this recipe. (Recipe: Chef Madan Lal Jaiswal/Jiggs Kalra, Bukhara Restaurant)*

1

Set the *paneer* on a flat counter top and cut it into 16 cubes, 2 inches x 2 inches x 1 inch. Combine the black cuminseed, *ajwain,* 1½ teaspoons of the *garam masala,* white pepper, turmeric, and salt. Sprinkle the seasoning evenly over the cubes and set aside.

2

In a mixing bowl, combine the batter ingredients. Place the *paneer* in this mixture, turning to cover, and let it soak for 45 minutes.

3

Thread the cubes on 2 metal skewers, leaving 1 inch between cubes, and place a whole raw onion at the end of each skewer so the *paneer* does not slide off.

4

Grill the *paneer* by the indirect method (page xxix) over medium-hot coals for about 10 to 12 minutes, turning 2 or 3 times to cook evenly. Remove from the fire and arrange on a platter. Sprinkle with a combination of the remaining ½ teaspoon *garam masala* and the fenugreek. Serve immediately.

ACCOMPANIMENTS

Garam Masala

1 whole nutmeg
1 teaspoon whole cloves
2 teaspoons cardamom
Two 1-inch sticks cinnamon
6 bay leaves
1 tablespoon black peppercorns
4 teaspoons coriander seeds
2 teaspoons ground cumin

Many years ago, an Indian friend taught me how to make her family's version of this ubiquitous seasoning, but I have changed it slightly to suit my taste. The trick to making a successful dry masala is the slow and careful dry-roasting of the spices. Since each spice cooks at a different rate, each must be dry-roasted individually. Use a heavy skillet, preferably cast iron, but do not grease it. A proper Indian cook would pound or grind the spices for a dry masala with a mortar and pestle or in a coffee grinder. A masala mixture is usually made fresh each day, but it retains at least some of its flavor for several weeks if stored in an airtight container. This makes about 1/2 cup.

1
Dry-roast each of the spices individually and stir them as they cook so they do not scorch.

2
Grind them in a processor or blender, or crush them with a mortar and pestle or in a coffee grinder. Combine ground spices. Store the spices in a jar with a tightly sealed lid.

Samosas

One 17¼-ounce package frozen puff
   pastry sheets
1 tablespoon vegetable oil
1 large onion, peeled and chopped
1 pound lean ground beef
1 large tomato, minced
1 teaspoon cayenne pepper
Pinch salt
½ bunch of fresh coriander, rinsed
   and chopped

Anyone who is at all familiar with Indian food will know about samosas, *the meat- or vegetable-filled pastries eaten as snacks or appetizers. This particular version is apparently quite popular with the Indian embassy crowd in Washington, D.C., probably because the recipe's author offers an easy alternative for making the pastry crust by using commercially prepared puff pastry dough available in the freezer sections of well-stocked supermarkets. If you wish to be authentic, follow the directions for making the* samosa *dough at the end of the basic recipe. These are delicious served with the Coriander Chutney (page 35) for dipping. This recipe makes about 16 to 24* samosas. *(Recipe: Janky Bhandoola)*

1
Preheat the oven to 350°. Thaw the puff pastry dough.

2
Heat the vegetable oil in a 10-inch skillet. Brown the onion, then drain off any excess oil. Add the remaining ingredients, stirring well, and continue cooking over medium heat until the meat is thoroughly cooked through. Drain off any excess fat and set the meat mixture aside.

3
Place one rectangular sheet of the puff pastry dough on a flat surface and cut it in thirds lengthwise. Working with 1 of the portions, roll it out on a lightly floured surface. Cover the 2 remaining sections with a damp paper towel. Use a sharp paring knife to cut the dough into triangles, starting at an upper corner and cutting diagonally down the dough. Repeat until you have cut out all the triangles from this section. (Cut the triangles to desired size.)

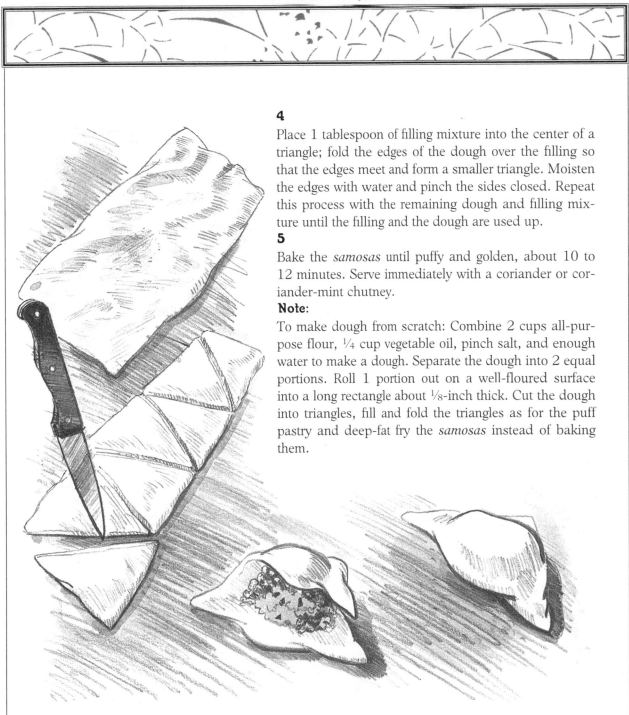

4

Place 1 tablespoon of filling mixture into the center of a triangle; fold the edges of the dough over the filling so that the edges meet and form a smaller triangle. Moisten the edges with water and pinch the sides closed. Repeat this process with the remaining dough and filling mixture until the filling and the dough are used up.

5

Bake the *samosas* until puffy and golden, about 10 to 12 minutes. Serve immediately with a coriander or coriander-mint chutney.

Note:

To make dough from scratch: Combine 2 cups all-purpose flour, ¼ cup vegetable oil, pinch salt, and enough water to make a dough. Separate the dough into 2 equal portions. Roll 1 portion out on a well-floured surface into a long rectangle about ⅛-inch thick. Cut the dough into triangles, fill and fold the triangles as for the puff pastry and deep-fat fry the *samosas* instead of baking them.

Kofta Curry

2 tablespoons vegetable oil
1 large onion, peeled and chopped
2 fresh green chilies, chopped
1 teaspoon grated fresh ginger
½ teaspoon chopped garlic
Salt to taste
2 tablespoons ground coriander
2 tablespoons red chili powder
1 teaspoon ground turmeric
1 teaspoon freshly ground black
    pepper
2 pinches cuminseed
2 pinches aniseed
2 pounds lean ground beef
½ cup milk
¾ cup water
Chopped coriander leaves for
    garnish

Unlike most Indian dishes, this is one you can prepare ahead and reheat at mealtime. (Recipe: Suku Nair)

1

Heat the oil in a large skillet. Sauté the onion, and when golden, add the fresh chilies, ginger, garlic, and salt. Spoon into a large saucepan and set aside.

2

Combine 1 tablespoon of ground coriander, 1 tablespoon of chili powder, ½ teaspoon of ground turmeric, ½ teaspoon of ground pepper, and a pinch each of cumin and anise seeds, and pulverize into a fine powder. Put the ground meat into a large mixing bowl and stir in the seasonings. Shape the meat into small balls and set aside.

3

Add the remaining tablespoon of ground coriander, tablespoon of chili powder, ½ teaspoon of ground turmeric, ½ teaspoon of ground pepper, and another pinch each of cumin and anise seeds to the onion mixture. Continue to cook over low heat for about 10 minutes. Add the milk and water and bring to a boil. Carefully put the meatballs into the liquid and simmer for about 30 minutes, stirring occasionally, or until the gravy has thickened. Remove from the heat and serve immediately, or refrigerate and reheat when needed. Garnish with coriander.

Dal Bukhara

²⁄₃ cup whole urad dal
3 tablespoons red kidney beans
Salt to taste
1 quart water
3½ teaspoons ginger paste
3½ teaspoons garlic paste
½ cup tomato puree
1 teaspoon red chili powder
8 tablespoons sweet butter
½ cup heavy cream

Chef Madan Lal Jaiswal at the Bukhara Restaurant slow cooks this dal *for hours over a temperate charcoal fire. Maybe it is imagination, maybe it is reality, but this rich, creamy dal seems to pick up the smoky flavor of the cook fires. At any rate, this is an exquisite dish for vegetarians and a perfect accompaniment for any grilled meat dish. It is easy to reproduce in any Western kitchen without benefit of a* tandoori *fire. The original recipe calls for frying the* dal *in a* handi, *an Indian cookpot that resembles the Chinese wok; however, you may use a skillet instead. Although extremely rich, this* dal *serves a scant 4 hungry people. (Recipe: Chef Madan Lal Jaiswal/Jiggs Kalra, Bukhara Restaurant)*

1

Wash the *dal* and beans in running water and soak overnight. Drain.

2

Put the *dal* and beans in a large skillet and add salt and the water. Bring to a boil, cover, and simmer until the *dal* and beans are tender and about two thirds of the liquid has evaporated, about 1 hour. Mash them with a spoon against the sides of the skillet. Stir in the ginger and garlic pastes, the tomato puree, chili powder, and all but 1 tablespoon of the butter. Stir and simmer for 45 minutes.

3

Stir in the cream and cook for 10 more minutes. Adjust seasonings. Spoon into a serving bowl and garnish with the remaining butter. Serve immediately.

Black Dal

2 cups urad dal
2 quarts water
Salt to taste
1 teaspoon ground turmeric
1 teaspoon vegetable oil
2 tablespoons butter or ghee
1 large onion, peeled and chopped
4 cloves garlic, peeled and
    chopped
One 2-inch piece fresh ginger,
    chopped or shredded
2 medium tomatoes, chopped
1 green chili, sliced
½ cup heavy cream
1 teaspoon garam masala
    (see page 27)
Coriander leaves for garnish

An Indian acquaintance who lives in New Delhi spent hours with me sharing several family recipes. This is one of them, and it has a slightly different and more piquant flavor than the one from the Bukhara Restaurant. (Recipe: Kitty Dugal)

1

Combine the *urad dal,* water, salt, and ground turmeric in a large saucepan. Bring the water to a boil, then lower the temperature and simmer for 2 hours, or until all the water has been absorbed.

2

Meanwhile, heat the oil and butter or *ghee* in a skillet and sauté the onion and garlic until golden. Add the ginger, tomatoes, and chili and fry for about 10 minutes. Stir this into the *dal* mixture and heat thoroughly. Just before serving, stir in the cream and *garam masala* and garnish with coriander leaves.

Eggplant Bhartha

2 large eggplants
8 tablespoons vegetable oil
2 large onions, peeled and chopped
2 large tomatoes, chopped
1 green chili, thinly sliced
Salt to taste
½ cup rinsed and chopped
    coriander leaves

Grilling the eggplants over a charcoal fire is the preferred cooking method. This gives the pulp a delicate smoky flavor. But you can brown the eggplant skin on a gas burner instead, though that may create a mess on your stove top. (Recipe: Kitty Dugal)

1

Rub the eggplants with 4 tablespoons of vegetable oil and place them over a hot charcoal fire or on the gas burners of a stove. Cook them until the flesh softens, for about 15 minutes, turning often. Remove the eggplants from the fire and run them under cool water to remove the blackened skins.

2

Scrape the pulp into a large skillet and mash thoroughly. Add the chopped onions and the remaining 4 tablespoons of vegetable oil. Sauté over medium heat, stirring frequently, for about 15 minutes.

3

Add the tomatoes, chili, and salt. Cover the skillet with a lid and lower the heat. Continue cooking for another 10 minutes, stirring occasionally. At serving time, garnish with coriander leaves.

Pea Pulao

1 cup basmati rice
2 teaspoons vegetable oil
1 small onion, peeled and cubed
1 cardamom
One 1-inch stick cinnamon
½ teaspoon cuminseed
1 cup fresh or frozen peas
1 teaspoon salt
2 cups water
Garnishes
Crisp fried onions
Chopped hard-boiled eggs

Pilaf, or pulao, is a rice dish as ancient as India. It originated in Northern India, where it was customarily served to the nabobs, or Persian princes. Many varieties of rice grow in India, but the best and the costliest is a fragrant, long-grained rice known as basmati, which has an unforgettable, slightly sweet taste and a delicate perfumed aroma. Pilafs usually contain meat; this meatless version is perfect for vegetarians but most especially as an accompaniment to grilled meats. (Recipe: Kitty Dugal)

1
Soak the rice in cold water for at least half an hour—1 hour is preferable. Soaking tenderizes the rice.
2
Meanwhile, heat the oil in a heavy skillet and fry the onion, cardamom, cinnamon, and cumin until the onion turns transparent and golden.
3
Drain the rice and add it to the skillet to sauté for about 3 minutes. Add the peas, the salt and the 2 cups of water and cover the skillet with a tight-fitting lid. Lower the heat and simmer for about 15 minutes, or until the rice is tender and the water has evaporated. Scoop the rice onto a serving platter and garnish it with fried onions and chopped hard-boiled eggs. Serve immediately.

Raita

2 cups plain yogurt, slightly drained
1 teaspoon salt
Freshly ground black pepper
¼ teaspoon roasted and ground
  cuminseed
2 whole potatoes, boiled and cubed
  (optional)
½ cup slivered almonds
½ cup trimmed and washed mint
  leaves
¼ to ½ cup raisins
1 cucumber, peeled and grated

Fresh yogurt is made and eaten daily in Indian homes. Note that 2 cups of yogurt, when drained, are reduced in volume, so start with more than 2 cups. This salad, or a variation of it, is almost a mealtime staple. This recipe yields about 4 cups without the potatoes. (Recipe: Kitty Dugal)

Beat the yogurt with an eggbeater until smooth. Add the remaining ingredients and serve chilled.

Coriander Chutney

2 cups rinsed and chopped
  coriander leaves
3 tablespoons grated coconut
1 tablespoon vinegar
1 fresh green chili, chopped
1 tablespoon sugar
2 tablespoons lemon juice
1 teaspoon cuminseed
Salt to taste

Chutneys—and not from the ubiquitous bottle of Major Grey's—are indispensable to most Indian meals. Considered digestives and an appetite stimulant, as well as a flavor accent, chutneys come in many different varieties and degrees of sweet, sour, and hot. This version—a chutney whose flavor should be familiar to many Westerners—is easy to make and delicious with meats and vegetables. I learned this in Hong Kong at an Indian cooking class taught by an American. This recipe makes about 1 cup (Recipe: Alma Koch)

Place all the ingredients in the container of a food processor or blender. Process until ingredients form a smooth paste.

Paneer

1 gallon whole milk
½ cup fresh lemon juice, or ½ cup
   white vinegar

This Indian-style cottage cheese, a staple of the Indian diet, is very easy to make. Be sure to continue stirring the milk once it begins to separate and to remove the hot milk from the heat immediately after it has separated—overcooking can toughen the cheese. Rinsing it under cold water once it is wrapped in the cheesecloth eliminates any acidic taste. (Recipe: Kitty Dugal; Suku Nair)

1

Pour the milk into a saucepan and bring it to a full rolling boil, stirring often. Lower the heat and add the lemon juice or vinegar, stirring constantly. When all the milk has curdled and the whey has separated—about 2 to 3 minutes—remove from the heat. Pour the cheese into a colander lined with several layers of cheesecloth or a kitchen towel and drain well. Rinse the curds with cold water to remove any trace of acidity and to help set the curds. Wring the cheese out to eliminate any whey or water. (For making kebabs, at this stage try to shape the cheese into a square or rectangle so you will have straight edges for cutting cubes.)

2

Keep the *paneer* wrapped in cheesecloth and place a heavy bowl or other weight on top. Press the *paneer* for about 3 hours. At this time, you can cut it into cubes for immediate use or store it in a container in the refrigerator for up to 2 days.

Fiery Fried Potatoes

2 tablespoons vegetable oil
10 large potatoes, cooked, peeled,
    and cubed
1 tablespoon mustard seeds
5 to 10 dried red chilies
1 teaspoon ground turmeric
1 teaspoon red chili powder
Salt and freshly ground black
    pepper to taste
1 teaspoon ground coriander

The recipe for this unusual potato dish was given to me many years ago, and it is certainly a brazen composition of hot, mild, and dusky flavors. (Recipe: Surinder Singh/Coco Vaish)

Heat the oil in a wok or heavy skillet. Add the potatoes, mustard seeds, chilies, turmeric, chili powder, and salt and pepper and fry the potatoes, stirring often, until they are crisp and browned. At the last moment, stir in the coriander, then scoop out and serve immediately.

Fried Chickpeas

2 tablespoons vegetable oil
One 3-inch piece fresh ginger,
   shredded
1 to 2 fresh green chilies, thinly sliced
3 15-ounce cans chick-peas,
   drained, with liquid reserved
1 large ripe tomato, cubed

Seasoning Paste

3 teaspoons ground coriander
4 teaspoons ground cumin
1 teaspoon amchor
1 teaspoon red chili powder
1 teaspoon ground allspice

This can accompany a grilled meat or it can be eaten without any other accompaniment. (Recipe: Surinder Singh/Coco Vaish)

1
Pour the oil into a heavy skillet and heat. Add the ginger and chilies and fry, stirring often, for 1 to 2 minutes.

2
Combine the ingredients for the seasoning paste, adding enough liquid from the chick-peas to make a paste. Pour mixture into the skillet and stir well. Continue cooking.

3
Add the chick-peas, tomato, and 1 cup of liquid from the chick-peas and cook for about 30 minutes, or until the mixture begins to thicken. Remove from the heat and serve hot or cold.

Green Beans with Coconut

½ cup sweet butter
1 teaspoon black mustard seeds
4 tablespoons cooked urad dal
1 teaspoon minced onion
One 1-inch piece ginger, freshly
    grated
2 teaspoons cayenne
Salt and freshly ground black
    pepper to taste
1 pound green beans, washed and
    trimmed
5 tablespoons grated coconut
1 tablespoon chopped coriander
    leaves
Juice of 1 lemon

This dish comes from Nepal, and although Nepal is not part of India, it neighbors India's northeastern borders. In some respects the food of the two countries is similar. I am including this dish because it complements grilled foods, and because it came into my hands in an offbeat way—while I was reviewing a Gurkha cooking contest in Hong Kong many years ago. (Gurkhas are the fierce, British-trained Nepalese soldiers.) The day was memorable, and so are these beans. (Recipe: Cooking Contest, Brigade of Gurkhas, British Army Catering Corps)

1

Heat the butter in a heavy skillet and, when it is bubbly, add the mustard seeds and *dal* and fry for 3 minutes. Stir in the onion, ginger, cayenne, salt, pepper, and beans and fry for 5 minutes, stirring often.

2

Add the coconut and coriander, lower the heat, cover, and cook for about 10 minutes, stirring occasionally, until the beans are tender. Spoon into a serving dish and sprinkle with the lemon juice. Serve immediately.

Sautéed Mixed Vegetables

1 cup cauliflower flowerettes
1 cup sliced carrots
1 large potato, peeled and cubed
½ pound green beans, cleaned and
    trimmed
1 cup fresh or frozen peas
20 spinach leaves
2 teaspoons vegetable oil
1 tablespoon mixed seasonings:
    cuminseed, coriander seeds,
    aniseed, fenugreek
1 tablespoon black mustard seeds
1 fresh green chili
Salt to taste

Over an elegant at-home tea in New Delhi, a friend's sister shared this easy mixed-vegetable dish that she says is very popular among her friends as an accompaniment for grilled foods. You can vary the amounts and varieties of vegetables according to what is fresh and seasonal. (Recipe: Prabeen Garewal)

1
Cut all vegetables except the peas and spinach leaves into uniform pieces.

2
Pour the oil into a skillet and heat till bubbly. Fry the seasoning mixture. Then add the vegetables except for the peas and spinach. When the vegetables are tender, add the peas.

3
Meanwhile, put the black mustard seeds, chili, and salt in the container of a food processor. Add enough water to make a paste—about ¼ to ½ cup—and process. Pour this paste over the vegetables, stirring thoroughly. Add the spinach leaves and cook briefly until wilted. Serve immediately.

Chapati

1 cup chapati *flour, or* ½ *cup each white flour and whole-wheat flour*

These flat whole-wheat breads are staples of the Indian table and are made fresh every day. They are very simple to mix and cook: I stood in Mrs. Sinha's kitchen in Jaipur and watched as she mixed the dough, baked the breads on a special ungreased griddle set aside just for cooking chapati, *and flipped them off. We ate several of these after dunking them into a warmed vegetable stew. The combination was delicious and a meal in itself. (Recipe: Mrs. Narain Sinha)*

1

Place the flour in a large mixing bowl and add enough water—about ⅓ to ½ cup—to make a soft but not sticky dough. Knead the dough on a lightly floured surface for about 10 minutes. Pinch off 8 equal portions of the dough and roll them into balls—they will be about the size of golf balls.

2

Set the dough aside for about 30 minutes. Then roll each ball out on a lightly floured surface, rolling and turning so the ball becomes an even round shape, to a 5- or 6-inch disc.

3

Heat an ungreased skillet and when the surface is hot enough for drops of water to skitter across it, place the flattened dough down on it. Let it bake for 30 seconds and then flip it over to cook on the other side for 20 seconds. Remove the skillet and put the cooked bread directly on the burner on medium heat. It puffs up in just a few seconds. Remove from the burner and stack the breads on a plate.

Potato Paratha

3 cups chapati *flour,* or 1½ cups each whole wheat flour and white flour
Vegetable oil
1 cup mashed potatoes
1 large onion, peeled and minced
2 fresh green chilies, minced
1 tablespoon chopped coriander leaves
Pinch salt
1 teaspoon red chili powder
1 teaspoon amchor
½ cup butter or ghee

Indian cooks make this bread look easy to assemble and grill, and in fact, it really is. With some practice, you can turn out a finished bread in about 1 minute. You can use fresh or leftover mashed potatoes, or you can use mashed cooked peas or cauliflower, seasoned with snipped coriander leaves or a sprinkle of garam masala. This is a flavorful and substantial bread, delicious served with dal *and meat. (Recipe: Vicky Varma)*

1
Combine the flour with enough water—about ¼ to ½ cup—to make a pliable dough. Lightly grease your hands with oil or butter and knead the dough until soft. Place the dough in a large bowl and cover with a damp cloth. Set aside for 30 minutes.

2
Combine the mashed potatoes with the onion, chilies, coriander leaves, salt, chili powder, and *amchor.*

3
Separate the dough into 7 or 8 equal-sized balls, setting aside a small portion of dough—about 4 tablespoonfuls—to use for sealing each *paratha* as you make it. Roll each ball out on a floured surface to a 4-inch round disc. Spread 1 teaspoon of softened butter or *ghee* on the surface, then place 2 tablespoonfuls of potato mixture onto the buttered surface. Fold the sides into the center and flatten the *paratha* with the palm of your hand. Use some of the excess dough set aside to seal in the potato mixture. Use a rolling pin to roll the *paratha* out into a 6-inch round disc. It will be about ⅛ inch thick.

4
Heat a skillet or griddle and lightly oil the surface. Place the *paratha* on the skillet and cook until the bottom becomes golden, about 30 seconds. Flip the bread over

with a large spatula and when the second side has cooked smear the top with butter. Turn the bread over one more time for a final browning on the first side, spread on more butter, and turn for the final browning of the second side. Cook until the bread is crisped. Remove from the griddle and serve immediately.

Naan

8¼ to 8½ cups all-purpose flour
½ cup plain yogurt
3 eggs
1 cup milk
3 teaspoons sugar
1 teaspoon baking powder
½ teaspoon baking soda
1½ teaspoons salt
About 1 cup water
2 teaspoons vegetable oil or ghee

This tandoori bread is a delicate—and popular—accompaniment to grilled meats. Although typically cooked on the clay insides of the tandoor oven, this can also be baked on a stove-top griddle with almost the same results. (Recipe: Ranjit Rai, Tandoor—The Great Indian Bar-Be-Cue)

1
Combine all the ingredients in a large mixing bowl and knead well. Set the dough aside for 4 to 6 hours.

2
The dough should have risen slightly. Punch it down and knead for several minutes. Divide the dough into 20 equal portions and roll them into balls. Cover them with a cloth.

3
Wet your hands and, working with 1 ball of dough at a time, roll out the dough on a floured pastry board until it is about ⅛ inch thick.

4
With moist hands, lift the flattened bread and press it against the side of a *tandoor* or put it on top of a hot, ungreased griddle. When the bread has puffed up and brown spots appear on the underside—in about 2 to 3 minutes—remove it from the *tandoor* or griddle. Repeat the process with the remaining dough.

DESSERTS

Phirni

¼ cup basmati rice
2 tablespoons water
2 teaspoons, or less, saffron threads
4 cups whole milk
1¼ cups sugar
1 teaspoon green cardamom
    powder
2 drops rose essence
2 teaspoons slivered pistachios
2 teaspoons slivered almonds

An elegant rice custard flavored with saffron and rose essence—and served typically in earthenware cups called shikoras *that impart an earthy taste to the custard—this dessert requires some time and labor, but it is worth every moment you spend. If a dessert could be called lyrical or poetic, this would be it. (Recipe: Jiggs Kalra,* Prashad, Cooking with Indian Masters)

1

Rinse the rice and soak it in cold water for 30 minutes. Drain and put the rice in the container of a blender with the 2 tablespoons water. Process to make a fine paste—do not underprocess or the rice will remain granular and the pudding will not thicken properly.

2

Soak the saffron threads in 1 tablespoon of warmed milk.

3

Add the remaining milk to a heavy saucepan and bring to a boil, stirring often to prevent scorching. Stir in the sugar and rice paste, then lower the heat. Continue cooking until the milk reduces by half and the mixture thickens into a custardlike consistency. Stir constantly to prevent lumping. Add the saffron, cardamom powder, and rose essence, and remove from the heat.

4

Pour the mixture into individual heat-resistant custard or dessert cups or into a large heat-resistant serving bowl. Garnish with the slivered nuts and refrigerate until the pudding sets.

Carrot Halvah

2 pounds carrots, scraped and
    shredded
1½ quarts whole milk
Vegetable oil
½ cup ghee
½ cup or more of each of the
    following: raisins, slivered
    almonds, and cashews
10 green cardamoms, ground
Sugar to taste
8 ounces ricotta cheese (or 4 cups
    skim milk powder)
Several sheets of varaq (optional—
    see Note)

This carrot pudding looks and tastes like a substantial dessert, but according to the Indian friend who gave me the recipe, families also use spoonfuls of this pudding to wrap in bread for a winter breakfast in Northern India. Or family members eat a tablespoon or two with hot milk as a kind of breakfast porridge. Leftovers stored in a tightly closed container keep well in the refrigerator for up to 4 months. (Recipe: Janky Bhandoola)

1

Place the carrots and milk in a large saucepan and bring to a boil. Lower the heat, cover the pan, and simmer until the carrots are soft and the milk and water from the carrots have almost completely evaporated, about 4 hours. Remove from the heat and set aside.

2

Heat 1 tablespoon each of oil and *ghee* in a heavy skillet. Fry the raisins and nuts for 3 to 4 minutes and add the ground cardamom, stirring well. Add the cooked carrots and sugar and fry for another 3 to 4 minutes. Add the ricotta and continue frying until the oil separates from the carrot mixture. Scoop the mixture into a serving dish. Decorate it with the silverleaf and with extra nuts, if desired. Serve hot.

Note:

These are paper-thin sheets of edible silver that Northern Indians use to adorn special dishes. When placing them on foods, you must handle them carefully so they do not tear or crumple. These fragile sheets are available at Indian markets.

Saffron Mango Kulfi

¼ teaspoon saffron threads
¼ teaspoon cardamom seeds
1½ cups low-fat milk, or 1½ cups
    half and half
2 large ripe mangoes (2½ pounds
    total), or about 2 cups mango
    pulp (see Note)
2 medium bananas
Juice of 1 lime
3 teaspoons maple syrup, maple
    sugar, or sugar
¼ cup heavy cream
⅓ cup blanched pistachios
2 to 3 drops rose essence, or
    1 teaspoon rose water

Kulfi *is a supremely dense, sweet ice cream that satisfies a lingering sweet tooth after just a few bites. Cookbook author and Indian vegetarian specialist Yamuna Devi created this low-fat version of the more traditional calorie-laden Indian ice cream which is made from full-fat buffalo milk. The ingredient categories of this recipe are the same, she explains, but the fat grams are not. Fresh ripe, sweet mangoes are preferable, but canned mango pulp is a satisfactory substitute for use in this frozen treat. (Recipe: Yamuna Devi)*

1
Toast the saffron threads in a dry pan over low heat for about 2 minutes. When they become brittle, remove and crush them to a powder. Combine the saffron, cardamom, and milk or half and half in a saucepan and slowly heat to the boiling point. Set aside and cool.

2
Peel and seed the fresh mangoes, cut about 1½ cups into ¼-inch dice, and set aside in the refrigerator for garnish. Puree the remaining mangoes, fresh or canned, with the bananas in a food processor or blender. Add the saffron milk, lime juice, maple syrup or sugar, cream, half the pistachios, and rose essence or rose water and blend.

3
Freeze in an ice cream machine following the manufacturer's instructions. Or freeze in ice-cube trays in your freezer—this produces an ice cream with an almost typically Indian texture. Garnish with remaining pistachios before serving.

Note:
If using canned mango pulp, buy 2 (15 ounce) cans to have enough fruit for this recipe. If you use the canned pulp you will not have any cubes to garnish the ice cream.

Mango Lassi

1 cup plain yogurt
2 slices fresh mango, or ¼ cup
   mango pulp
¼ cup milk
Pinch ground cardamom
2 drops rose water
2 teaspoons sugar
5 ice cubes

Whether you consider it drink or dessert, this refreshing mixture is just pure delight. (Recipe: Suku Nair)

Place all ingredients in the container of a food processor or blender and puree. Serve immediately.

Vermicelli Pudding

3 tablespoons butter or ghee
1 cup uncooked vermicelli, cut
    into 1-inch lengths
1 tablespoon raisins
2 tablespoons cashews, halved
    lengthwise
2 cups water
3 cups milk
¼ cup sweetened condensed milk
¼ cup sugar
2 drops yellow food coloring
Pinch ground cardamom
Drop or 2 rose essence

A popular Indian sweet, this pudding is made with vermicelli—the medium-fine Indian variety is preferable, but you can substitute the Italian, if you wish. It looks at first as if the mixture will never thicken, but once the milk reduces and the pasta absorbs the liquid, the pudding begins to firm and set. You may adjust the sweetness to suit your taste. (Recipe: Suku Nair)

1

Heat the butter or *ghee* in a large skillet and when bubbly, add the vermicelli and cook until it turns a golden brown. Remove the vermicelli from the skillet and sauté the raisins and cashews in the *ghee*. Set aside.

2

Put the water in a saucepan and bring to a boil. Add the vermicelli and let it cook. Drain and return the vermicelli to the saucepan. Add the whole and condensed milks and bring to a simmer. Add the sugar and simmer over medium heat, stirring constantly, until the vermicelli thickens and the milk reduces and thickens, about 30 minutes. Remove from the heat and stir in the raisins, cashews, food coloring, cardamom, and rose essence. Pour into a serving dish and refrigerate until set and cold.

*Chapter
2*

THAI

FIRES

THAILAND IS A LAND OF CONTRADICTIONS: IS IT FAIRY-TALE KING-
dom or pleasure dome? The Golden Triangle or unspoiled beaches? Modern congestion
or the remote teak forest? Ancient hill tribes or millions of tourists? Elephants in the wild
or peacocks in captivity? The truth is, Thailand is all of these—and more. For the gastronome in search of the ultimate culinary adventure, Thailand may well be the exotic
Promised Land, filled not only with coconut milk and honey, but with every sort of edible
creature and plant life, all of which will eventually find their way to a local cookpot or
grill. I learned from a guide in Northern Thailand—and saw some of this at markets and
food stalls in Chiang Mai—that country locals eat grilled snakes, ants, crickets, and
worms. And on everyone's dining table, the produce—from familiar beans and marble-
sized eggplants to unfamiliar leaves and roots and stalks—is unparalleled in its freshness.

Cooking up everything that may be edible sounds very Chinese in its waste-not,
want-not pragmatism. But the Thais carry off their cooking in a slightly different way—
that is, Thai flavors always seem much more intense and lively, which may have something
to do with the Thai obsession with chilies. Newcomers may be surprised to discover how
"chilied" authentic Thai dishes really are. A Thai will shrug and move on to the next
mouthful, while a Westerner could be stuck doing a slow burn. That is not to say that
everything is intolerably hot. To the contrary, Thai cooks play with taste combinations,
and a single dish may be simultaneously sweet, sour, salty—and, of course, hot. To
achieve these ends, they rely on such basic seasonings as Thai fish sauce, garlic, lemongrass, coconut milk, sugar, ginger, galangal, coriander, shallots—and chilies. Thais are
incredibly fussy about their chilies and incorporate several varieties in their cuisine, each
chili hotter than the next. The "rat dropping" chili—obviously named because of its
shape—is one of the hottest in the world, says Bangkok food writer Bob Halliday.

No dish is humble and straightforward or unadorned and unseasoned. Nothing is
ever as simple as it seems. In fact, much of the food is breathtaking in its sophistication
and cleverness. Take the rose petal and watercress salad, for example, with its mix of

meat, seafood, nuts, fish sauce, and rose petals. Edwardian cooks would envy its class. Or the delectable dish called *rume,* which is nothing more than seasoned ground pork wrapped in a net of egg yolk threads.

The Thai table, set with a multicourse celebratory meal, can resemble an Alice-in-Wonderland artwork that would tempt the most jaded palate. Ice and butter sculptures adorn formal settings, and even for simpler meals, serving platters are garnished with one or many fanciful and frilly vegetable and fruit carvings, fooling the eye and seducing the hungry to feast. In short, Thai food, like much of the country itself, is a sensual and addictive experience.

Sociable Thais prefer communal eating, so main meals consist of many courses, including a soup; a curry; a grilled, stir-fried, or steamed meat or seafood; assorted condiments; and fruit or a sweet for dessert. Breakfasts and lunches are lighter, and may center on fried rice or noodles with a meat or vegetable garnish. (As elsewhere in Asia, rice—usually eaten morning, noon, and night—is basic to the cuisine, and it provides a bland counterpoint and welcome relief to the rich, savory—and hot—stir-fries, curries, and grills.) When not at the table, Thais snack on portable goodies offered, so it seems, at every turn. Vendors with their baskets, stands, and grills full of treats and sweets are a common sight on Bangkok sidewalks.

Although Thai cooks are versatile, and can as easily stir-fry as steam, they have certainly perfected the art of grilling. As nowhere else in Asia, grilling seems omnipresent. One young Thai lady, Sanee Maphungphong, remembers learning how to cook—as a child, she took her set of cookpots, the ingredients, and some burning charcoal and practiced making family dishes. Just looking out a hotel window in Chiang Mai, you might glimpse a vendor pushing his mobile grill cart down the sidewalk, offering wedges of charcoaled chicken and sticks of *satays* for sale. In the capital city Bangkok, you will see grill vendors hawking charcoaled bananas, peeled or unpeeled; crispy whole baby squid polka-dotted with chopped red chilies; flattened dried squid that puff up when cooked; and grilled morsels wrapped in banana leaves.

Bangkok is the perfect place to start a Thai eating spree, and the obvious place to find your culinary bearings. The curious traveler should make at least two market tours: one to the real floating market, many kilometers up the Chao Phraya river from Bangkok, where vendors on boats hawk their food wares much as Thais must have done before there were tourists and supermarkets; the other to Bangkok's famed weekend market out

near the airport. It seems that everyone in Bangkok goes there on Sunday to buy everything under the sun—from Pekingese puppies (for pets) and calves (probably not for pets) to straw hats, printed T-shirts, and peacock-feather fans. And shoppers will find all the raw ingredients for Thai cooking displayed in their pristine splendor. They might even, as I did once, catch sight of circular bamboo trays carefully arranged with overlapping layers of shiny cockroachlike bugs, the *mangda,* considered a desirable seasoning ingredient. A market has opened across the street, I understand from Bob Halliday, where regional cooks come to sell the specialties of their area—and one of these is indigo-blue pastries, tinted by the intense color of the flour (made from a relative of the Western sweet-pea flower) they use.

Bangkok also offers what is reputedly the largest restaurant in the world—the Tum Nak Thai, a ten-acre sprawl that seats 3,000 and features waiters on roller skates. This may have gastronomic value only as a curiosity, and Thai food is only one of several cuisines offered.

Those tourists who are serious about Thai food should enroll in local cooking classes, and there are several programs set up for visitors. Perhaps the best known are those at The Thai Cooking School at The Oriental Bangkok hotel. A week-long course in its tropical —and elegant—bungalow classroom setting, across the Chao Phraya river from the hotel, should provide a basic knowledge about one of the world's most interesting—and hottest —cuisines. Besides, after class, you get to eat everything you have learned how to cook. Splendid.

And after Bangkok? All of Thailand is your oyster.

THE GRILLS

Chicken Satay Panang

▗▚▖▚▗▚▖▚▗▚▖▚▗▚▖▚

1½ pounds boneless, skinless chicken
    breast, cut into strips 5 inches long
    x 1½ inches wide x ¼ inch thick
Bamboo skewers
Marinade
7 shallots
3 cloves garlic
5 dried chilies, seeds removed,
    soaked in water
1 teaspoon salt
2 teaspoons minced galangal
1 stalk lemongrass, thinly sliced
1½ cups coconut milk
2 tablespoons finely chopped
    coriander root
1 teaspoon finely chopped kaffir or
    regular lime rind
5 peppercorns
1 teaspoon shrimp paste

Satays *in Thailand are really snack foods or appetizers, and are never, or rarely, eaten as the main course. But, several skewersful of satay with accompaniments would make a meal. Here, chicken strips are literally threaded on skewers for a succulent grilled dish. (Recipe: Sanee Maphungphong)*

1
Put the unpeeled shallots and garlic in an ungreased skillet and dry-roast them until they are softened. Alternatively, you may wrap them in foil and grill them by the direct method (page xxix) over hot coals.
2
Put the chicken strips in a mixing bowl and set aside. Put the chilies, salt, galangal, and lemongrass in the container of a food processor or blender and puree. You may need to add some of the coconut milk to help process. Add the roasted shallots and garlic, the coriander root, lime rind, peppercorns, shrimp paste, and the remaining coconut milk. Pour this over the chicken, cover with foil or plastic wrap, and marinate for at least 1 hour, preferably longer.
3
Thread the chicken lengthwise along the skewers. Pour the marinade into a saucepan and heat it to serve as a gravy. Grill the chicken by the direct method (page xxix) over medium-hot coals for 8 to 10 minutes, turning often to brown evenly. Remove from the fire and serve immediately with the hot coconut mixture.

Pork Satay

2 pounds boneless pork loin or
   Boston butt, cut into thin 3-inch-
   long, 2-inch-wide strips
Bamboo skewers
Marinade
1 to 1½ tablespoons curry powder,
   or to taste
¼ cup white vinegar
3 tablespoons water
1 teaspoon salt
1 tablespoon sugar
½ cup coconut milk
Peanut Sauce
1½ to 2 tablespoons Thai red curry
   paste
Two 13½-ounce cans coconut milk
1 cup unsalted peanuts, ground
1½ teaspoons salt
⅔ cup sugar

This recipe calls for Indian curry powder, which the chef uses for its yellow coloring. (Recipe: Chef Duangrudee Zier, Bangkok West Restaurant)

1
Put the pork strips in a shallow baking dish. Mix the marinade ingredients and pour over the meat. Cover with foil or plastic wrap and refrigerate overnight.

2
Make the peanut sauce by combining the curry paste with 1 can coconut milk in a saucepan. Heat until the mixture appears oily, about 6 to 10 minutes. Add the remaining coconut milk, ground peanuts, salt, and sugar. Bring the mixture to a boil. Lower the heat to medium and stir constantly until the sauce becomes thick and appears slightly oily, 20 to 30 minutes. Be careful not to overheat because the sauce will scorch.

3
Thread the pork strips on skewers. Grill the pork by the direct method (page xxix) over medium-hot coals for 8 to 10 minutes, turning once and brushing the meat with the marinade. Remove from the fire and serve with the peanut sauce.

Chicken Satay

4 *whole chicken breasts, skinned, boned, and cubed*
Bamboo skewers

Marinade
2 *tablespoons curry powder*
10 *cloves garlic, peeled and minced*
Freshly ground black pepper to taste
½ *cup white vinegar*
¼ *cup vegetable oil*
Salt to taste

Peanut Sauce
1 *tablespoon vegetable oil*
3 *tablespoons Thai red curry paste*
1 *tablespoon Thai Masaman curry paste*
2 *cups chopped roasted peanuts*
1 *cup coconut milk*
1 *cup palm sugar or brown sugar*
1 *cup tamarind juice*

(Recipe: Royal Orchid Sheraton Hotel & Towers, adapted)

1
Put the cubed chicken in a shallow baking dish. Combine the marinade ingredients in the container of a food processor or blender and puree. Pour the marinade over the chicken and set aside for at least 30 minutes.

2
To make the peanut sauce, pour the oil in a skillet and heat. Add both curry pastes, the peanuts, and coconut milk. Heat until the mixture comes to a boil, then add the sugar and tamarind juice. Remove from heat.

3
Thread the chicken onto skewers. Grill by the direct method (page xxix) over medium-hot coals for 8 to 10 minutes, turning once. Remove from the fire and serve immediately with the peanut sauce.

Beef Satay

36 *thin slices of top round steak,*
   1 inch wide and 3 to 4 inches long,
   fat removed
Bamboo skewers
Marinade
½ teaspoon ground turmeric
Pinch salt
1 cup coconut milk

Yet another dazzling Thai satay. Use the peanut sauce of your choice, such as the generic Indonesian sauce on page 145. (Recipe: Chef Sarayuth Atibodhi, The Thai Cooking School, The Oriental Bangkok hotel)

1
Put the meat into a roasting pan. Dissolve the turmeric powder and salt in the coconut milk. Pour the marinade on the meat, turning the meat to be sure all pieces are coated. Set aside for at least 1 hour.

2
Thread the meat on the bamboo skewers—since the pieces are long and not cubed, insert the skewer at least twice along the length of the meat. Grill the meat by the direct method (page xxix) over medium-hot coals, for 8 to 10 minutes, turning once and basting with the marinade. Serve immediately with a peanut sauce.

Grilled Beef Salad

¼ to ½ pound top round
1 teaspoon sliced lemongrass
1 lime leaf, julienned
10 fresh mint leaves, washed and dried
3 dried red chilies, thinly sliced

Sauce
2 tablespoons tamarind juice
1 tablespoon chili oil
¼ tablespoon fresh lemon juice
¼ tablespoon Thai fish sauce
¼ teaspoon sugar

A popular salad, this can be varied by arranging the sliced beef on several overlapping lettuce leaves, and garnishing with sliced fresh green chilies, sliced cucumbers, coriander leaves, and thinly sliced onions. The flavor of the beef improves after marinating in the sauce before serving. This recipe makes 2 servings. (Recipe: Royal Orchid Sheraton Hotel & Towers)

1
Grill the beef by the direct method (page xxix) over medium-hot coals, turning often. Remove from the fire and slice into thin strips. Set aside in a large dish.

2
Combine the sauce ingredients and pour over the meat. Garnish with the lemongrass and lime leaf. Pass the mint leaves and chilies on the side.

Grilled Spiced Chicken

One 3½- to 4-pound frying chicken,
  cut into serving pieces
¼ cup chopped spring onions
Marinade
5 large cloves garlic
20 black peppercorns
4 long pieces coriander root,
  chopped
4 to 5 tablespoons Thai fish sauce
¼ cup shredded fresh ginger
One 13½-ounce can coconut milk

There are countless variations on this well-known grilled chicken dish, known as Kai Yang. Some cooks would omit the ginger and add a touch of turmeric for color. This version is very simple but keeps the Thai flavor. (Recipe: Chef Duangrudee Zier, Bangkok West Restaurant)

1

Wash the chicken pieces and pat dry. Make equally spaced horizontal slashes in each piece—this allows the marinade to penetrate and the chicken to cook faster. Put the chicken in a shallow baking dish and set aside.

2

Combine the marinade ingredients in the container of a food processor or blender and puree. Pour this marinade over the chicken. Sprinkle with the spring onions. Cover with foil or plastic wrap and refrigerate for at least 2 hours.

3

Grill the chicken by the indirect method (page xxix) over medium-hot coals for about 15 minutes on each side, basting with the marinade. Remove from the fire. Serve immediately.

Grilled Squid

1 pound fresh or thawed squid, cut
into bite-sized pieces
Bamboo skewers
1 bottle (25 fluid ounces) chili sauce
(see Note)

This dish is so simple it's hard even to call it a recipe. According to Mr. Visith Laohapant, this is a favorite way for Thais to enjoy squid—the grilling enhances its taste and texture. These tidbits can be served as hors d'oeuvres or as part of the main meal. He uses a bottled Thai sweet chili sauce for dipping. (Recipe: Visith Laohapant, Bangkok Garden Restaurant)

1

Clean the raw squid by removing the ink sac, beak, head, and intestines. Remove the purple skin and rinse the pouch and tentacles before slicing. Thread the squid onto skewers and grill by the direct method (page xxix) over medium-hot coals for 4 to 5 minutes, turning often. Remove from the fire.

2

Serve immediately with the chili sauce, for dipping.

Note:

Mr. Laohapant says to use the sauce made by the Thep Padungporn Coconut Co., Thailand. This sauce is both sweet and hot. It is readily available.

Grilled Freshwater Fish with Curry

1½ pounds freshwater fish fillets,
   such as catfish, thinly sliced
¼ pound ground pork, cooked and
   cooled
2 large eggs, beaten
2 tablespoons sliced lime leaves
1 teaspoon salt
2 tablespoons Thai fish sauce
Banana leaf or foil for wrapping

Curry paste

8 to 10 dried red chilies
14 shallots, peeled and chopped
4 to 6 cloves garlic, peeled and
   chopped
1½ tablespoons minced galangal
1 stalk lemongrass, thinly sliced
2 teaspoons minced lime rind
2 or more teaspoons chopped fresh
   coriander
1 teaspoon shrimp paste
Salt to taste
One 13½-ounce can coconut milk

The fish picks up intense flavors from the curry and subtler ones from the banana leaves. (Recipe: Rungnapa Routh, adapted)

1

Rinse the fish fillets and pat dry. Slice them into long, thin strips and set aside in a shallow baking dish. Combine the curry paste ingredients in the container of a food processor or blender and puree. Pour over the fish, and add the pork, eggs, lime leaves, salt, and fish sauce.

2

If you are using a banana leaf, soften it according to directions in the Glossary. Put the fish mixture in the center of the leaf and wrap to cover. You may need to use more than 1 leaf. Fold the sides to the center to cover the fish. Secure both ends shut with toothpicks. If using foil, crimp the ends closed. Brush the banana leaf packet with oil, if desired.

3

Grill the fish by the direct method (page xxix) over medium-hot coals for 10 minutes. Remove from the fire. Unwrap and serve immediately.

Grilled Duck in Red Curry

1 tablespoon vegetable oil
1 tablespoon Thai red curry paste
¾ pound grilled duck meat, cut into 1½-inch cubes
3 cups coconut milk
½ cup canned crushed pineapple, drained
2 lime leaves
5 to 6 Thai basil leaves, chopped
2 tablespoons Thai fish sauce
1 tablespoon palm sugar or brown sugar
8 to 10 cherry tomatoes

The chef recommends serving this spectacular dish with hot rice and pickled ginger. For a meatier curry, double the amount of duck meat. The recipe tester used both duck breast and a whole duck. The breast grills in about 30 minutes; the whole duck grills in about 1½ hours. (Recipe: Royal Orchid Sheraton Hotel & Towers)

Heat the oil in a saucepan. Add the red curry paste and sauté it over low heat for about 10 minutes. Add the remaining ingredients and cook over low heat, stirring often, about 10 minutes. Serve immediately.

Tiger Cry

1 pound round steak, trimmed of fat
Marinade
2 tablespoons white or light soy
    sauce
2 teaspoons Thai fish sauce
Seasoning Sauce
2 teaspoons or more red chili
    powder or crushed red chilies
6 tablespoons Thai fish sauce
4 tablespoons fresh lemon juice

This dish, also known as Crying Tiger, is supposedly so hot it would make tigers cry. I first tasted it at a very casual grill restaurant on the outskirts of Bangkok. Although the food was delicious, the most memorable part of the meal was watching a young boy riding an elephant down the street. This is a composite of 2 recipes. (Recipe: Rungnapa Routh/Visith Laohapant, Bangkok Garden Restaurant)

1
Put the steak in a large baking dish. Combine the marinade ingredients and pour over the meat. Cover with foil or plastic wrap and set aside for 1 to 2 hours.
2
Meanwhile, combine the ingredients for the seasoning sauce and set aside in a small serving dish.
3
Grill the steak by the direct method (page xxix) over medium-hot coals, turning at least once, for 7 to 10 minutes or until cooked to desired doneness. Transfer the meat to a serving platter, slice thin, and serve immediately with the sauce to the side or poured on top.

Grilled Lobster

1 tablespoon lemon juice
1 tablespoon Worcestershire sauce
Salt and freshly ground pepper to
  taste
One 1-pound cooked lobster, split in
  half lengthwise
Seasoning Sauce
2 cloves garlic, minced
2 fresh chilies, minced
4 tablespoons lemon juice
2 tablespoons Thai fish sauce
¼ cup chopped fresh coriander

Chef Khun Satit gave me this recipe without any mea-surements, so I combined ingredients to taste. You can cook your own lobster or buy it precooked, before bar-becuing. This recipe makes 1 serving. (Recipe: Chef Khun Satit, Dusit Inn, adapted)

1

Combine the lemon juice, Worcestershire sauce, and salt and pepper and brush on the cut halves of the lobster. Combine the ingredients for the seasoning sauce and set aside.

2

Grill the lobster shell side up over medium-hot coals for 2 minutes. Turn over to grill for 4 to 5 minutes with the shell side down and brush the flesh with some of the seasoning sauce. Remove from the fire. Serve immediately with the seasoning sauce.

ACCOMPANIMENTS

Chili Jam

1 teaspoon shrimp paste
10 cloves garlic, peeled and left
    whole
10 shallots, peeled and sliced
10 dried or fresh red chilies
1 cup ground dried shrimp
1 tablespoon Thai fish sauce
2 tablespoons sugar
2 tablespoons tamarind juice
3 tablespoons vegetable oil

Served as a seasoning with many Thai meals, this relish is normally blended with a mortar and pestle. (Recipe: Chef Sarayuth Atibodhi, The Thai Cooking School, The Oriental Bangkok hotel)

1

Dry-roast the shrimp paste, garlic, shallots, chilies, and dried shrimp in an ungreased skillet. Put these in the container of a food processor or blender with the fish sauce, sugar, and tamarind juice and puree.

2

Heat the oil in the same skillet and stir-fry the paste until it is fragrant. Continue cooking until it reduces in volume slightly. Remove from heat and cool before serving.

3

Refrigerate the jam in a glass or plastic container with a tight-fitting lid. It lasts for several weeks.

Soft Thai Spring Rolls

Filling
⅔ pound shrimp, cooked, peeled, deveined, and quartered
Zest of 1 lemon
1 cup julienned red bell pepper
½ cup julienned green bell pepper
¼ cup chopped fresh coriander leaves
1 cup minced scallions
8 mint leaves, julienned
8 basil leaves, julienned
⅛ cup shredded fresh ginger
⅛ cup fresh lime juice
2 tablespoons Thai fish sauce
1 teaspoon chili oil

Dipping Sauce
½ cup soy sauce
⅛ cup Thai fish sauce
2 teaspoons chili oil
40 triangular rice paper wrappers

The filling of these uncooked spring rolls resembles a coarsely chopped vegetable salad—with shrimp. Serve these as an appetizer or an hors d'oeuvre. Makes about 40 pieces. (Recipe: Chef Joyce Piotrowski, Epicurean Events)

1
Combine the filling ingredients, including shrimp, in a large bowl. In a separate bowl, combine the dipping sauce ingredients.

2
To wrap, dip each wrapper in warm water to soften and lay it on a flat surface. Starting from the wide end, put 1 tablespoon of filling on the wrapper, making sure to include a piece of shrimp. Fold the sides in to the middle and roll tightly toward the pointed end. Set aside on a baking tray and keep covered with a damp towel until all the spring rolls are finished. Serve the rolls with the dipping sauce.

Spicy Seafood Soup

8 cups chicken stock
2 stalks lemongrass, thinly sliced
One 1-inch piece galangal
2 cloves garlic, peeled and crushed
2 to 3 fresh green chilies, or to taste,
   thinly sliced
1 tablespoon Thai fish sauce
¼ cup fresh lime juice
1½ to 2 pounds large raw shrimp,
   shelled and deveined
½ pound squid, cleaned (see Note)
   and cut into thin pieces
4 lime leaves, thinly sliced
Garnish
6 scallions, thinly sliced
1 cup rinsed and chopped coriander
   leaves

This is my version of a very special, very fiery shrimp and lemongrass soup eaten beachside at a Pattaya restaurant in Thailand many years ago. The soup was remarkable for many reasons: It was thick with whole and sliced fresh chilies and was the hottest dish I've ever eaten anywhere. It was chunky with fresh prawns with a few baby squid and octopus tossed in. And the broth was intensely flavored. There are many versions of this popular Thai soup—known as the shrimp-only version, tom yam kung—*but they are often thin and lacking spirit. Many include straw or fresh mushrooms, but I don't remember their presence in the Pattaya soup.*

1
Combine the stock, lemongrass, galangal, garlic, chilies, fish sauce, and lime juice in a large saucepan, and heat until the liquid simmers. Cook for 10 minutes.

2
Add the cleaned shrimp, squid, and lime leaves to the hot broth and simmer another 5 minutes. Serve immediately, garnished with chopped scallions and coriander leaves.

Note:
To clean squid, remove the beak (or mouth), the eyes, ink sac, cartilagelike backbone, and the intestines and outer skin. Rinse the body and tentacles thoroughly before slicing. Squid is also available frozen.

Herbed Soup

5 shallots, peeled
1 tablespoon chopped coriander
    root
1 teaspoon black peppercorns
1 teaspoon salt
½ cup ground dried shrimp
½ cup minced fresh shrimp
5 cups chicken broth or water
¼ pound whole raw shrimp, shelled
    and deveined
2 cups sliced fresh vegetables, such
    as green beans, squash, spinach,
    and mushrooms

Seasoning Mixture
2 tablespoons Thai fish sauce
1 tablespoon whole black
    peppercorns
2 cups basil leaves, preferably Thai
    or any sweet (Asian, not Western)
    basil

(Recipe: Chef Sarayuth Atibodhi, The Thai Cooking School, The Oriental Bangkok hotel)

1
Combine the shallots, coriander root, peppercorns, and salt in the container of a food processor or blender and rough chop. You may need to add a little of the broth to process. Pour this mixture into a large mixing bowl and add the dried shrimp and the minced fresh shrimp, stirring to combine.

2
Put the broth or water into a large saucepan and bring to a boil. Stir in the shallot/shrimp mixture until well combined and bring to a boil again.

3
Lower the heat and add the whole shrimp and sliced vegetables. Combine the fish sauce, peppercorns, and basil leaves and add to the soup. Cook gently for a few minutes, stir, and serve immediately.

Chicken in Coconut Milk Soup

½ pound boneless chicken breast
   meat, cut into bite-sized cubes
2 cups coconut milk
Ten ½-inch-thick slices galangal
3 lime leaves
3 stalks lemongrass, cut into 1-inch
   lengths and crushed
3 tablespoons Thai fish sauce
Juice of 2 limes
5 fresh green or red chilies, finely
   minced
¼ cup chopped fresh coriander for
   garnish

This recipe is a composite of 2 very similar dishes and the results are lovely. (Recipe: Rungnapa Routh/Chef Khun Satit, Dusit Inn)

Put the chicken cubes in a large saucepan and add the coconut milk. Bring to a boil. Add all the remaining ingredients except the garnish. Lower heat, and simmer until the chicken is cooked, about 10 minutes. Remove from heat and ladle into individual soup bowls. Sprinkle each portion with coriander. Serve immediately.

Hot and Sour Glass Noodle Salad

1 head leaf lettuce, trimmed, rinsed, and dried
1 tablespoon pickled garlic
½ pound cooked "glass" or bean thread noodles
½ cup thinly sliced scallions
½ cup chopped coriander leaves
1 tablespoon lime juice
1 tablespoon Thai fish sauce
1 to 2 tablespoons ground dried chilies (Thais use "rat dropping" chilies)
Sugar to taste
½ pound ground pork, cooked with garlic, and cooled

The 60-year-old Saw Ying Thai Restaurant in Bangkok serves very authentic Thai food. The place is packed daily by hungry Thais—and this salad is a wonderful find. (Recipe: Chef Somboon Phulek, Saw Ying Thai Restaurant/Bob Halliday)

Place the lettuce leaves in a large salad bowl. Combine the remaining ingredients in a large mixing bowl, stirring well. Scoop on top of the lettuce and serve immediately.

Stir-fried Noodles, Thai Style

3 tablespoons vegetable oil
2 tablespoons total red chilies and
  shallots, pounded together
3 tablespoons Thai fish sauce
1 tablespoon sugar
3 tablespoons tamarind water (1½
  tablespoons tamarind paste mixed
  with ¼ cup hot water)
1 teaspoon lime juice
1 cup minced or whole cooked
  shrimp
½ pound thin rice noodles (soaked
  in hot water and drained to soften)

Garnish
2 large eggs, beaten
2 tablespoons fried crushed peanuts
2 tablespoons deep-fried diced tofu
2 tablespoons deep-fried dried
  shrimp
2 cups bean sprouts
Shredded fresh red or green chilies
Coriander leaves

Known as paad Thai *(also spelled* pad Thai *and* pud Thai)*, these spectacular noodles almost demand to be included in a Thai meal. There are infinite variations on this dish, and it can include pork or chicken. This particular recipe originally called for wrapping the noodles in an egg crepe, but I have changed this to the more common and easier way of garnishing the noodles with shredded, cooked egg. (Recipe: Chef Sarayuth Atibodhi, The Thai Cooking School, The Oriental Bangkok hotel, adapted)*

1

Pour the oil into a skillet and heat. Add the chilies and shallots, the fish sauce, sugar, tamarind water, and lime juice and sauté until fragrant. Add the shrimp and stir until well combined. Add the softened noodles and stir well again. Set aside.

2

Heat a nonstick or lightly greased skillet and pour in the beaten eggs, swirling them out to make a flat layer, or crepe. Carefully remove the crepe from the pan in a single sheet and place on a large serving platter. Fold it over several times and shred fine. Set aside.

3

Scoop the noodle and shrimp mixture onto a platter. Garnish with the peanuts, tofu, shrimp, bean sprouts, chilies, shredded egg, and coriander leaves. Serve immediately.

Fried Spicy Fish

½ cup plus 2 tablespoons vegetable
  oil
2 pounds whole fish, such as flounder
  or sea trout, cleaned, head and
  tail intact
½ pound boneless pork roast, thinly
  sliced
1 clove garlic, peeled and minced
One 1-inch piece fresh ginger, sliced
2 tablespoons black bean sauce (see
  Note)
3 tablespoons vinegar
2 tablespoons sugar
5 scallions, sliced
1 large onion, peeled and diced
1 cup chopped celery
½ cup straw mushrooms (see Note)
1 carrot, peeled and sliced
1 cup water
3 tablespoons cornstarch mixed with
  3 tablespoons water

(Recipe: Visith Laohapant, Bangkok Garden Restaurant)

1

Heat ½ cup of vegetable oil in a skillet large enough to hold the fish. Add the fish and fry until crispy and golden on both sides. Transfer the fish to a serving platter.

2

Add 2 tablespoons vegetable oil to the same skillet and add the pork, garlic, ginger, black bean sauce, vinegar, and sugar. Sauté until the pork is cooked. Add the vegetables and water and continue cooking. Add the cornstarch mixture and stir until the sauce is thickened. Pour over the fish and serve immediately.

Note:

Black bean sauce is readily available in cans at Asian markets. Straw mushrooms have a pronounced flavor that accents many Asian dishes. These are rarely available fresh but are readily available in cans at Asian markets.

Green Chicken Curry

35 *fresh chilies (25 whole, 10 thinly sliced)*
1 *stalk lemongrass, sliced*
1 *tablespoon chopped kaffir or regular lime rind*
7 *thin slices galangal*
1 *tablespoon chopped coriander root*
2 *cloves garlic, peeled*
5 *shallots, peeled*
1 *teaspoon ground toasted coriander seeds*
1 *teaspoon ground toasted cuminseed*
½ *teaspoon fresh turmeric, or 1 teaspoon ground turmeric (optional)*
1 *teaspoon shrimp paste*
4 *cups coconut milk*
2 *cups cubed raw chicken breast or thigh meat*
3 *to 4 tablespoons Thai fish sauce*
1 *teaspoon palm sugar or brown sugar*
7 *kaffir lime leaves, julienned*
1 *cup Thai basil leaves*

This version of Thai green curry with chicken is one of the outstanding dishes of any cuisine. The recipe calls for 2 different kinds of Thai chilies, prig khee nu *and* prig kee fa, *but the recipe tester just used the chilies she had at hand. If you decide to use the full complement of chilies, this will be very hot—you may wish to halve or quarter the amount, depending on your taste. You may also want to use the slightly cooler, longer chilies. The original recipe calls for sliced chicken; the tester cubed the meat instead. (Recipe: Chef Sarayuth Atibodhi, The Thai Cooking School, The Oriental Bangkok hotel)*

1
Combine the whole chilies, lemongrass, lime rind, galangal, coriander root, garlic, shallots, coriander seeds, cuminseed, and turmeric in the container of a food processor or blender to chop and mix well. Add the shrimp paste and puree. You may need to add some of the coconut milk to process.

2
Pour 1 cup of the coconut milk in a saucepan and bring to a boil. Continue to boil until the milk thickens and an oil slick appears on the surface. This may splatter, so you may want to keep the pan partially covered. When the slick appears, add the chili mixture and cook until it is fragrant and thick. Stir regularly to keep the mixture from sticking and burning. Continue cooking until oil seeps out from the fried mixture.

3
Meanwhile, pour the remaining coconut milk into a large saucepan and add the chicken. Simmer until the meat is cooked, for about 15 minutes.

4

Add the fish sauce, sugar, cooked chicken and its coconut milk to the seasoning mixture. Add the lime and
basil leaves and sliced chilies just before serving. Serve
while hot.

Chicken with Basil Leaves and Hot Chilies

4 tablespoons vegetable oil
1 clove garlic, peeled and chopped
½ pound chicken breast meat, sliced
  into 5-inch x 2-inch strips
2 fresh red chilies, sliced
1 whole stem Thai basil, leaves only
2 tablespoons Thai fish sauce
¼ teaspoon sugar
¼ cup chicken stock or water

*The owner of the Bangkok Garden Restaurant says
that this has become the signature dish of his establish-
ment. He adds that you can use pork or beef instead of
chicken with equally good results. (Recipe: Visith Laohapant, Bangkok Garden Restaurant)*

1

Heat the oil in a skillet. Add the garlic and chicken and
sauté until the meat is partially cooked, about 5 to 6
minutes.

2

Add the chilies, basil leaves, fish sauce, sugar, and stock
or water and stir together until the chicken is cooked
through, 8 to 10 minutes.

3

Remove from the heat and serve immediately.

Green Papaya Salad

1 large whole green papaya (see Note)
1 to 2 cloves garlic, peeled and minced
5 to 6 fresh green chilies, crushed or finely sliced
2 tablespoons dried shrimp
1 large ripe tomato, sliced
1 to 2 tablespoons lemon juice
1 to 2 tablespoons Thai fish sauce
Sugar to taste

This is one time—Thai and Lao cooks assure me—when you must not use a food processor or hand grater for shredding. They would be much easier, of course, but would destroy the crisp texture of the papaya. To mix and crush the ingredients, use a mortar and pestle and/or your hands. (Recipe: Muttika Setatayak Gladson, Thai Luang Restaurant)

1

With a very sharp paring knife, peel off and discard the tough outer skin of the papaya. Hold the papaya in one hand and, using a very sharp cleaver, make chopping slashes into the papaya lengthwise along the fruit. Take the knife and shave off the slashed flesh lengthwise—do this often during the slashing process—and let the shreds fall into a large bowl. Continue slashing and shaving the papaya all the way around until you have about 4 to 5 cups of shreds. If you wish, you can shred the entire papaya and adjust the seasonings to suit your taste.

2

Add all the remaining ingredients. Traditionally, the ingredients should be pounded together with a mortar and pestle and stirred together by hand. Without a pestle, use a heavy wooden spoon and your hands to crush and mix the ingredients together. You want this to be very juicy. Serve chilled or at room temperature.

Note:

The large green papayas that the Thais and Lao use for this salad are readily available at most Asian markets. I have not tried the small, unripe papayas from the supermarket so I do not know if these are suitable substitutes. I don't think they have the same crisp-juicy texture.

Green Mango Salad

½ cup sliced, cooked, and cooled
   pork loin
½ cup sliced, cooked shrimp,
   cooled
3 tablespoons coarsely chopped
   roasted peanuts
½ tablespoon ground dried shrimp
½ tablespoon minced garlic
2 shallots, peeled and minced
1½ cups peeled, chopped green
   mango
Lettuce leaves
½ cup fresh coriander leaves for
   garnish

Dressing

3 tablespoons palm sugar or brown
   sugar dissolved in a little water
3 tablespoons Thai fish sauce
2 tablespoons fresh lemon juice
8 small fresh chilies, pounded or
   minced

Similar to, yet very different from, the Green Papaya Salad above—and a stunning dish. Do not make this in advance because the mango shreds may become soggy—they should be very crisp. The cook who gave me this recipe said it would be very typical for a Thai cook to experiment with amounts and flavors to come up with a pleasing combination, and I took her at her word. This recipe makes 2 to 3 servings. (Recipe: Rungnapa Routh, adapted)

1

Combine the pork, cooked shrimp, peanuts, dried shrimp, garlic, and shallots in a large mixing bowl and stir together. Combine the dressing ingredients. Put the chopped mango in a large salad bowl. Add the dressing and mix well.

2

Arrange the lettuce leaves on a platter or individual serving plates and mound the salad on top. Garnish with the coriander and serve immediately.

DESSERTS

Sticky Rice and Mango

2 cups coconut milk
Sugar to taste
3 cups cooked and warm sticky, or
    glutinous, rice (see page 253 for
    cooking instructions)
6 ripe mangoes, peeled and sliced

This simple yet elegant dessert is served in Thailand only during mango season when the fruits are ripe and sweet. (Recipe: Rungnapa Routh/Visith Laohapant, Bangkok Garden Restaurant)

1
Pour the coconut milk into a saucepan and bring to a boil. Lower the heat and add the sugar. Stir until the sugar is dissolved and remove from the heat.

2
Scoop the rice into a large serving bowl and pour the coconut milk over it. Cover the bowl with a lid or plastic wrap until the rice absorbs the coconut milk. Divide the rice among 6 individual bowls or plates and cover each serving with slices of mango, allowing 1 mango per person.

Thai Coconut Custard

½ cup palm sugar or brown sugar
3 large eggs
Meat from 3 young coconuts, grated,
    or about 2 cups dried shredded
    coconut
¾ cup coconut milk

This sweet can be served with coffee for breakfast or as a dessert. For dessert, it can also be eaten on top of sticky, or glutinous, rice. If you eat it as is, you may want to reduce the amount of sugar. (Recipe: Mrs. Charles Wilding-White)

1
Preheat the oven to 350°. Grease a 9-inch baking dish and set aside.

2
If you use palm sugar in a block, crumble or crush it to make it granular. Crack the eggs into a large mixing bowl

and add the sugar. Beat for 1 minute, then add the shredded coconut and coconut milk.

3

Pour the mixture into the baking dish and bake for 45 minutes. Serve warm or cold.

Grilled Bananas

Street vendors in Northern Thailand—probably every-where in the country—have these hot sugary bananas for sale all day and all night long. Visith Laohapant, owner of the Bangkok Garden Restaurant in Maryland, and Muttika Setatayak Gladson, owner of the Thai Luang Restaurant in Virginia, explained how this dessert is cooked. Both warned that Westerners may have problems duplicating the dish because the short, fat Thai bananas are not available here. For best results, use any short sweet bananas—their texture is much firmer and stickier than that of the regular long banana, which burns and almost melts before it's heated through. Thread the peeled bananas on bamboo skewers and grill them by the direct method (page xxix) over medium-hot coals for 10 minutes or until browned. Turn them often. You can prevent their sticking by placing the skewers on a metal barbecue screen placed directly on the barbecue rack. After cooking, flatten them slightly, and dip them into a syrup of palm sugar dissolved in coconut milk.

Grilled Coconut Rice Cakes

1 cup raw jasmine rice
1½ to 2 cups cold water
2 tablespoons cold cooked rice
Pinch salt
½ cup coconut milk
½ cup palm sugar or brown sugar
Vegetable oil

A sensational gooey treat, these grilled cakes—known in Thailand as Khanom Krok—are a popular snack food, delicious for breakfast as well as for an after-dinner sweet. Bangkok food writer Bob Halliday walked me through Bangkok's Chinatown one morning and pointed out a street vendor grilling these little treats on his portable barbecue and doing a brisk business. The cakes call for a special cast-iron mold available at some Asian markets—quite possibly you could substitute a cast-iron muffin or popover tin, instead. Cooking this over a charcoal fire requires some skill because you have little control over the heat—but it can be done successfully. If you get impatient, use your stove-top burner. Although this is sweet, Thais like to garnish it with chopped garlic and onion, or grated pumpkin, sweet potato, or taro root mixed with shredded coconut. The Thai lady who gave me this recipe says that the addition of the cooked rice assures success. Makes about 25 to 30 cakes. (Recipe: Darunee Kunchai)

1

Soak the jasmine rice in 1½ cups water for at least 8 hours. Put the soaked rice and its water, the cooked rice, and the salt into the container of a blender—do not use a food processor because it does not puree the mixture smoothly enough. After blending, the batter should have the viscosity of white house paint. If the batter is too thick, add a little more water, but no more than ½ cup, to thin it out.

2

Start a barbecue fire far enough in advance of cooking time to let the coals burn down to the white-ash stage.

3

In another mixing bowl, combine the coconut milk with the palm or brown sugar and set aside.

4

Grease the insides of the indentations of the *khanom krok* mold or muffin tins with the vegetable oil. Put the mold on the rack over the hot coals. Test the batter and the heat of the fire by making a trial cake. If that cooks and browns without burning, then fill the remaining indentations three quarters of the way to the top with the rice batter. After about 30 seconds, pour in the sugar mixture to fill up each indentation to the top. Put the special lid over the mold. If you use muffin tins, use foil or a large saucepan lid to cover.

5

Grill for about 5 minutes, checking that the bottoms of the little cakes are not getting burned as they cook. To do this, use a spoon to lift them up slightly from the mold. As the cakes cook, most of the sugar sinks into the batter to sweeten it. The coconut milk and the remaining sugar form a top layer that firms slightly. To remove the cakes, scoop around the sides of the indentations with a spoon to loosen the cakes. When the bottoms are browned and firm, the cakes should slip out easily. You can layer these like a round sandwich, putting the 2 flat sides together, or serve them as single cakes. Oil the indentations again and repeat the process until all the batter has been cooked. Serve and eat immediately.

Chapter
3

SAILING

THE

STRAITS

TOURS AND TRAVEL AGENTS OFTEN LUMP MALAYSIA AND SINGAPORE
together, selling them to visitors as if the two countries were still loosely joined under the
British colonial flag, and as if each could not be enjoyed for its own unique pleasures. Of
course, these two countries are only a causeway apart—tiny Singapore sits right on the
very edge of the Malay Peninsula, separated from the mainland by a curling ribbon of
water. At first glance, many of the foods, peoples, and customs of the two countries seem
surprisingly alike. But the two are worlds apart.

Size alone makes the difference. Malaysia consists of thirteen states and two federal
territories on a land area about the size of England. Two of its states, Sabah and Sarawak,
are located across the South China Sea on the coastal fringe of Borneo, and have a distinct
culture and history of their own. Malaysia's 18 million people are a potpourri of many
different races—primarily Malays and the other indigenous peoples, the Chinese, and
Indians. Stretching from Thailand in the north down to Singapore and the South China
Sea, Malaysia includes desolate coastal areas and glamorous beach resorts, inland cities
and wild lush jungles, emerald mountains and remote waterways. Perhaps the easiest way
to grasp its diversity is to take a quick tour of the National Museum in the capital city,
Kuala Lumpur. The museum's graphic displays show the cultural and political history of
this Asian region, and also give a breathtaking view of the country's wildlife: weird and
wonderful mammals, iridescent insects, and venomous snakes that look as if they all
crawled out from someone's fevered fantasy.

Singapore, on the other hand, comprises only 618 square kilometers that are home
to 2.7 million racially and culturally diverse people. Exciting, glamorous, and steaming
hot, Singapore dazzles with its clean streets; colonial, Chinese, and Arab architecture; and
sensory overload. It's the miniature dragon of Asia, poised for a brilliant leap into the
future with its claws still clinging to Asian tradition. But subtle changes are reshaping this
tiny city-state: the old Chinatown, where laundry dries on bamboo poles poking out
windows, is becoming gentrified. The tangle of alleys that separate Little India from Arab

Street look less cluttered on each visit. Old Change Alley for bargain-hunting curios is gone. And much of the famous waterfront Satay Club—an open-air collection of food stalls specializing in *satays*—has been plowed over. At least the graceful Raffles Hotel—with its legends of poets and of tigers prowling in the billiard room—remains, restored before tropical decay and bulldozers crumbled it forever. Yet, of Singapore's many delights, none is more compelling than finding tradition linked with the here-and-now: Singaporeans still parade the Lion Dance through Chinatown, still sell perfumed flower necklaces and bags of fresh spices in Little India, and still display exotic straw goods and gaudy woven rugs on Arab Street sidewalks, while no more than one mile away one finds the sleekest luxury stores in the world.

Malaysia

OUTSIDERS MAY DEFINE MALAYSIAN COOKING AS I ONCE DID, BY THE prodigious use of chilies, which provide a pervasive and pleasant sting to many dishes. But one could argue that what really defines Malaysian food is a far gentler ingredient: coconut, both its meat and its milk. Coconut milk turns up somewhere in virtually every course, from the rich coconut rice, to the marinades, meat and vegetable curries, and finally the pastries and puddings. And coconut meat is almost as omnipresent.

Beyond the lavish use of chilies and coconut milk, Malaysian cooking is hard to pin down, because the cuisine is composed of foods from three distinctly different cooking traditions: Malay (58 percent), Chinese (32 percent), and Indian (basically, South Indian, 10 percent). Somewhere in there you will find Malaysian dishes, which—explains Mrs. Abdul Jabar, the wife of a Malaysian official, formerly stationed at the Embassy of Malaysia in Washington—are dishes that all three ethnic groups have come to serve at their family tables. These may include fried noodles, *satays* (pieces of meat threaded on skewers), coconut rice, *po piah* (a type of spring roll), the refreshing drink *ais kacang,* or a fried meat dish that may be Indian in origin but is now universally popular. Of course, each ethnic group has its strict eating taboos: the Muslims (Malays) do not eat pork. The Hindus (Indians) do not eat beef. And the Chinese generally do not eat mutton, but not for any particular religious reason. And in a strict Chinese household, the cook would use very little coconut milk.

To complicate the picture, each community in each Malaysian state puts its own stamp on a dish—a *rojak* (fresh vegetable salad) you eat in Johore, for example, may not much resemble a *rojak* you can buy from a beach-side hawker in Penang. And the dishes of the *nyonya*—the Malay-Chinese peoples, also known as the Straits Chinese, or Peranakans—add their own special emphasis to Malaysian cooking. These foods combine the lemongrass, galangal, and pandan flavors Malays love with more orthodox Chinese ingredients. But to confuse matters even more, *nyonya* cooking has both Singaporean and Melakan variations. And individual tribal groups have their own cooking styles as well.

In less than a day's time touring Kuala Lumpur, the gastronomically curious can sample all three major styles of cooking, and maybe some minority foods, too. There's lunch at Yazmin Restaurant—call ahead for reservations—for a truly authentic Malay meal: rich curries, coconut fried rice, *rendang, mee goreng, satays,* and banana desserts sweetened with palm sugar and accented with pandan.

A stop at one of the many hawkers' stalls at an outdoor food center sheltered from the sun and rain by a permanent roof might give you a different taste. (The government widely supports food centers because this casual way of eating is part of Malaysian life.) An afternoon snack might consist of grilled chicken legs seasoned with turmeric, or Indian *dal,* or Indian *masala dosai* (pancakelike bread filled with a richly spiced vegetable), or a plate of noodles speckled with chilies.

An evening stroll through Chinatown would present the hungry with endless opportunities to sample a bowl of fried rice or fish porridge, or a plate of chili crabs or steamed prawns and rice. Since Chinatown closes down to traffic at night to convert to a crowded marketplace, it is a grand place to wind up a day of eating.

But everywhere in Malaysia, people take their food seriously. Consider the island of Penang, for example. Most visitors come with ideas of spectacular sunsets, romantic trysts, and poolside lounging. But for anyone who loves food, Penang is just this side of paradise. The central food markets and streets in downtown Georgetown, the island's main city, impress visitors with their astonishing variety, sights, and aromas. Penang, however, saves up its real gustatory salvos for its hawkers' stalls. Even in the pounding rain one night, the stretch of stalls beachside on Gurney Drive were crowded as people waited for their gingery fish soup, Penang *laksa,* and fiery prawn curry.

If grilling is not always visible in Malaysia—and this is speculation—it may be that much Malaysian grilling has gone underground or indoors to suit Western tastes. One chef noted that only poor people still grilled at home, but that might have been a personal opinion. There was ample enough evidence of grilling: hawkers sell *satay* in many places, and on the streets of Penang I watched a vendor grilling a coiled meat product and saw hardware stores selling stacks of concrete charcoal pots and metal grilling stands.

Certainly Malaysia gives the world some memorable grilled foods. For that matter, Malaysian food is, on the whole, remarkably delicious. This may be because Malaysians simply love good food. As the chef at Yazmin Restaurant observes, "We Malaysians are gluttons. We eat all the time."

THE GRILLS

Grilled Chicken

One 3- to 4-pound roasting chicken, quartered

Marinade
One 2-inch piece galangal
1 tablespoon ground coriander
1 tablespoon ground turmeric
Pinch salt
1 tablespoon tamarind pulp, mixed with ½ cup hot water

Seasoning Mixture
1 large onion, peeled and chopped
3 tablespoons grated fresh ginger
3 tablespoons minced garlic
6 candlenuts or macadamia nuts
5 dried red chilies
2 tablespoons vegetable oil
2 stalks lemongrass, thinly sliced
1 to 2 cups coconut milk, depending on how fiery you want the mixture

Mrs. Abdul Jabar, the wife of a Malaysian government official and a practiced cook, says that this is a wonderful grilled dinner. (Recipe: Mrs. Abdul Jabar)

1
Put the chicken pieces in a large baking pan. Combine the marinade ingredients in the container of a food processor or blender and puree. Pour this mixture over the chicken. Cover the pan with foil or plastic wrap and set aside for 1 hour.

2
Combine the onion, ginger, garlic, nuts, and chilies in the container of a food processor or blender and puree. You may need to add some water to help process. Add the oil to a skillet and heat. Add the paste and fry over medium heat, stirring constantly until fragrant, about 10 minutes. Add the lemongrass and sauté for 5 minutes or so, or until fragrant. Transfer these ingredients to a large saucepan and add the coconut milk. Bring the mixture to a boil.

3
Add the chicken, return to a boil, and cook for about 10 minutes. Remove the chicken and set aside. Lower the heat and continue cooking the coconut-milk mixture at a gentle boil until the liquid thickens and reduces, about 30 minutes.

4
Grill the chicken quarters by the indirect method (page xxix) over hot coals for 20 to 30 minutes, brushing them occasionally with the reduced coconut-milk mixture and turning them several times. Test for doneness before removing them from the fire. Heat the remaining coconut-milk mixture to serve with the chicken as a gravy. Remove the chicken from the fire and serve immediately.

Grilled Pomfret

One 1½-pound pomfret, cleaned, or
   any other small whole fish, such as
   mackerel, head and tail intact
Vegetable oil for greasing
Marinade
8 dried red chilies
4 shallots, peeled and sliced
2 cloves garlic, peeled
½ to 1 teaspoon ground turmeric
One ½-inch piece fresh ginger
One ½-inch piece galangal
5 candlenuts or macadamia nuts
Salt and lime juice to taste

As an alternative to grilling, you can sprinkle the fish with grated coconut and bake it in the oven at 350° for about 20 minutes. (Recipe: Chef Noorhayati Shafie, Shangri-La Hotel)

1
Make horizontal slits along both sides of the fish. Set it aside in a shallow baking dish. Combine the marinade ingredients in the container of a food processor or blender and puree. You may need to add some water to help process. Spoon the marinade over the fish, turning the fish so that both sides are fully covered. Set aside for 1 hour.

2
Brush the rack on the grill with oil. Or, if you use a special fish rack for grilling, brush it with oil. This prevents the fish from sticking. Grill the fish by the direct method (page xxix) over medium-hot coals for 7 to 10 minutes, or until done, turning once. Remove from the fire and serve immediately.

Grilled Pomfret in Banana Leaf

One 1¼-pound whole pomfret,
   cleaned, or any other small whole
   fish such as mackerel, head and
   tail intact
Banana leaves or foil for wrapping
Vegetable oil for brushing
Seasoning Paste
1 tablespoon diced red chilies
2 teaspoons minced garlic
6 tablespoons minced shallots
1 tablespoon minced fresh turmeric,
   or 2 tablespoons ground turmeric
1 teaspoon shredded turmeric leaf
   (optional)
2 lime leaves
2 stalks lemongrass
1 teaspoon lime juice
Salt and pepper to taste
¾ cup grated coconut

This is a slightly different version of the previous Grilled Pomfret recipe because it comes wrapped in and scented by banana leaf. The filling is moist but the skin is crispy. You can bake this in the oven but then wrap it in foil. (Recipe: Chef Mok Tai Heng, Palm Beach Hotel)

1

Put the fish in a shallow baking dish and set aside. Combine all the seasoning ingredients except the coconut in the container of a food processor or blender and puree. You may need to add some water to help process. Stir in the coconut. Stuff half this mixture into the cavity of the fish and spread the remainder on top.

2

If you are using a banana leaf, soften it according to the directions in the Glossary. Put the fish in the center of one or more banana leaves. Fold the sides to the center to cover the fish. Secure both ends shut with toothpicks. If using foil, crimp the ends closed. Brush the banana-leaf packets with oil, if desired.

3

Grill the fish by the direct method (page xxix) over medium-hot coals for 10 minutes, turning once. Remove from the fire. Serve the fish immediately, scooping out the filling to use as garnish.

Grilled Fish

1½ pounds whole fish, such as
   striped bass, cleaned, rinsed, and
   dried, head and tail intact
Banana leaves or foil for wrapping
Vegetable oil for brushing

Seasoning Mixture

2 tablespoons vegetable oil
6 tablespoons crushed dried chilies
5 fresh green chilies, minced
2 teaspoons shrimp paste
2 stalks lemongrass, finely diced
10 tablespoons chopped shallots
2½ tablespoons minced garlic
Salt, pepper, and tamarind paste
   to taste
Juice of 2 limes

Chili Sauce

5 fresh red chilies, minced
5 fresh green chilies, minced
10 shallots, peeled and chopped
5 cloves garlic, peeled
Juice of 2 limes
2 tablespoons sugar
Salt

This is a general recipe that is appropriate for any whole fish. (Recipe: Mrs. Abdul Jabar)

1

Put the oil in a skillet and heat. Add the chilies, shrimp paste, lemongrass, shallots, and garlic and fry the mixture until fragrant, about 15 minutes. Remove from the heat and add salt, pepper, and tamarind paste, stirring well. Rub the mixture all over the fish and then add the lime juice. Put the fish in a baking dish. Cover with foil or plastic wrap, and set aside.

2

Combine all the chili sauce ingredients in the container of a food processor or blender and puree. Set aside.

3

Brush the rack on the grill with oil. Or, if you use a special fish rack for grilling, brush it with oil. This prevents the fish from sticking. Grill the fish by the direct method (page xxix) over medium-hot coals for 7 to 10 minutes, turning once. Remove from the fire and wrap in banana leaves or foil.

4

If you are using banana leaves, soften them according to the directions in the Glossary. Put the fish in the center of one or more leaves and fold the sides to the center to cover the fish. Secure both ends shut with toothpicks. If using foil, crimp the ends closed. Brush the banana-leaf packets with oil, if desired. Return the fish to the grill and cook by the direct method (page xxix) over medium-hot coals for 5 minutes more, turning once. Remove from the fire and serve immediately with the chili sauce.

ASIAN GRILLS

Beef Satay

1¼ pounds lean beef, such as top
    round, cut into 1-inch cubes
Bamboo skewers
Marinade
4 cloves garlic, peeled and minced
2 shallots, peeled and minced
1 teaspoon curry powder
1 teaspoon ground turmeric
½ teaspoon ground cumin
½ teaspoon ground coriander
½ teaspoon pandan leaves, finely
    chopped, or 1 teaspoon pandan
    extract
1 stalk lemongrass, minced
2 teaspoons soy sauce
½ teaspoon freshly ground black
    pepper
1 teaspoon fresh lemon juice
2 teaspoons sugar
1 teaspoon salt

This Penang version of the popular skewered and grilled meat is just one of the many ways Malaysians eat satay. Use the best cuts of beef or the satay will not be appropriately tender—this is finger food eaten without knife or fork. The chef says you can also use lamb or chicken. This is so delicious that you might want to double the recipe. (Recipe: Chef Mok Tai Heng, Palm Beach Hotel)

1
Put the beef in a shallow baking dish. Combine all the marinade ingredients and pour over the beef. Cover with foil or plastic wrap and set aside for at least 1 hour.
2
Meanwhile, make the peanut sauce by combining the chilies, lemongrass, ginger, candlenut or macadamia nut, galangal, shallots, and shrimp paste in the container of a food processor or blender and puree. You may need to add some water to help process. Pour the oil into a skillet and heat. Sauté the pureed ingredients until fragrant. Then add the coconut, peanut butter, peanuts, and stock or water, and stir until well blended. Add the sugar, soy sauce, lemon juice, and salt. Simmer the sauce over low heat, stirring often, for about 15 minutes. Keep warm until ready to serve.

Peanut Sauce

4 *dried chilies, soaked in water and*
  deep-fried
1 *stalk lemongrass, minced*
1 *teaspoon grated fresh ginger*
1 *candlenut or macadamia nut*
1 *teaspoon minced galangal*
4 *shallots, peeled and chopped*
1 *teaspoon shrimp paste*
¼ *cup vegetable oil*
4 *tablespoons fried shredded*
  coconut
4 *tablespoons peanut butter*
8 *tablespoons chopped peanuts*
½ *cup beef stock or water*
1½ *tablespoons sugar*
1 *tablespoon soy sauce*
1 *teaspoon lemon juice*
Salt to taste

3

Thread the beef on the bamboo skewers, about 4 pieces per skewer. Grill by the direct method (page xxix) over medium-hot coals for 7 to 10 minutes, turning once. Remove from the fire and serve with the peanut sauce. Sliced cucumbers and onions make a nice accompaniment.

Satay Kajang

3 pounds chicken breast, deboned
   and cubed
Bamboo skewers
Marinade
1 teaspoon ground cumin
½ teaspoon ground cinnamon
8 shallots, peeled and diced
1 teaspoon ground coriander
2 teaspoons ground turmeric
¼ cup sugar
1 stalk lemongrass, thinly sliced
2 teaspoons roasted peanuts
Salt to taste
2 tablespoons vegetable oil
Peanut Sauce
About 2 cups roasted peanuts
One 1-inch piece fresh ginger
One 1-inch piece fresh galangal
3 tablespoons crushed dried chilies
2 stalks lemongrass, thinly sliced
¼ to ½ cup sugar
1 large onion
½ cup tamarind juice
1 tablespoon vegetable oil

For many years, the town of Kajang, about 20 miles from Malaysia's capital, Kuala Lumpur, has been famous for its satay. *People, including tourists, would drive there, even late in the evening, for a satay snack. Now Kajang-style* satay *is sold in Kuala Lumpur and elsewhere—but the roads to Kajang still lead* satay *devotees to their favorite snack. Baste the* satay *during grilling with ½ cup coconut milk and 1 tablespoon oil, if desired. (Recipe: Mrs. Abdul Jabar)*

1

Put the chicken cubes in a shallow baking dish. Combine all the marinade ingredients in the container of a food processor and puree. Spread the puree over the chicken cubes. Cover the dish with foil or plastic wrap and refrigerate for several hours. Remove the chicken at least 30 minutes before cooking to bring it to room temperature.

2

Meanwhile, make the peanut sauce by combining all the sauce ingredients in the container of a food processor or blender and pureeing. If you need extra liquid for processing, use more tamarind juice rather than water.

3

Thread the chicken cubes on bamboo skewers and grill the *satays* by the direct method (page xxix) over medium-hot coals for 5 to 7 minutes, turning at least once. Remove from the fire and serve immediately with the peanut sauce.

Spicy Grilled Prawns in Banana Leaf

1 teaspoon ground turmeric
1 tablespoon fresh lime juice
Salt and pepper to taste
1 pound jumbo prawns, cleaned and
    shelled
Banana leaves or foil for wrapping
Vegetable oil for brushing
Seasoning Mixture
½ cup plus 2 tablespoons thick
    coconut milk
One 2½-inch piece Malaysian palm
    sugar, crushed, or ¼ cup brown
    sugar
½ tablespoon shrimp paste
10 shallots, peeled
4 cloves garlic, peeled and
    chopped
4 candlenuts or macadamia nuts
One 1-inch piece galangal
4 red chilies

This is a wonderful way to prepare shrimp. The recipe calls for "king" prawns; buy the largest size you can afford—it will be worth the cost. (Recipe: Chef Mok Tai Heng, Palm Beach Hotel)

1
Place the prawns in a shallow baking dish. Combine the turmeric, lime juice, and salt and pepper and season the prawns with this mixture. Put the seasoning mixture ingredients in the container of a food processor or blender and puree. Pour the mixture over the prawns.

2
If you are using a banana leaf, soften it according to the directions in the Glossary. Place equal portions of the seasoned prawns into the center of each leaf. Fold the sides to the center to cover the filling. Secure both ends with toothpicks. If using foil, crimp the ends closed. Brush the outside of the banana-leaf packets with oil, if desired.

3
Grill the prawns by the direct method (page xxix) over hot coals for 7 to 10 minutes, turning often. Remove from the fire and serve the prawns immediately, in their wrappers.

Grilled Glutinous Rice with Prawn Filling

2½ cups sticky, or glutinous, rice, soaked in water overnight
2 cups coconut milk
½ cup water
Pinch salt
Banana leaves or foil, cut into sixteen 7-inch x 7-inch squares, for wrapping
Vegetable oil for brushing

Filling

¼ cup vegetable oil
½ cup plus 2 tablespoons grated fresh coconut or shredded dry
½ pound raw prawns, shelled, deveined, rinsed, and chopped
2 tablespoons ground red chilies
1 teaspoon minced garlic
1 teaspoon minced fresh ginger
Salt and pepper to taste

(Recipe: Chef Mok Tai Heng, Palm Beach Hotel)

1
Drain the rice and add the coconut milk, water, and salt. Mix well and steam until the rice is tender. (For instructions on steaming, see page 253.)

2
Meanwhile, put 2 tablespoons of the vegetable oil in a skillet and fry the grated coconut until lightly browned, or about 10 to 15 minutes. Crush the coconut and set it aside.

3
Add the remaining oil to the skillet and sauté the prawns over low heat for several minutes. Add the chilies, garlic, ginger, and coconut and sauté the mixture until fragrant, for about 10 minutes. Add the salt and pepper and stir well.

4
If you are using a banana leaf, soften it according to the directions in the Glossary. Place a tablespoon of cooked rice on a leaf or a foil strip and spread it out. Spoon 1 teaspoon of the filling in the center of the rice, and spoon another tablespoon of rice on top. Fold the sides of the leaf or foil to the center to cover the filling. Secure both ends shut with toothpicks if you are using a banana leaf. If using foil, crimp the ends closed. Repeat the process until all the rice is used up. Brush the banana-leaf packets with oil, if desired.

5
Grill the packets by the direct method (page xxix) over medium-hot coals for 10 minutes, or until the leaves are browned. Turn the packets over several times so they cook evenly. Remove from the fire and serve the rice balls immediately in their packets.

ACCOMPANIMENTS

Penang Po Piah

3 tablespoons vegetable oil
1 teaspoon minced garlic
¼ pound raw prawns, cleaned,
    shelled, deveined, and diced
¼ pound ground pork
2 cups shredded yam bean or
    jicama
8 leaves Chinese cabbage,
    shredded
2 tablespoons fried shallots
1 cup chicken stock or water
1 tablespoon sweet soy sauce
2 large eggs, made into a thin
    pancake and cut into shreds (see
    Pork Noodle Soup, step 2,
    page 198)
½ pound tofu, thinly sliced and fried
    crisp (see Rojak, page 96)
½ pound cleaned crab meat
1 package po piah skins or spring
    roll wrappers (see Note)

These stuffed vegetable rolls are very similar to the universally popular Chinese spring rolls. But unlike spring rolls, these are not fried, but served uncooked. This recipe makes about 24 pieces. (Recipe: Chef Mok Tai Heng, Palm Beach Hotel)

1

Pour the vegetable oil into a skillet and heat. Add the garlic and fry until golden. Add the prawns and pork, stirring well. Add the shredded yam bean and fry until it is tender and the pork is cooked through. Add the cabbage, shallots, and chicken stock or water and cook for about 2 minutes. Season with soy sauce.

2

Scoop the cooked mixture into a large mixing bowl, letting the excess liquid drain off. Add the shredded eggs, tofu, and crab meat and stir well.

3

Thaw frozen wrappers according to package directions. Working with 1 *po piah* or spring roll wrapper at a time, place the wrapper flat on a clean surface and put 1 or 2 tablespoons of filling mixture into the center of the wrapper. Fold into a roll and place the filled wrappers on a serving platter. Serve with your favorite dipping or chili sauce.

Note:

Spring roll wrappers are readily available at supermarkets and at Asian markets. *Po piah* or the similar *lumpia* wrappers are sold frozen at many Asian markets.

Rojak

1 pound firm tofu, sliced and fried
¼ cup vegetable oil
¼ pound bean sprouts, blanched
¼ pound watercress, blanched
¼ pound yam bean or jicama
2 cups diced fresh pineapple
1 cucumber, peeled and diced
Salad Dressing
5 to 10 red chilies, to taste
2 teaspoons shrimp paste
¾ cup roasted peanuts
1 teaspoon tamarind paste, stirred with 1 cup water
¼ to ½ cup Malaysian palm sugar or brown sugar
Salt to taste

There are several variations of this very popular salad; Chinese, Indian, and Malaysian, and of course, the numerous individual variations, to say nothing of the rojak *that Singaporeans serve. This makes a wonderful accompaniment for a grilled seafood dinner. (Recipe: The Embassy of Malaysia, Washington, D.C.)*

1

Blot excess moisture from the tofu with paper towels. Heat the vegetable oil in skillet and when bubbly, add the tofu slices. Fry until golden on all sides—you may need to add more oil. Remove from the pan and drain on paper towels.

2

Combine the salad ingredients in a large serving bowl and set aside.

3

Place all the dressing ingredients in the container of a food processor or blender and process until smooth. Adjust seasonings to taste.

4

Pour the dressing over the salad and toss. Serve immediately or refrigerate until ready to use.

Cabbage Braised in Coconut Milk

1 small head green cabbage, cored
   and shredded
1 large onion, peeled and thinly
   sliced
2 green chilies, thinly sliced
2 shallots, peeled and sliced
Pinch saffron threads
Salt and freshly ground black
   pepper to taste
2 tablespoons vegetable oil
1½ cups coconut milk
1 pound raw prawns, shelled and
   deveined, left whole or
   sliced in half lengthwise

This savory cabbage mixture is almost a daily fixture on Malaysian tables. Usually it is served with rice as an accompaniment. This would be appropriate to serve at a buffet barbecue party. (Recipe: Mrs. Abdul Jabar, adapted)

1
Wash the cabbage well and soak it in cold water to cover for 30 minutes. Combine the onion, chilies, shallots, saffron, and salt and pepper with the oil in a large skillet and sauté until the mixture becomes fragrant, for about 10 minutes.

2
Drain the cabbage and place it in a large saucepan with the coconut milk and bring to a boil over medium high heat. Add the fried seasonings. Lower the heat and simmer, covered, until the cabbage is tender, about 15 minutes. Add the prawns to the saucepan for the last 5 minutes of cooking time.

Coconut Rice

4 cups long-grain rice
4 cups coconut milk
Pinch salt
Several drops of pandan extract, or
    1 to 2 pandan leaves
One 1-inch piece of ginger, thinly
    sliced

Known as nasi lemak, *this popular rice dish is a Malaysian staple and is often served at breakfast or for snacks. But really, says Mrs. Jabar,* nasi lemak *is eaten at any time of day or night, and is often served with an assortment of its own garnishes. (For suggestions, see below). It is also accented with spoonfuls of the popular Malaysian relish,* sambal ikan bilis—*see recipe below. This is an ideal accompaniment for grilled fish. (Recipe: Mrs. Abdul Jabar)*

1

Combine all the ingredients in a large saucepan, bring to a boil, lower the heat, and simmer the rice, covered, over low heat until all the milk has been absorbed or for about 10 to 15 minutes. Stir to loosen the rice grains and spoon into a large serving dish.

2

Serve it immediately and pass as accompaniments the following: steamed green beans, quartered hard-boiled eggs, sliced cucumbers, quartered boiled potatoes, and roasted peanuts. Pass the *Sambal* (recipe follows) in a separate dish.

Sambal Ikan Bilis

8 ounces dried anchovies (see Note)
2 ounces dried chilies
6 shallots, peeled
2 cloves garlic, peeled
½ teaspoon shrimp paste
½ cup tamarind juice
Salt and sugar to taste
½ cup vegetable oil

For Malaysian cooks, this is a standard seasoning condiment made from dried anchovies. But you can also use fresh prawns or squid for a very different taste.

1

Fry the anchovies in 2 tablespoons of the vegetable oil until crisp. Drain and set aside. Combine the chilies, shallots, garlic, and shrimp paste in the container of a food processor or blender and chop fine.

2

Heat the remaining oil in a skillet and fry the chopped ingredients until fragrant, about 10 minutes. Add the tamarind juice, salt, and sugar, lower the heat, and simmer until thick. Add the reserved anchovies and cook until the oil separates. Remove from the heat and spoon into a serving dish. Leftovers store well in a tightly covered container.

Note:

Dried anchovies in Malaysia are known as *ikan bilis* and are used to season many Malaysian dishes. These anchovies are readily available at Asian markets. Do not use tins of oily Western anchovies as a substitute.

Cucumber Salad

2 cucumbers, peeled and thinly
    sliced
½ fresh pineapple, peeled and
    diced
1 medium onion, peeled and thinly
    sliced
1 green and 1 red chili (or more,
    if desired)

Dressing
1 teaspoon shrimp paste
2 to 3 tablespoons dried shrimp
2 to 3 red chilies, sliced
Juice of 1 lime or lemon
¼ to ½ cup water
Salt and sugar to taste

This light, refreshing salad is a popular Malaysian dish and is served often, even at festival meals. You may use fewer chilies for a milder salad. (Recipe: Mrs. Abdul Jabar)

1
Place the cucumbers, pineapple, and onion in a large mixing or salad bowl. Seed and slice the chilies and add them to the bowl—use more or fewer chilies, depending on how hot you would like the dish.

2
Place the shrimp paste in an ungreased skillet and cook over medium heat for 5 to 10 minutes to bring out its flavor. Then put the shrimp paste, dried shrimp, and seeded red chilies in the container of a food processor or blender with the lime or lemon juice, water, salt, and sugar and process to make a paste. Pour over the salad ingredients. Serve immediately or chill until serving time.

DESSERTS

Ais Kacang

1 cup cubed grass jelly (see Note)
1 small can sweet red beans
1 cup sweet corn kernels
1 cup evaporated milk
1 to 2 cups sugar syrup (made from
    boiling sugar and water together
    in a 1:1 ratio)
2 cups water
Shaved ice

A perfect hot-weather refreshment with shaved or crushed ice and a variety of other unusual ingredients, ais kacang, or ice beans, is normally sold at hawkers' stalls. But Mrs. Jabar served this as dessert for a Sunday brunch, and it was a perfect conclusion to a chilied meal. You may color the syrup red, if desired. This recipe makes 2 to 3 servings. (Recipe: Mrs. Abdul Jabar)

1

Place a spoonful of the grass jelly, red beans, and corn into each serving dish. Add a scoop of shaved ice to each dish.

2

Combine the milk, sugar syrup, and water, stirring well. Pour over the ice to fill the dishes.

Note:

Grass jelly is a black seaweed-based product that looks like gelatin cubes and is thickened with cornstarch. You must cut it into cubes before serving. It is available canned at most Asian markets. You can store leftovers in the refrigerator for several days.

Sugar-filled Pastry Balls

½ cup glutinous rice flour
Pinch salt
Few drops of pandan extract
Green food coloring (optional)
¼ to ½ cup palm sugar or brown
   sugar
1 cup freshly grated or shredded
   dry coconut, sprinkled lightly with
   salt

Known as onde-onde, *these are simple to make and delicious to eat, like popping a puff of crunchy-chewy sugar in your mouth. In fact, these are so good you may want to double the recipe. You should use freshly grated coconut, if possible. This recipe makes about 20 balls. (Recipe: Mrs. Abdul Jabar)*

1
Combine the rice flour and enough water to make a soft, pliable dough. Add salt, a few drops of pandan extract, and green coloring, if you wish.

2
Pinch off small pieces of dough and shape them into one-inch round balls. If you are using the solid Malaysian palm sugar, chop the sugar block into small pieces. Make a hole in the center of the dough and fill the hole with ½ teaspoon sugar. Pinch the dough shut to seal it and set the ball aside. Repeat this process until all the dough is used up.

3
Meanwhile, bring a pot of water to a boil. Drop several dough balls at a time into the boiling water. The balls are done when they float to the surface of the water. Scoop them out with a slotted spoon and drain very well.

4
When cool, roll the balls in grated coconut and arrange them on a platter. Serve immediately. If you make these ahead, store them in a tightly covered container, otherwise they will dry out and become hard.

Steamed Rice Pudding

5 tablespoons brown sugar
2½ cups water
1½ cups rice flour
1½ teaspoons cornstarch
1 tablespoon pandan extract
Variety of food coloring
1 tablespoon lime water (see Note)
Grated coconut

(Recipe: Mrs. Abdul Jabar)

1
Combine the sugar and 1 cup of water in a saucepan and bring to a boil. When the sugar is dissolved, add the remaining water, and stir in the rest of the ingredients except the coconut.

2
Pour the hot mixture into small custard cups and color each differently. Place the cups in a vegetable steamer over water and bring to a boil. Cover and steam for 15 minutes or until firm. When cool, turn out the individual puddings onto serving plates and serve with grated coconut.

Note:
Powdered limestone, also known as white lime paste, is an alkali paste used in minute amounts to add body to many Malaysian and Southeast Asian desserts. This is available in tiny plastic jars in many Asian markets. Mix 1 pinch in 1 tablespoon water.

Sago Pudding

2 cups small sago granules
4 to 5 cups water
2 egg whites
Pinch salt
Sauces
One 13-½ ounce can coconut milk
½ pound Malaysian palm sugar, or
   1 cup brown sugar
1½ cups water

*T*his dessert is a version of Western tapioca pudding, except that sago is not tapioca and here the sweetness comes from a dark sugar syrup added at the table. This is a popular dessert everywhere in Malaysia and, for that matter, in Singapore as well—but with a difference. Singaporeans do not rinse their sago during the cooking process. One old Malaysian cookbook says this dessert is also known as Singapore, Penang, Malacca, Straits Settlements, or Palm Pudding. It cools the palate after a piquant main course. Sliced fresh fruit is a traditional topping. (Recipe: The Embassy of Malaysia, Washington, D.C.)

1

Rinse and drain the sago. Set it aside to soak in cold water to cover for about 10 minutes and drain again. Meanwhile, pour the 4 or 5 cups water into a large saucepan and bring to a boil. Slowly add the sago granules, stirring well, and cook over low heat until the sago become clear, about 20 minutes. Stir often and keep heat low to prevent the sago from scorching.

2

Pour the sago into a small-mesh wire strainer and rinse under cool water to remove any remaining starch. It may seem as if all the granules are washing away—do not be alarmed. Drain well.

3

Beat the egg whites with the salt until stiff, then fold into the sago. Pout the mixture into a 2-quart mold or serving dish and refrigerate until chilled. Scoop directly from the mold to serve.

4

Meanwhile, make the sauces: Pour the coconut milk into a serving pitcher, and dilute with water, to a desired consistency. Combine the sugar and 1½ cups water in a

saucepan and bring to a boil. Continue cooking over medium heat, stirring constantly, until the sugar is dissolved and the syrup thickens slightly. Pour into the serving pitcher. Pass the sauces with the chilled sago.

Banana Porridge

4 tablespoons small sago granules
1½ cups water
½ cup Malaysian palm sugar or brown sugar
½ cup granulated sugar
3 large ripe bananas, peeled and sliced
1 cup coconut milk

By adding a layer of vanilla wafers, you might think you were eating an old-fashioned Southern vanilla pudding made chunky with sliced bananas. But you are not. Think instead "tropics" and imagine yourself sitting by a gentle, rolling surf. (Recipe: Chef Mok Tai Heng, Palm Beach Hotel, adapted)

1
Wash and drain the sago granules. Then soak them in cold water to cover for 20 minutes.

2
Place the 1½ cups water in a large saucepan and bring to a boil. Add the palm or brown sugar and granulated sugar and cook, stirring well, until the sugars are dissolved and form a slightly thick syrup, 15 to 20 minutes. Strain the syrup.

3
Add the banana slices to the syrup and simmer until the bananas are cooked, about 5 minutes. Then add the coconut milk and sago.

4
Simmer the mixture until the sago becomes transparent, 30 to 35 minutes. Watch carefully so the mixture does not scorch. Remove from the heat and allow the porridge to thicken and cool slightly. Serve at once or refrigerate and serve chilled. Garnish with additional sliced bananas, if desired.

Singapore

SOME PEOPLE ARE BORN TO SHOP; OTHERS ARE BORN TO EAT. SINGA-poreans are born to do both. By an accident of birth, they live in the world's most luxurious shopping mall. They also live with the world's most exciting smorgasbord. Singaporeans can sample an exotic turtle soup or a platter of fried snake. Or if they prefer, order Japanese *teriyaki,* take their children for an American hamburger, treat aunties and uncles to a Taiwanese steamboat dinner, or pick up their chopsticks for a Cantonese, Teochew, Szechwanese, Hunanese, Hainanese, Hakka, Hokkien, or Pekingese Chinese meal. They can dine at the restored Raffles Hotel in British colonial splendor, splurge on *la grande cuisine,* or tighten their purse strings for a modest hawker's meal. And they can do all this twenty-four hours a day.

And of course, if Singaporeans choose to stay home and cook—though with so much bargain food on hand home cooking might become obsolete—they need only to shop for the raw ingredients at any one of the many food markets scattered across the city. Clothing, sprays of fragrant flowers, fancy trinkets, practical kitchenwares, and food in every guise make up the merchandise at most major centers. My favorite is the Chinatown Complex at the corner of Trengganu and Smith streets in Chinatown. Most interesting sight? The table stacked with quivering, shimmering piles of tofu in every imaginable shape, texture, and style.

The quest for food never stops. Booklets, brochures, magazines, and the monthly *Food Paper* feature current food stories; reviews of what's hot, what's not; and articles to educate Singaporeans about their own culinary roots. Although streams of outsiders have inundated tiny Singapore during its colorful past, those who have settled—the Malays, the Straits Chinese *(nyonyas),* the English, the Indians, and mainland Chinese—have each contributed to the local kitchen. Favorite flavors come from such staples as coconut milk, lemongrass, chilies, shrimp paste, and more chilies. A true Singaporean meal might include a platter of chili crabs, a bowl of Hainanese chicken soup, a scoop of fried noodles, an Indian *murtabagh* (flat bread with curried stuffing), *po piahs,* fish head curry, and *satay.*

Ah yes, the *satays*. Arguably the best *satays* are grilled at the Satay Club—not a club at all, but a shrinking collection of outdoor food vendors. The bosses have hired their own men to fan the blazing cookfires—and probably themselves, as they sweat by the crackling heat—while they grill handfuls and handfuls of skewered chicken, beef, prawn, and mutton *satays*. Tourists and locals start to congregate at dusk and go from stand to stand to select their evening meal, which will undoubtedly include dozens of *satays* served with a fiery-sweet peanut sauce. If Singaporeans could claim no other barbecuing success—and few native dishes are grilled—they can boast about their *satays*. Of course, Singaporeans do grill other foods, but more as a lure for the foreigners who want a Korean barbecue, Malaysian-style grilled chicken, Chinese roast duck, or freshly grilled king prawns at Newton Circus Food Center.

Singapore's leading food lady and editor of the monthly *Food Paper,* Violet Oon, summarizes her country's food by calling the local cuisine more "an attitude, a state of mind." Exposed from birth to multiethnic cooking, Singaporeans take for granted that they may breakfast on Chinese congee, lunch on English lamb cutlets, snack on Malay rice flour cakes, and dine on Indian curries. That's if they stick only to the foods of their own home base. But the world of food is theirs for the sampling, and, as Ms. Oon concludes: "Everyone is used to culinary excitement. I used to say that union problems in any factory [in Singapore] always revolved around the canteen food. You can have thirty varieties [of food] for tea . . . But if you try to feed them like an American canteen—sandwiches and hamburgers—they will go on strike."

As you can see, food is on everyone's mind in Singapore.

Grilled Whole Sea Bass in Turmeric Marinade

1 whole sea bass, 2 to 2½ pounds, cleaned and scaled, head and tail intact
Banana leaves or foil for wrapping
Vegetable oil for brushing
Marinade
3 tablespoons onion paste
2 tablespoons chili paste
5 teaspoons garlic paste
2 tablespoons ground turmeric
2 stalks lemongrass, thinly sliced
3 lime leaves
¼ cup tamarind juice
Salt and sugar to taste
2 tablespoons vegetable oil
Chili-Lime Dipping Sauce
2½ cups fish sauce
1 cup fresh lime juice
1 cup water
½ cup sugar
2½ tablespoons minced garlic
1½ cups fresh coriander leaves, packed
¾ cup chopped green chilies

Besides bass, you can use any other fatty fish, such as garoupa (grouper) or snapper. Or you may use an equivalent amount of squid, skewered either whole or cut into circles. (Recipe: Chef Jimmy Lim, Hyatt Regency Singapore)

1
Put the fish in a shallow baking dish. Combine all the marinade ingredients in the container of a food processor or blender and puree. Pour the marinade over the fish, turning the fish so that both sides are fully covered. Cover with foil or plastic wrap and set aside for 30 minutes.

2
Meanwhile, combine all the ingredients for the chili-lime dip in the container of a food processor or blender and puree. Pour into a serving container and set aside until ready to eat.

3
If you are using banana leaves, soften them according to the directions in the Glossary. Put the fish in the center of the leaf and fold the leaf over to cover the fish. You may need to use several leaves to be sure the fish is covered. Secure both ends with toothpicks. If using foil, crimp the ends closed. Brush the banana-leaf package with oil, if desired.

4
Grill the fish by the direct method (page xxix) over medium-hot coals for 10 to 15 minutes. Remove from the fire and unwrap the fish. Serve immediately with the chili-lime dipping sauce.

Singaporean Shrimp Satay

1 pound large raw shrimp, shelled
   and deveined
Bamboo skewers

Marinade
2 large shallots, peeled and
   chopped
12 cloves garlic, peeled and
   chopped
One 2-inch piece fresh ginger
1 stalk lemongrass, thinly sliced
1 cup sugar
1 teaspoon salt

Peanut Sauce
1 pound roasted salted peanuts
⅔ cup vegetable oil
2½ tablespoons minced garlic
One 1-inch piece fresh ginger,
   minced
2½ tablespoons minced shallots
1 stalk lemongrass, thinly sliced
5 tablespoons shrimp paste
2 tablespoons chili paste
2 tablespoons ground turmeric
Tamarind juice from 1 tablespoon
   tamarind paste stirred into ½ cup
   water
Sugar and salt to taste

As with most satays—which are addictive—one skewer per person will certainly not be enough, so you may want to double, even triple, this recipe. Serve this with peanut sauce and sliced onions and cucumbers. The sauce recipe should give you enough for plenty of leftovers, and leftovers will freeze well in an airtight container. Experiment with the sauce to find what proportions of ingredients and thickness you like. (Recipe: Chef Jimmy Lim, Hyatt Regency Singapore)

1
Put the shrimp into a large baking dish. Combine all the marinade ingredients in the container of a food processor or blender and puree. You may need to add some water to help process. Pour the marinade over the shrimp. Cover the baking dish with foil or plastic wrap and refrigerate for at least 6 hours.

2
Put the peanuts in the container of a food processor or blender and process quickly. Avoid overprocessing or the peanuts will turn into peanut butter. Heat the oil in a skillet and fry the garlic, ginger, shallots, and lemongrass for 5 minutes. Add the shrimp paste, chili paste, and ground turmeric. Stir thoroughly. Add the peanuts, tamarind juice, sugar, and salt. This is a very thick mixture—you may need to dilute it with water. Simmer the mixture uncovered for about 1 hour. Serve the sauce hot.

3
While the sauce simmers, thread the shrimp on skewers, and grill by direct method, page xxix, over medium-hot coals for about 7 minutes, turning at least once. Remove from the fire. Serve the *satay* with rice cakes (see recipe for *lontong,* Compressed Rice, page 147) and the hot peanut sauce. You may also pass around sliced onions and cucumbers.

Prawn Otak Otak in Banana Leaf

2¼ pounds mackerel fillets

3 tablespoons chopped fresh or
   frozen turmeric root

6½ teaspoons finely minced garlic

4 tablespoons finely minced shallots

6 tablespoons finely minced
   lemongrass

4 tablespoons crushed candlenuts or
   macadamia nuts

2 tablespoons chili paste

2¼ cups thick coconut milk

2 tablespoons salt, or to taste

Pinch MSG, optional

¼ cup sugar

½ pound raw small or minced large
   shrimp

Banana leaves or foil for wrapping,
   80 pieces cut into 8-inch x 4-inch
   strips

This fish puree is wrapped in a leaf before grilling and is popular with both Malaysians and Singaporeans. The original recipe for this version calls for wrapping the mixture in coconut leaves, but I have substituted banana leaves or foil. The chef notes that the flavor will not be the same if you use foil. These quantities should yield about 40 pieces. This is a somewhat tedious recipe to prepare since you must fill and fold innumerable packets with a piping of fish paste, but it is certain to be a conversation stopper at any gathering. (Recipe: Chef Jimmy Lim, Hyatt Regency Singapore)

1

Put the fish on a chopping board, and with a sharp clever, mince the meat finely. Set aside.

2

Put the turmeric, garlic, shallots, lemongrass, and candlenuts or macadamia nuts into the container of a food processor or blender and puree. Add the minced fish and chili paste and puree. Do not overprocess—this should have some texture.

3

Transfer the mixture to a large mixing bowl. Slowly stir in the coconut milk, salt, MSG, and sugar. Stir in the minced shrimp.

4

If you are using banana leaves, soften them according to the directions in the Glossary. Lay two pieces on top of each other to make a layer. Spoon 2 tablespoons of filling mixture into the center of the wrapper. Fold the wrapper from each side to the center—this covers the filling. Secure the ends by sealing them closed with toothpicks. If using foil, crimp the ends. Repeat this process until all the paste is used up. Brush the banana-leaf packets with oil, if desired.

5

Grill the packets by the direct method (page xxix) over medium-hot coals for 10 minutes, turning them once. Remove from the fire and serve immediately. Let your guests unwrap the packets.

THE ACCOMPANIMENTS

Singaporean Spring Rolls

Vegetable oil for frying
1 teaspoon minced garlic
½ pound total of the following:
  ground pork, minced shrimp, and
  cleaned crab meat
2 cups shredded jicama
6 cabbage leaves, shredded
1 carrot, shredded
2 tablespoons minced shallots
¼ cup crushed tofu
1 tablespoon soy sauce
1 egg, made into a flat omelet and
  shredded (see Pork Noodle Soup,
  step 2, page 198)
1 package 8-inch square spring roll
  wrappers (see Note)

Sweet and Sour Dipping Sauce

1 cup tomato ketchup
¼ cup rice vinegar
¼ cup water
1 whole red chili, minced
Juice of ½ lemon
2 cloves garlic, peeled and minced
¼ cup sugar
½ teaspoon salt
1 tablespoon cornstarch

Almost every Asian country has its version of these popular snacks—with almost as many variations of the dipping sauce. For a crispier spring roll, use the leaves from the round Western cabbage because they contain less water so produce less juice during cooking. Makes 24 rolls. (Recipe: Chef Jimmy Lim, Hyatt Regency Singapore)

1

Heat the oil in a skillet and fry the minced garlic until fragrant and golden, then add the pork, shrimp, and crab meat. Add the shredded jicama and fry until tender. Add the cabbage, carrot, shallots, tofu, and soy sauce and cook for about 2 minutes. Set aside.

2

Combine the ingredients for the sweet and sour dipping sauce and set aside.

3

Transfer the cooked filling mixture to a large mixing bowl. Stir in the shredded egg, then place 1 spring roll wrapper on a clean surface. Scoop 1 tablespoon of filling mixture onto one end of the wrapper and fold the wrapper toward the other end, tucking the sides in tightly as you fold. Repeat until all the mixture has been used.

4

Pour about 1 cup of oil into a heavy skillet and heat. Add the rolls, 2 or 3 at a time, and fry until they are brown and crispy on both sides. You may have to add extra oil as you continue to fry the rolls. Serve with the sweet and sour dipping sauce.

Note:

Square spring roll wrappers are available fresh or frozen at most Asian markets. If you buy frozen, thaw before separating them. Follow the manufacturer's directions for folding. Seal by wetting the edges with water.

Prawn Mee Soup

2 quarts water
1 pound raw prawns in their shells
2 tablespoons vegetable oil
6 cloves garlic, peeled and minced
One 2-inch piece fresh ginger
4 shallots, peeled and minced
1 stalk lemongrass, thinly sliced
2 tablespoons rock sugar
2 tablespoons fish sauce
3 tablespoons soy sauce
Freshly ground black pepper to
    taste
1 pound dried or fresh egg noodles,
    preferably Chinese
1 bunch watercress
⅓ pound bean sprouts

This dish leaves a lingering hint of citrus along with the more assertive flavor of the shrimp and is almost substantial enough to serve as a light main course for luncheon. (Recipe: Chef Jimmy Lim, Hyatt Regency Singapore)

1

Bring the water to a boil and cook the prawns for 3 to 4 minutes. Strain the prawns, reserving the cooking liquid for later use. When the prawns are cool enough to handle, peel off the shells.

2

Put the shells in a large skillet. Add the oil and sauté the prawn shells until they are browned. Add the garlic, ginger, shallots, lemongrass, sugar, and fish sauce, stirring to combine well. Add the reserved water and boil uncovered for about 30 minutes. Add the soy sauce and pepper.

3

Meanwhile, cook and drain the noodles according to package directions and set aside.

4

Just before serving, use tongs to lift the prawn shells out of the stock. Discard the shells. To serve the soup, combine the watercress and bean sprouts with the noodles in a large soup tureen and cover with the shrimp stock. The heat from the stock will "cook" the vegetables just enough to soften them. Garnish with the cooked prawns.

Singaporean Laksa

1 stalk lemongrass, thinly sliced
2 teaspoons ground turmeric
4 dried chilies
1 tablespoon to ½ cup dried shrimp,
   according to taste
2 shallots, peeled and chopped
4 cloves garlic, peeled and minced
1 teaspoon shrimp paste (optional)
Salt, pepper, and sugar to taste
1 quart water
¼ cup vegetable oil
1 quart coconut milk
½ pound thick rice vermicelli, dried
   and soaked in hot water to soften,
   or fresh, cooked according to
   package directions
¼ pound bean sprouts

Garnish

6 small squares dried tofu (see Note)
30 fish balls, cooked (see Note)
1 pound large shrimp, cooked,
   cleaned, and peeled

The Singaporean version of this noodle-and-seafood soup is made with a coconut milk base, unlike the Malaysian version, which is usually made of a clear broth seasoned with lemongrass. For the best flavor, be sure your coconut milk is not too thick. (Recipe: Chef Jimmy Lim, Hyatt Regency Singapore)

1

Combine the lemongrass, turmeric, chilies, dried shrimp, shallots, garlic, shrimp paste, seasonings, and ½ cup of the water in the container of a food processor or blender, and process to make a chunky paste.

2

Heat the oil in a wok or skillet and sauté the lemongrass mixture to bring out the flavors, about 10 minutes. Transfer the mixture to a large saucepan, add the coconut milk and remaining water and simmer uncovered for 2 hours.

3

Half an hour before serving, soak the noodles or cook the noodles in boiling water according to package directions and drain. Just before serving, add the bean sprouts to the soup to soften them. To serve, place generous portions of the noodles in individual serving bowls. Then top with the hot soup mixture. Garnish with tofu, fish balls, and shrimp.

Note:

Dried tofu used as a garnish acts like a sponge to soak up any excess oil on the surface of the soup. Fish balls are available fresh or frozen at Asian markets. These should be simmered in water until they float to the surface.

Chili Crabs

4 to 4½ pounds live crabs, about 18
   Maryland blue crabs
1 cup vegetable oil
6 tablespoons minced garlic
1¼ cups diced onions
¾ cup chili sauce (see Note)
¾ cup tomato ketchup
¼ cup soy sauce
Pinch MSG (optional)
Salt and freshly ground pepper to
   taste
1 cup chopped fresh coriander for
   garnish

This is one of Singapore's best dishes. In Singapore, the most enjoyable way to eat these messy crabs is at a hawker's stand where nobody minds how many shells drop to the ground or how covered with drippings you get. Live crabs may need to be steamed or boiled for about 1 minute to quiet them and make them easy to handle. A perfect barbecue accompaniment, this should be enjoyed with very cold beer. If you wish to add more fire to the sauce, the chef suggests a dash of powdered chilies. (Recipe: Chef Jimmy Lim, Hyatt Regency Singapore)

1

Peel off the top shells and clean out the gills and innards. Using a large cleaver, cut each crab in half lengthwise and, if desired, cut it into quarters. Set them aside.

2

Heat the oil in a large wok. Deep-fry the crabs for 5 to 10 minutes, or until the crabs turn orange. Remove from the oil and set aside. Add onion and garlic and stir-fry until golden. Add the chili sauce, ketchup, soy sauce, and salt and pepper and stir-fry for 2 to 3 minutes.

3

Put the crab pieces back into the wok and toss crabs and sauce together. If the sauce is too thick, add some stock or water to thin it. When the crabs are heated through, scoop crabs and sauce from wok onto a large serving platter and garnish with coriander. Serve immediately.

Note:

An Asian market may offer a bewildering number of chili sauces. For this recipe, select a Malaysian or Singaporean brand that is described as both hot and sweet. You can always add sliced chilies to make it hotter. Store leftover chili sauce in the refrigerator.

Fried Carrot Cake

4 cups water
2 cups rice flour
1 heaping tablespoon sago flour
   (see Note)
1 teaspoon sugar
½ teaspoon salt
2 tablespoons vegetable oil
1 cup shredded daikon

Garnish
3 tablespoons vegetable oil
2 cloves garlic, peeled and minced
2 large eggs, beaten
6 scallions, trimmed and sliced
2 teaspoons light soy sauce
Freshly ground black pepper to
   taste
4 ounces chopped preserved, salted
   radish (see Note)

This is a curious name for an accompaniment that is not a cake and does not contain carrots. Instead, it contains shredded daikon, which is Japanese radish. According to my Singaporean friend, carrot cake is a popular snack in Singapore and elsewhere. The Thais and Cambodians usually serve it with fresh bean sprouts and ground chilies, a habit the Singaporeans are gradually adopting. (Recipe: Anna Leow)

1

Put a 2-quart glass baking dish on a steamer rack in a large saucepan over boiling water and heat the dish before adding the batter.

2

Put 2 cups of the water in a saucepan and bring to a boil. Mix the remaining 2 cups of water with the flours, sugar, and salt in a bowl. Add the oil and daikon and beat well with a fork until well blended. Pour the boiling water slowly into the flour mixture, stirring to prevent lumps. Immediately pour the flour mixture into the hot pan and continue to stir. If you do not do this for the first few minutes, the flour will become hard and grainy. Cover the saucepan and let the mixture steam until firm, about 15 minutes. When firm, remove from the heat and set aside to cool before slicing into cubes. You can cover and refrigerate the cake overnight, if you wish.

3

To make the garnish, heat the vegetable oil in a frying pan and sauté the garlic until brown. Add the cubed flour mixture and stir-fry for several minutes. Remove from the heat. Make a thin omelet by combining the eggs, scallions, soy sauce, and pepper and cooking this in a single layer in a frying pan until firm. Shred the eggs. Serve the rice cubes hot, and pass the shredded

egg and radish for garnish. You may also serve this with crushed red chili, if you wish.

Note:

If you cannot find sago flour, use tapioca flour instead. You can find the salted radish condiment at most Asian markets.

Fried Spicy Okra

1 tablespoon shrimp paste
3 fresh red chilies
2 tablespoons dried shrimp
2 cloves garlic, peeled
6 tablespoons water
¼ cup vegetable oil
1 pound fresh okra, or two 10½-
  ounce boxes frozen, sliced in half
  lengthwise
Salt and sugar to taste
Pinch MSG (optional)

A Singaporean-nyonya *dish, this spicy okra mixture pairs well with grilled chicken or beef. (Recipe: Anna Leow)*

1

Combine the shrimp paste, chilies, dried shrimp, garlic, and 3 tablespoons of the water in the container of a blender or a spice grinder and puree. Heat a wok or heavy skillet until hot, then add the oil. Fry the shrimp paste mixture in the oil for about 5 minutes, stirring often.

2

Add the okra, salt, sugar, and MSG and stir-fry over high heat for 1 minute. Add the remaining water and simmer the mixture, stirring often, for 5 minutes, or until the okra is soft. Serve immediately.

DESSERTS

Almond Bean Curd with Lychees

2 cups condensed milk
3 cups plus 1 tablespoon water
¾ cup sugar
Dash of almond extract
One 0.9-ounce packet agar-agar
   powder
Two 1-pound, 4-ounce cans lychees
   or longan fruits, drained, for
   garnish

This Chinese dessert is a refreshing custardlike concoction that, despite its name, does not contain bean curd, or tofu. (Recipe: Chef Jimmy Lim, Hyatt Regency Singapore)

1

Put the milk and 3 cups water into a large saucepan and bring to a boil. Add the sugar and almond extract, and stir.

2

Mix the agar-agar powder with the 1 tablespoon water to soften, then stir it into the boiling liquid, mixing well. Remove from the heat and continue stirring for a few minutes as the mixture cools.

3

When it is cool, pour into a serving dish and refrigerate for several hours until chilled. Before serving, cut the pudding into cubes, put the cubes in individual dessert dishes, and garnish with the fruit.

Coconut Pandan Cake

9 egg whites
1 cup superfine sugar
1 teaspoon cream of tartar
8 egg yolks
2 tablespoons corn oil
1 teaspoon vanilla extract
¾ cup self-rising flour
1 teaspoon baking powder
Pinch salt
1 teaspoon pandan extract
2 tablespoons thick coconut milk

Anna Leow created this spongy cake which includes two typical Singaporean ingredients: coconut milk and pandan flavoring. The cake does not need any frosting. (Recipe: Anna Leow)

1
Preheat the oven to 350°.

2
Put the egg whites into a large mixing bowl and beat them until frothy. Gradually stir in ½ cup of the sugar and the cream of tartar. Continue beating the egg whites until very stiff. Set aside.

3
Put the egg yolks, the remaining ½ cup of sugar, the corn oil, and vanilla extract in a mixing bowl and beat well. Gradually stir in the flour, baking powder, and salt until the mixture is smooth. Stir in the pandan extract and coconut milk. Stir the egg yolk mixture into the beaten whites, folding in gently from the bottom of the bowl up to incorporate well.

4
Pour into an ungreased 10-inch round cake tin. Bake in the preheated oven for 50 minutes. Raise the oven temperature to 375° and bake for 10 minutes longer. Remove from the oven and invert the cake pan upside down to cool in the pan. Cool completely before slicing.

Egg and Coconut Jelly

1 to 2 ounces agar-agar
2 quarts water
3 cups sugar
3 large eggs
One 13½-ounce can coconut milk
Few drops food coloring of your
    choice
Drop vanilla extract

A delightful and refreshing dessert that makes 8 to 10 servings. (Recipe: Mahani Mohamad)

1

Mix the agar-agar and water in a large saucepan—these contents should fill the pan about one third to one half of the way to the top. The jelly expands once it is mixed with water. Heat the mixture over medium heat. When it begins to boil, stir in the sugar and continue stirring until the sugar dissolves, or about 5 minutes. Bring the mixture to a boil again.

2

Meanwhile, beat the eggs for 3 to 4 minutes. Slowly stir in the coconut milk and mix well. Slowly pour the egg and coconut milk mixture into the boiling jelly. Stir several times. Add the food coloring and vanilla and continue to stir. Bring the mixture to a boil again.

3

Once it boils, the egg and coconut milk mixture will float to the top. Taste for sweetness and add more sugar, if desired.

4

Remove from the heat and pour the hot mixture into a 10-inch x 15-inch (or larger) baking pan and refrigerate until chilled. The final product will have 2 layers: a top egg-coconut layer and a bottom clear-jelly layer. Slice and serve.

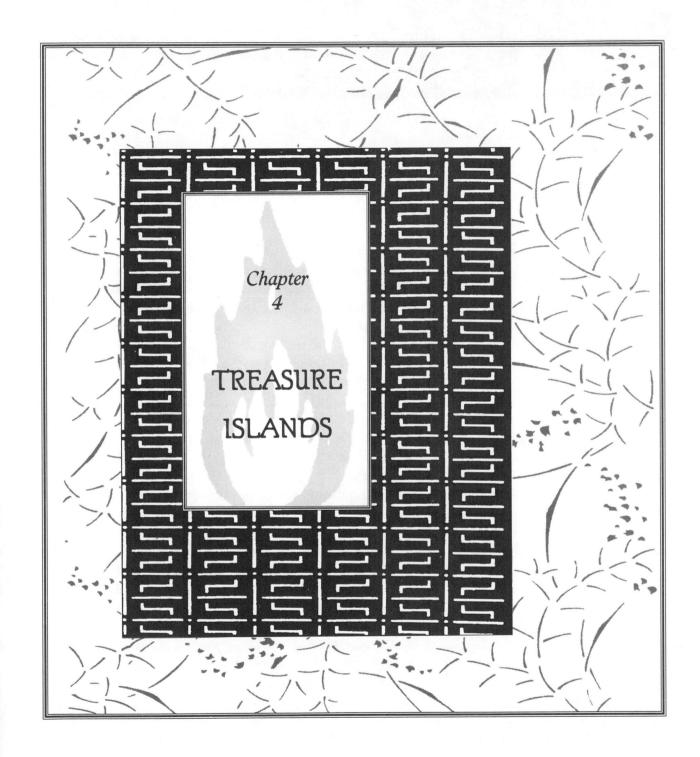

Chapter
4

TREASURE

ISLANDS

TO VISIT THE ISLAND OF BALI IS NOT TO KNOW INDONESIA. IT IS NOT
even to know Bali. Even if you get past the stone walls that protect the villagers from evil
spirits and strangers, you are not Balinese and may never understand the local mind and
soul. The lure of this verdant and sculptured paradise draws planeloads of visitors in
search of some sort of tropical nirvana. But in their motorized island crisscrossing, tourists
often shatter the calm of this still enchanting, still enchanted place. And in their wake,
they leave an island and people with one foot in antiquity and the other in the twenty-first
century. Can Bali survive television and Colonel Sanders? One Westerner I talked to, Chef
Hubert Lorenz, then at the Bali Hyatt, was hopeful, though he talked about a modern
blight—street litter—that puts the island's changes in a certain perspective: In the past,
the Balinese used banana leaves and coconut shells for wrapping or carrying foods. When
discarded, these decomposed in time and disappeared. Today, the Balinese often use
plastic and Styrofoam, which may last forever.

No matter which Indonesian destination travel agents offer, many Western tourists
still define Indonesia as Bali. Yet the two are fundamentally different and the difference is
basic: religion. Unlike most other Indonesians, who are Muslims, the Balinese are very
serious Hindus and their beliefs permeate every aspect of their life and calendar. Ancient
festivals, stone temples, and fantastic statuary to Hindu deities are all stitched into the
seams of daily Balinese life. Where else, for example, might one find a temple deity
guarding a food market, as does goddess Rambut Suddana with her fragrant floral offerings in Denpasar's central square? Where else, in fact, would you find a food market quite
like this one?

Tourists often pass up this extraordinary open bazaar in the island's capital in favor
of more glamorous destinations. But the market offers a candid view of the real Balinese
and of their food: Ancient women in traditional sarong *kabayas* and young girls with short
skirts and plastic sandals crowd in everywhere to sell dark green, orange, and crimson
chilies; live chickens bound together by their legs; dusky spices ground to fire, to accent,

or to sweeten; just-picked fruits exotic to the Western eye; baskets of wriggly fresh fish and shellfish, and silvery dried fish, speckled white with salt; thousands of green, brown, and white eggs; bottles of jewel-toned fresh fruit juices; and chunks of brown sugar and pressed sea salt. All this is set against a backdrop of nonstop bargaining; the skronking of caged animals; and the whoosh of foods being chopped, blended, sizzled, or wrapped in banana leaves. And that's only the first of three floors of merchandise. Because few tourists will ever be invited to a Balinese village home to eat a native meal of grilled fish *sates* (the Indonesian spelling of *satay*) or spicy pork stew cooked in coconut milk, they need to seek out the restaurants that offer traditional meals not stripped of island flavor and fire.

This three-story market seems very Balinese, but other Indonesian cooks also rely on these same ingredients. A generic Indonesian pantry is stocked with candlenuts and lemongrass, nutmeg and papayas, taro and torch ginger, chili *sambals* and sweet soy sauce, to name just a few. Indonesian Sri Owen, in her famous cookbook *Indonesian Food and Cookery,* devotes fifty-one pages to describing the country's staples. That suggests that any Indonesian meal is a series of complex flavors and textures.

But what is a typical Indonesian meal? It is a shared experience of many dishes, which at dinner might start with several sticks of *sate,* and include occasionally a soup, then two or three or four (maybe even twenty) meat, seafood, and vegetable dishes, condiments, and fruit or a fruit-based dessert. The central point of any meal is always rice: white rice or red rice or black rice. Long-grain rice or glutinous rice. Steamed rice, boiled rice, or fried rice. Or boiled and then steamed rice. Indonesians have a love affair with rice and they work with it in magical ways, transforming it from plain to elegant. The inventive Balinese, for example, enjoy a simple Black Rice Pudding (see recipe, page 151) with a sweet, subtle flavor that could stand up proudly against the most daring of French pastries. Rice is so important to Indonesians that many islanders have even deified the grain, treating it with reverence lest they offend the rice grains and cause them not to grow properly. That a rice-based recipe—*nasi goreng,* or fried rice—is the closest thing to a national dish is not surprising. Yet everywhere I ordered it, I got a slightly different taste and collection of garnishings, and given the islands' diversity, that is not surprising either.

Dishes and flavors vary dramatically because the cuisine is not defined by a stack of national recipes. Instead, it belongs to the cooks of the 13,000-plus islands that comprise the nation, making this a regional cuisine linked by certain common dishes and common ingredients. For example, no matter where you eat, coconut oil or coconut milk would

probably be folded in somewhere. Few Indonesian meals would be complete without a shot of fire from one of the varieties of local chilies, inserted in the recipe or served as a *sambal* (relish) on the side. Indonesians love chilies as much as they do rice, and apparently consume them by the gross. A color photo in Chef Detlef Skrobanek's book, *The New Art of Indonesian Cooking,* captures this chili obsession: A portly vendor in a local market sits by her supply of red chilies, mounded in a three-foot tangle at her side.

Indonesian ingredients taste oddly familiar if you have eaten in Thailand or Malaysia. Yet one element sets Indonesian cooking apart: the spicing—luxurious blends that may include cinnamon, cloves, cardamom, and nutmeg—that an Indonesian cook uses to shade and smooth flavors. Indonesia was, after all, in an earlier incarnation of the fabled East Indies, the Spice Islands, which generated centuries of pirate raids and plunder.

Despite the availability for city dwellers of a few modern gadgets and conveniences, Indonesian cooking looks as if it is still very much rooted in village life. Few Indonesian cooks function without a mortar and pestle, a coconut grater, and a charcoal stove. In fact, in many Indonesian kitchens, everything is cooked—if not grilled—over charcoal. In the villages, says Chef Skrobanek, coconut husks are popular fuel because they burn hot and retain their heat. Indonesian grilling starts with *sates,* and goes on to fish wrapped in banana leaves, prawns on bamboo skewers, suckling pigs, cuts of lamb, and fowl. Perhaps Indonesian grilling reaches its zenith with its *sates,* however, as these are certainly among the most unusual skewered foods in the world. Their appeal does not particularly come from the marinades—as these are often very bland—but from the rich accompanying sauces, which may be thickened with peanuts, rice, tapioca root, or sweet potatoes. The appeal also comes from the choice of ingredients to skewer, which run the gamut from chicken and goat intestines, beef tongue, and unhatched chicken eggs, to the more familiar (at least, to Westerners) meats, seafood, and fowl.

Westerners who skirt the rest of Indonesia in favor of a trip to Bali will never get to savor and enjoy the full range of Indonesian cooking. And that would be a pity because, as Chef Skrobanek points out, "We have so much beautiful food here."

THE·GRILLS

Lamb Sate

2 pounds boneless leg of lamb, cut into 1-inch cubes
Bamboo skewers
Fried sliced shallots for garnish (see Glossary)

Marinade
½ cup sweet soy sauce
2 tablespoons soy sauce
½ teaspoon ground white pepper
½ teaspoon ground cumin
Salt to taste
3 cloves garlic, peeled
One 1-inch piece fresh ginger, peeled and grated

Dipping Sauce
6 cloves garlic, peeled and mashed
1 green chili, thinly sliced and seeds removed
¾ cup roasted peanuts
¼ cup boiling water
Juice of ½ lemon
Sweet soy sauce to thin mixture

(Recipe: Chefs Hubert Lorenz and Nenjah Sujartha, Bali Hyatt)

1
Place the lamb in a shallow baking dish. Combine the marinade ingredients in the container of a food processor or blender and puree. Pour the mixture over the lamb. Cover the dish with foil or plastic wrap and set aside for 1 hour.

2
Meanwhile, make the dipping sauce by combining the garlic, chili, peanuts, water, and lemon juice in the container of a food processor or blender and pureeing. Thin with a bit of sweet soy sauce if necessary. Pour the sauce into a small serving dish.

3
Thread 4 pieces of lamb onto a bamboo skewer. Repeat this process until all the meat is skewered. Grill the lamb by the direct method (page xxix) over medium-hot coals for 7 to 10 minutes, turning once to brown the meat evenly. Remove from the fire and serve immediately with the sauce and fried shallots.

West Sumatran Sate

8 to 10 pounds beef, including
   tongue, heart, and meat
1½ tablespoons vegetable oil
Bamboo skewers
Fried shallots for garnish (see
   Glossary)

Seasoning Mixture
1½ shallots, peeled
¾ tablespoon grated fresh turmeric
   root or ground turmeric
One 1-inch piece ginger
One 1-inch piece galangal
6 to 7 cloves garlic, peeled
6 to 10 fresh red chilies
½ tablespoon coriander seeds
Freshly ground black pepper to
   taste
1 stalk lemongrass
¼ tablespoon cuminseed
1 teaspoon MSG (optional)
Salt to taste
3 Indonesian or other Oriental bay
   leaves, thinly sliced
½ turmeric leaf, thinly sliced
   (optional)
2 lime leaves, thinly sliced

This is a Padang-style sate *that uses less familiar cuts of beef, such as tongue and heart, as well as the meat itself. And it is always served for special celebrations, such as the end of Ramadan. Serve this* sate *with* lontong *(rice cubes, see Compressed Rice, page 147); steamed rice; pickles; and a simple salad of sliced onions, grated carrots, and sliced green peppers dressed with vinegar, salt, and sugar. Unlike other* sates, *the meat is boiled first before grilling to give it flavor. And unlike the familiar peanut dipping sauces, this sauce is made with ground rice and coconut milk. The cooks who showed me this dish say they prepare it by instinct and without using strict measurements. They insist that grinding the ingredients together with a white stone mortar and pestle is important, but failing that, you can use a food processor. They also say that turmeric leaf provides an important flavor and that there is no substitute. Turmeric leaves are not readily available in the United States, however, so they are optional in this recipe. This recipe serves about 10. (Recipe: Rachmi and Rasuna Musa)*

1
Combine the seasoning mixture ingredients, except the leaves, in the container of a food processor or blender and puree. You may need to add some oil or water to help process. Stir in the leaves.

2
Put the tongue, hearts, and meat into a large stockpot with water to cover and 1 tablespoon of seasoning mixture and bring to a boil. Lower the heat and simmer for about 1 hour, or until the meat is medium well done. Drain the meat, reserving the cooking water. Cool the meat and cut it into ¾-inch cubes. Remove the skin from the beef hearts.

Dipping Sauce

1 cup raw long-grain rice, soaked in
    water to cover for 3 hours
1 cup coconut milk
¼ cup vegetable oil
½ turmeric leaf, thinly sliced
    (optional)
1 Indonesian bay leaf, thinly sliced
2 lime leaves, thinly sliced

3

Combine ¾ tablespoon of the seasoning mixture with the 1½ tablespoons vegetable oil and rub this mixture over the beef. Thread the beef on skewers and set aside.

4

To make the dipping sauce, drain the rice and put it into the container of a food processor or blender with the coconut milk and puree. Combine the remaining seasoning mixture with the ¼ cup vegetable oil in a saucepan and heat until fragrant, or about 20 to 30 minutes. Pour the rice mixture into this and slowly add the water from cooking the meat. Add the turmeric, bay, and lime leaves. Keep stirring the rice and adding water until the consistency of the sauce is thin but not soupy. Set aside.

5

Grill the meat by the direct method (page xxix) over hot coals for 3 to 4 minutes, basting with any meat drippings. Transfer to a serving platter, garnish with the fried shallots, and pass the sauce separately.

Sweet Beef Sate

1½ pounds sirloin or flank steak, cut
     into ½-inch x 1-inch x 2-inch cubes
Bamboo skewers
1 tablespoon sweet soy sauce
1 tablespoon margarine
Seasoning Paste
5 red chilies
5 tablespoons fried shallots (see
     Glossary)
5 cloves garlic, peeled
½ teaspoon whole peppercorns
½ teaspoon coriander seeds
5 fennel seeds
8 candlenuts or macadamia nuts
One 1-inch piece fresh turmeric, or
     1 tablespoon ground
One 1-inch piece galangal
½ stalk lemongrass, white part only
Salt to taste
Pinch sugar
3 tablespoons vegetable oil, plus
     extra for processing paste if
     needed

(Recipe: Indonesian Dishes and Desserts, *Gaya Favorit Press)*

1
Combine the seasoning paste ingredients except the oil in the container of a food processor or blender and puree. You may need to add some oil to help process.

2
Pour the 3 tablespoons of oil into a skillet and heat. Fry the seasoning paste until fragrant, about 10 minutes. Remove from the heat and set aside.

3
Put the meat into a shallow baking dish and add the seasoning paste, stirring to coat the meat well. Thread the meat on the skewers, about 3 to 4 pieces per skewer. Mix the seasoning paste remaining in the pan with the soy sauce and margarine to make a basting sauce.

4
Grill the beef by the direct method (page xxix) over medium-hot coals for 8 to 10 minutes, turning several times and brushing the meat often with the basting sauce. Remove from the fire and serve immediately.

Ground Meat Sate

2 pounds lean ground beef
5 tablespoons minced shallots
Salt and freshly ground black
   pepper to taste
Bamboo skewers
Basting Sauce
1 tablespoon vegetable oil
4 shallots, peeled and minced
6 cloves garlic, peeled and minced
1 cup coconut milk
Salt and freshly ground black
   pepper to taste
1 teaspoon cornstarch
2 tablespoons sweet bean paste

(Recipe: Sahid Jaya Hotel & Tower, adapted)

1

Mix the meat with the shallots, salt, and pepper. Pinch off 2 tablespoons of meat and shape into a small flattened ball. Repeat until all the meat is formed. Thread the meat onto bamboo skewers, 2 or 3 balls per skewer, and set aside.

2

Make the basting sauce by heating the oil in a heavy skillet and frying the shallots and garlic for about 5 minutes. Add the coconut milk and salt and pepper. Transfer ¼ cup of liquid to a small mixing bowl and add the cornstarch, stirring well to make a thick paste. Pour this mixture back into the skillet and stir it in well. Continue cooking and stirring over medium heat until the mixture thickens. Stir in the sweet bean paste.

3

Grill the *sates* by the direct method (page xxix) over medium-hot coals for about 10 minutes, brushing them liberally and often with the basting sauce. Remove from the fire and serve immediately.

Grilled Balinese Duck

1 teaspoon tamarind paste mixed
  with 1 tablespoon water
Salt to taste
One 4- to 5-pound duck, as lean as
  possible
Banana leaves or foil for wrapping
Seasoning Mixture
6 large shallots, peeled and
  quartered
2 tablespoons crushed candlenuts or
  macadamia nuts
3 tablespoons minced fresh ginger,
  peeled
1½ ounces galangal
1 tablespoon ground turmeric
2 tablespoons minced fresh chilies,
  seeds removed
¼ teaspoon freshly ground black
  pepper
1 tablespoon shrimp paste
3 bay leaves
½ teaspoon ground nutmeg
Salt to taste
1 cup vegetable oil

There are at least two versions of this dish: One calls for using a whole duck, the other for using a quartered duck and boiling it in a seasoning mixture before grilling. For this recipe, use a whole duck wrapped in banana leaves. Its cooking is a lengthy process, so start very early in the day. The chefs call for using two different varieties of galangal—the greater and the lesser galangals, known as laos *and* kencur, *respectively. You will probably find only greater galangal at your local Asian grocers and it will probably be frozen. The chefs recommend cooking the duck in a low fire of rice chaff and coconut husks, or smoking it—but slow-cooking it by the indirect method produces delectable results. When the cooked duck is finally unwrapped, the intermingled fragrance of seasonings and banana leaves is remarkable, and the duck is butter tender. This recipe may serve only 2 people, it is that good. (Recipe: Chefs Hubert Lorenz and Nenjah Sujartha, Bali Hyatt)*

1
Combine the tamarind mixture with salt to taste and rub the duck with this mixture. Put the duck in a large baking pan. Cover it with aluminum foil or plastic wrap and set aside for 2 hours.

2
Combine all the seasoning mixture ingredients except the oil in the container of a food processor or blender and puree. You may need to use some of the oil to help process. Sauté the seasoning mixture in the oil for at least 10 to 15 minutes, or until fragrant. Stuff the cavity with the mixture and skewer or stitch the cavity closed.

3
If you are using banana leaves, soften them according to the directions in the Glossary. Put the duck in the center

of a leaf and wrap to cover with several layers of leaves. Secure snugly with twine. If using foil, crimp the ends closed.

4

Grill the duck by the indirect method (page xxix) over warm—not hot—coals, for a total of 8 to 10 hours. You may have to replenish the fire as needed. Remove the duck from the fire and place on a large serving platter. Unwrap and serve immediately.

Grilled Rack of Lamb

One 1¼-pound rack of lamb
Seasoning Mixture
1 teaspoon ground nutmeg
1 clove garlic, peeled
1 teaspoon chopped shallots
½ tablespoon minced fresh ginger
1 tablespoon diced lemongrass
½ tablespoon ground turmeric
Salt and freshly ground black
   pepper to taste
1 cup vegetable oil

This recipe serves 2. (Recipe: Chef Detlef Greiert, Jakarta Hilton International)

1

Clean the rack and put it in a large baking dish.

2

Combine all the seasoning mixture ingredients except the oil in the container of a food processor or blender and puree. You may need to use some of the oil to help process them. Spoon the puree into a mixing bowl and add the oil, stirring well to combine thoroughly. Spread the mixture over the lamb and marinate for at least 30 minutes.

3

Prior to grilling, wrap the exposed rib ends in aluminum foil to prevent burning. Grill the lamb by the indirect method (page xxix) over hot coals for about 30 minutes. If you like well-done lamb, you may need to cook it another 10 to 20 minutes. Remove the rack from the fire and serve immediately.

Grilled Game Hens

2 Cornish game hens, about 1 pound
   each

Seasoning Rub

3 tablespoons butter
2 teaspoons salt
2 teaspoons garlic powder
2 teaspoons onion powder

Marinade

½ to 1 cup coconut milk
1 to 2 stalks lemongrass
1 to 2 lime leaves
3 to 4 fresh red chilies
¼ teaspoon ground turmeric
1 large onion, peeled and quartered
1 to 3 cloves garlic, peeled
One 1-inch piece fresh ginger
½ teaspoon ground coriander
2 candlenuts or macadamia nuts

This recipe serves 4. (Recipe: Mrs. Soetjepto, Sabang Restaurant)

1

Split the hens in half lengthwise. Combine the seasoning mix and rub on the hens. Grill the hens by the direct method (page xxix) over medium-hot coals for 20 minutes, turning several times to cook evenly. Remove from the fire and place in a shallow baking dish.

2

Meanwhile, prepare the marinade by combining the ingredients in the container of a food processor or blender and processing them until smooth. Pour the marinade mixture over the hens. Cover the baking dish with foil or plastic wrap and refrigerate the hens for at least 7 hours.

3

One hour before the second grilling, remove the hens from the refrigerator and bring them to room temperature. Twenty minutes before serving, grill the hens by the direct method over medium-hot coals for about 15 minutes, basting them with the marinade. Turn them at least once to brown and crisp both sides. Remove from the fire and serve immediately.

Grilled Suckling Pig

One 12- to 15-pound suckling pig

Stuffing Mixture

1¼ cups ground turmeric

11 large green chilies, rinsed, stems removed

⅔ pound galangal, cut into chunks

1¼ cups minced fresh ginger

3 large heads garlic, sectioned and peeled

2 cups chopped shallots

¼ cup tamarind paste mixed with ½ cup water

1¼ cups sliced lemongrass

5 Indonesian bay leaves

5 tablespoons coriander seeds

¼ cup shrimp paste

Freshly ground black pepper to taste

2 teaspoons freshly grated nutmeg

Coating

½ cup plus 2 tablespoons ground turmeric

5 tablespoons salt

¼ to ½ cup vegetable oil

Because the Balinese are Hindu and not Muslim, they are allowed to eat pork, and a suckling pig often figures prominently in a celebratory meal. This fabulous dish has served as the centerpiece of the Tandjung Sari Hotel's Saturday night Balinese feast, with island dancers performing during the meal. One chef says it should always be cooked in a pit, but you can also spit-roast it or cook it in a large covered barbecue. This recipe serves 8 to 10. (Recipe: Mrs. Tatie Wawo-Runtu, Tandjung Sari Hotel)

1

Puree all the ingredients for the stuffing mixture in the container of a food processor—the quantity may be too large for the container of a blender, and you may have to do this in stages.

2

Spoon the stuffing mixture into the cavity of the pig. Combine the coating ingredients and spread this mixture over the surface of the pig, coating it well.

3

Skewer the pig on a rotisserie, or place it on the rack of a large covered barbecue. Grill the pig by the indirect method (page xxix) over medium-hot coals for several hours, or until cooked through. You may have to replenish the fire as needed. To test for doneness, insert a skewer or sharp knife into the thigh. If the juices run clear, the meat is ready. Remove from the fire and place the pig on a large serving platter. Present the platter to your guests before carving the pig.

Spicy Grilled Chicken

30 to 40 red chilies (or slightly less
    than ½ pound total)
4 large shallots, peeled
12 cloves garlic, peeled
One 4-inch piece fresh ginger
2 teaspoons ground turmeric
1 teaspoon ground cumin
2 tablespoons crushed candlenuts or
    macadamia nuts
1 tablespoon vegetable oil
3 small frying chickens, quartered
2 stalks lemongrass, thinly sliced
4 to 5 lime leaves
3 Indonesian bay leaves
Salt and sugar to taste
2 cups chicken broth

Known as ayam rica-rica, *this is a chicken dish typical of Manado, a part of Indonesia known for its fiery foods. This recipe calls for a total of 30 to 40 chilies the way I weighed them out, and you may want to cut back on that unless you don't mind searing your mouth. It also called for both red chilies and small hot chilies—I just used the red chilies I had on hand. The staff at the hotel suggests using the larger red chilies because they are not as hot. This is certainly one dish for which you must experiment with chili quantities. This chicken may be served either fried or grilled and definitely with plenty of something cooling to drink. (Recipe: Sahid Jaya Hotel & Tower)*

1
Place the chilies, shallots, garlic, ginger, turmeric, cumin, and candlenuts in the container of a food processor or blender and puree. You may need to add some oil to help process. Heat the 1 tablespoon oil in a skillet and add the ground seasonings. Fry for about 10 minutes, or until fragrant and oily.

2
Add the chicken parts with the lemongrass, lime leaves, bay leaves, and the salt and sugar. Add the chicken broth and cook until the chicken is half-cooked, about 10 minutes.

3
Remove the chicken from the broth and grill by the direct method (page xxix) over medium-hot coals for about 15 to 20 minutes, turning once. Brush the chicken with the spiced broth during grilling. Remove from the fire and serve immediately.

Clipped Beef Sate

One ½-inch piece galangal
1 lime leaf
2⅛ cups thin coconut milk
1 pound sirloin or flank steak
1¼ cups thick coconut milk
Bamboo skewers
Seasoning Paste
6 shallots, peeled
3 cloves garlic, peeled
1 teaspoon coriander seeds
10 cuminseed
One ½-inch piece fresh turmeric, or
    about 1 tablespoon ground
Salt to taste
Pinch palm sugar or brown sugar
3 tablespoons vegetable oil

Also known as sate gapit, *this Javanese specialty is customarily served on sticks of bamboo that have been slit down the center so that the bamboo actually clips, or holds, the meat in place. The ends are tied together with twine. For a reasonable facsimile, just use standard bamboo skewers to hold the meat. (Recipe:* Indonesian Dishes and Desserts, *Gaya Favorit Press)*

1

Combine the ingredients of the seasoning paste except the oil in the container of a food processor or blender and puree. You may need to use some of the oil to help process. Heat the remaining oil in a skillet, add the seasoning paste, and fry until the mixture is fragrant, or about 10 minutes. Add the galangal, lime leaf, thin coconut milk, and beef and cook until the beef is tender.

2

Remove the beef and cut it into 2½-inch x 3½-inch x ¼-inch cubes. Pound the meat to flatten the pieces slightly. Put the meat back into the skillet and add the thick coconut milk. Simmer over low heat until all the liquid has evaporated and the oil forms a slick on the surface, about 1 hour.

3

Clip the pieces of beef on the skewers, or thread them on skewers. Grill by the direct method (page xxix) over hot coals for 1 minute on each side. Serve immediately.

Chicken in Bamboo

One 2-pound frying chicken,
   skinned, deboned, and cut into
   1½-inch cubes
1 tablespoon salt, or to taste
Juice of 1 lime
1 or 2 large eggs, well beaten
1 stalk lemongrass, thinly sliced
2 scallions, thinly sliced
1 basil leaf, sliced
1 tablespoon chopped shallots
1 pandan leaf, quartered lengthwise
Bamboo, cleaned
Banana leaves
Seasoning Paste
3 red chilies
8 shallots, peeled
One 1-inch piece fresh turmeric, or
   2 teaspoons ground
One 1-inch piece fresh ginger

From Java, this popular, special-occasion dish is characteristically grilled in bamboo tubes. Many Indonesians use bamboo segments as cooking utensils, and will make a distinction between which varieties of bamboo to use. In Sumatra, for example, the glutinous rice dish cooked in bamboo requires the thin-walled telang variety. Certainly a novelty for the Westerner, cooking with bamboo might be challenging—if you can find the bamboo. Alternatively, you can wrap the chicken mixture in banana-leaf packets, and grill or bake them. (Recipe: The Embassy of the Republic of Indonesia, Washington, D.C.)

1
Put the chicken into a baking dish. Season with salt and lime juice and set aside for 30 minutes. Meanwhile, combine the ingredients for the seasoning paste in the container of a food processor or blender and puree.

2
Combine the chicken with the eggs, lemongrass, scallions, basil, chopped shallots, pandan, and the seasoning paste.

3
Line the interior of the bamboo sections with banana leaves. Fill in the sections with the chicken mixture and seal the ends with folded banana leaves. Continue this process until all the mixture is used up. Grill by the indirect method (page xxix) for 30 minutes, or until cooked. (Alternatively, you can bake it in a 400° oven.) Scoop the chicken out of the bamboo and, if you wish, serve it on banana leaves.

Grilled Tofu in Banana Leaf

1 pound fresh, soft tofu
10 shallots, peeled and sliced
2 large tomatoes, thinly sliced
1 large egg
3 to 4 fresh red chilies, thinly sliced
Pinch MSG (optional)
½ teaspoon each salt and sugar
Banana leaf or foil for wrapping

Although traditionally served as a side dish, you may augment this with more tofu, pieces of fish, and extra vegetables to turn it into a full meal. A native of Jakarta, Douglas Lauw says that this dish has strong Chinese overtones and is an example of real home cooking, an inexpensive peasant food that would never turn up on a restaurant menu. (Recipe: Douglas Lauw)

1

Place the tofu in a mixing bowl and crumble it with your hands. Add the remaining ingredients except the banana leaf and mix together well.

2

If you are using a banana leaf, soften it according to the directions in the Glossary. Cut a square of banana leaf large enough to hold all the ingredients (or make smaller, individual-sized packets) and scoop the tofu into the center. Fold the sides to the center to cover the filling and secure both ends with toothpicks. If using foil, crimp the ends closed.

3

Grill by the direct method (page xxix) over medium-hot coals for 15 minutes, turning once. Remove from the fire and place the packet on a serving plate. Remove the toothpicks and open the folds of the leaf for easy serving. Serve immediately.

Grilled Tuna

2 pounds fresh tuna fillets
Vegetable oil for greasing
Marinade
Juice of 2 limes
Fresh or ground turmeric to taste
1 lime leaf
1 or 2 fresh turmeric leaves
    (optional)
1 tablespoon chopped shallots
3 cloves garlic, peeled and minced
Salt to taste
1 teaspoon sweet soy sauce

This recipe calls for limo *limes which, the chef says, are native to Indonesia, but you may use Western ones instead. Turmeric leaves are not readily available in the United States and there are no substitutes. (Recipe: Chef Detlef Greiert, Jakarta Hilton International)*

1

Cut the fish into thin slices and put into a baking dish. Combine and stir together all the marinade ingredients and pour this mixture over the fish. Cover the dish with foil or plastic wrap and set aside for 30 minutes.

2

Brush the rack on the grill with oil. Or, if you use a special fish rack for grilling, brush it with oil. This prevents the fish from sticking. Grill the fish by the direct method (page xxix) over medium-hot coals for 7 to 10 minutes, turning once. Remove from the fire and serve immediately.

Spicy-Hot Fish

*Vegetable oil for brushing and
    frying*
*One 1½ pound white or red
    snapper, cleaned and gutted,
    head and tail intact*
Seasoning Mixture
1 stalk lemongrass
3 to 4 candlenuts or macadamia nuts
*One ½-inch piece fresh ginger,
    grated*
1 whole tomato, quartered
7 to 8 fresh red chilies
1 tablespoon vegetable oil
1 tablespoon water

(Recipe: Mrs. Soetjepto, Sabang Restaurant)

1
Brush the rack on the grill with oil. Or, if you use a special fish rack for grilling, brush it with oil. This prevents the fish from sticking. Grill the fish by the direct method (page xxix) over medium-hot coals for 5 to 7 minutes, turning once and brushing it with vegetable oil.

2
Remove the fish from the fire and set aside. Put the seasoning mixture ingredients into the container of a food processor or blender and puree. Heat about 1 tablespoon oil in a skillet large enough to hold the fish. Add the seasoning ingredients and fry for a few minutes. Add the cooked fish and fry with the other ingredients for about 10 minutes. Serve immediately.

Jakarta Barbecued Chicken

1 quart water
4 whole chicken breasts, split
1 tablespoon butter
Juice of 1 lemon
1 tablespoon vegetable oil
3 shallots, peeled and diced
6 candlenuts or macadamia nuts
2 to 4 chilies, diced
2 cups sweet soy sauce
One 2-inch piece galangal,
    chopped, for garnish

Douglas Lauw says that this grilled chicken is found only in Jakarta. It should be served with steamed rice and vegetables. When serving, season it and the accompaniments with sweet soy sauce. (Recipe: Douglas Lauw)

1

Put the water and chicken in a saucepan and bring to a boil. Poach the breasts about 10 minutes and drain. Dot the chicken with the butter, sprinkle with the lemon juice, and set aside.

2

Heat the oil in a skillet, add the shallots, nuts, and chilies, and sauté until slightly browned, or about 10 minutes. Add the sweet soy sauce and simmer for about 5 minutes.

3

Mix about ¼ cup of this sauce with the chicken, being sure that all surfaces are covered. Grill the breasts by the direct method (page xxix) over medium-hot coals for about 15 minutes, turning once or twice. Remove the chicken to a serving platter and pour the remaining soy sauce mixture over the top. Garnish with the chopped galangal and serve immediately.

Grilled Spicy Fish Wrapped in Banana Leaf

Juice of 1 lemon
½ pound fish fillets, such as red
    snapper, sea bass, or grouper
Banana leaf or foil for wrapping
Seasoning Mixture
2 shallots, peeled and chopped
2 cloves garlic, peeled
2½ tablespoons chopped candlenuts
    or macadamia nuts
1 to 2 red chilies
¼ cup chopped fresh tomato
1 tablespoon diced fresh ginger
1 tablespoon vegetable oil

This unusual fish dish is delicious with plain white rice. (Recipe: Chefs Hubert Lorenz and Nenjah Sujartha, Bali Hyatt)

1

Combine all the seasoning mixture ingredients except the oil in the container of a food processor or blender and puree. You may need to add some oil to help process.

2

Put the oil in a skillet and add the seasoning mixture. Sauté for about 5 minutes, then remove from the heat.

3

Squeeze the lemon juice over the fish fillets. Coat them with the seasoning mixture.

4

If you are using a banana leaf, soften it according to the directions in the Glossary. Put the fish in the center of the leaf (you may need to use more than one) and fold the sides to the center to cover the fish. Secure both ends with toothpicks. If using foil, crimp the ends closed.

5

Grill the fish by the direct method (page xxix) over medium-hot coals for about 7 minutes, turning once to brown evenly. Remove from the fire and serve immediately.

Grilled Prawns

20 jumbo prawns in their shells
Juice of 3 limes
2 tablespoons vegetable oil
Salt to taste
Marinade
6 shallots, peeled
6 cloves garlic, peeled
3 candlenuts or macadamia nuts
3 to 5 red chilies, seeds removed
1 medium tomato, chopped
4 tablespoons freshly grated ginger
2 teaspoons ground turmeric
1 tablespoon vegetable oil

Use a pair of bamboo skewers to hold the prawns firmly in place so they do not slip around while grilling. (Recipe: Chefs Hubert Lorenz and Nenjah Sujartha, Bali Hyatt)

1
Combine all the marinade ingredients except the oil in the container of a food processor or blender and process to make a coarse paste. Heat the 1 tablespoon of oil in a heavy skillet and add the marinade paste. Sauté for about 5 minutes, then remove from the heat and cool.

2
Use a sharp paring knife to slit down the spine of each prawn to devein, but be careful not to pull the shell off. Pinch off the legs and tails. Place the prawns in a shallow baking dish. Combine the lime juice, 2 tablespoons oil, and salt and sprinkle this mixture over the prawns. Then coat them with the spice mixture. Cover the baking dish with foil or plastic wrap and refrigerate for at least 1 hour.

3
Thread the prawns on bamboo skewers and grill by the direct method (page xxix) over medium-hot coals for 7 minutes, brushing with marinade and turning once to cook evenly. Remove from the fire and serve immediately.

ACCOMPANIMENTS

Bakmie Ayam

One 2½- to 3-pound frying chicken
3 quarts water
4 large onions, peeled and diced
2 cloves garlic, peeled and minced
1 tablespoon vegetable oil
1½ tablespoons sweet soy sauce
Ground white pepper, salt, and
  sugar to taste
1 pound fresh Chinese egg noodles
1 bunch choi sam, rinsed and
  trimmed (see Note)
¼ pound bean sprouts
1 bunch scallions or spring onions,
  trimmed and thinly sliced
One jar preserved cabbage
  (optional—see Note)
One 12-ounce can whole straw
  mushrooms

Garnish
Fried or boiled won tons, or Chinese
  fish or meat balls, as desired

This dish is popular in the Chinese-Indonesian community in Jakarta and has a "Peranakan" taste (that is, a cross between Indonesian and Chinese). It is a peasant soup served in huge bowls and may be eaten with fried or boiled won tons or with Chinese meat or fish balls as a garnish. You can buy frozen, already made won tons at many supermarkets or Asian markets. Huge dollops of chili sambal are always stirred into the bowl before eating. It makes a good first course for a casual meal. (Recipe: Douglas Lauw)

1

Place the chicken in a large stockpot and add the water. Bring the water to a boil, lower the temperature, and simmer the chicken until cooked, about 1 hour. Remove the chicken from the stock and set it aside until it is cool enough to handle. Strain and set the stock aside. There should be about 10 cups of liquid.

2

Fry the onion and garlic in the vegetable oil, and when golden brown, add the soy sauce. Remove from the heat.

3

Remove chicken from the bone and cut it into bite-sized pieces. Combine with the onion and garlic mixture. Add the pepper, salt, and sugar, and stir to mix thoroughly.

4

Bring the chicken stock to a boil again and add the noodles, cooking them until tender, 4 to 5 minutes. Add the *choi sam,* bean sprouts, scallions, and straw mushrooms and simmer for 2 to 3 minutes. Ladle the stock with a portion of noodles and vegetables into individual serving bowls and stir in a spoonful of chicken and seasonings. Alternatively, pour the stock, noodles, and vegetables into a large soup tureen and stir in the chicken

and seasonings. Garnish with your choice of won tons or fish or meat balls and the cabbage.

Note:

Choi sam is a member of the Chinese cabbage family. It has long green stems, pointed green leaves, and sometimes little yellow flowers. It is available at Asian markets.

Preserved cabbage is a fermented vegetable that gives foods a certain punch. Use this in moderate amounts as a garnish. The cabbage is sold in jars or small, ceramic crocks with Chinese characters on it at most Asian markets. It lasts indefinitely if stored in the refrigerator after opening.

Sambal Kecap

1 quart sweet soy sauce
2½ tablespoons chopped shallots
2 tablespoons diced green chilies
2 tablespoons diced red chilies
Juice from 10 limo limes or
    5 regular limes

This makes enough for 15 servings. (Recipe: Chef Detlef Greiert, Jakarta Hilton International)

Combine all the ingredients and whisk together thoroughly. Store in a tightly sealed container in the refrigerator.

Generic Sate Sauce

One 1-pound jar of chunky peanut
 butter (preferably the kind without
 preservatives)
1 quart water
½ teaspoon salt
Sugar to taste
4 to 6 shallots, peeled and thinly
 sliced
3 to 4 tablespoons sweet soy sauce
2 to 3 tablespoons chili sambal
 (recipe follows)

Chili Sambal

¼ pound red chilies, sliced
1 teaspoon salt
1 teaspoon sugar
½ to 1 teaspoon shrimp paste

According to Douglas Lauw, the secret here is long, slow cooking to bring out and intensify all the flavors. (Recipe: Douglas Lauw)

Combine all the ingredients in a saucepan and cook on a low flame for about 1 to 1½ hours.

Douglas Lauw remembers his mother mixing up a chili sambal, or sambal ulek, every day, by following this basic recipe. You can grind the chilies in a mortar and pestle, or process them quickly—you want minced chilies, not a paste—with a food processor. For milder sambal, remove the interior membranes and seeds. This recipe makes about half a cup. (Recipe: Douglas Lauw)

1
Grind or mince the chilies very fine. Stir in the salt and sugar, adding more to taste, if desired.
2
Dry fry the shrimp paste and grind, or mix it with the chilies. Serve immediately or store in a covered container in the refrigerator until ready to use.

West Sumatran Rendang

2 pounds top round roast, trimmed
   of all fat, cut into 2-inch cubes
Four 13½-ounce cans coconut milk
2 tablespoons hot chili paste
   (see Note)
One 4-inch piece fresh ginger,
   grated
4 cloves garlic, peeled
2 large onions, peeled and
   quartered
2 tablespoons coriander seeds
2 stalks lemongrass, sliced
2 slices fresh lemon
Four to six ½-inch-thick slices
   galangal
4 to 6 turmeric leaves (optional)
4 to 6 lime leaves
Salt to taste

Rendangs are popular meat dishes in both Malaysia and Indonesia and it is anyone's guess which recipe is original and which is hotter. Because it cooks slowly for many hours, the meat (often beef) is not only extremely tender, it is also apparently somewhat preserved—according to one cook, all the meat juices are dried out so the meat does not require refrigeration and keeps, unspoiled, for up to 1 month if stored in a jar at room temperature. I can't vouch for that, but this is so tasty that it won't last beyond one meal. Rendangs are often served with sate, rice, and a vegetable dish like gado-gado (page 150). (Recipe: Aminah Lanif)

1

Wash and dry the meat cubes. This removes any trace of blood and any "beefy" aroma.

2

Combine all the ingredients, except the meat and 3 cans of the coconut milk, in the container of a food processor or blender and puree. Pour this mixture and the remaining cans of coconut milk into a large stockpot and bring to a boil. Adjust the heat so that the mixture continues to boil gently. Keep the pot partially covered so the contents do not splatter. Stir often so that the mixture does not curdle or scorch. Continue cooking for 2 to 3 hours —the mixture will reduce by half and the oil from the coconut milk will begin to separate—that is, the natural oils from the coconut milk will begin to form a slick on the surface of the mixture. You must not add the meat until this point in cooking. Once the surface of the mixture is covered with a thin coating of oil, it is ready for the meat cubes.

3

Add the meat, lower the heat slightly, and continue simmering for another 3 hours, or until the liquid mixture

cooks away and the meat is brown. Remove from the heat. You can serve immediately or refrigerate and re-heat to serve another day.

Note:

Mrs. Lanif uses a Vietnamese garlic chili paste that is very hot. You could probably use any type of very hot chili paste with good results.

Compressed Rice

4 cups raw long-grain rice
Salt to taste
Banana leaves or foil for wrapping

Lontong Daun *is the well-known log of compressed rice that is traditionally boiled in a banana leaf wrapper and, when cooked, is sliced and served cold with sates. Malaysian cooks have their own version. (Recipe: Chef Detlef Greiert, Jakarta Hilton International)*

1

Rinse the rice and soak it in well-salted water for about 30 minutes. Drain the rice.

2

If you are using banana leaves, soften them according to the directions in the Glossary. Lay 2 layers of leaves or foil about 8 inches long on a flat surface and spoon a portion of rice down the center of the wrapper. Fold the sides to the center to cover the rice. Secure both ends with toothpicks if you are using banana leaves. If using foil, crimp the ends closed. Repeat this process until all the rice is used up.

3

Place the "tubes" of rice into a saucepan with water to cover. Bring the water to a boil and cook the rice in boiling water for about 1 hour. Remove the rice tubes from the water and cool before unwrapping. After unwrapping, cut the rice into 2-inch-thick slices. Serve cold.

Sour Vegetables with Beef

1 pound top round roast
Pinch salt
3 tablespoons vegetable oil
6 shallots, peeled and thinly sliced
2 cloves garlic, peeled and
   thinly sliced
8 to 10 green chilies, thinly sliced
5 red chilies, thinly sliced
One 1-inch piece galangal
2 bay leaves
¼ pound green beans, trimmed and
   cut into 2-inch pieces
2 tomatoes, quartered
8 small star fruit, quartered
   (see Note)
1 to 2 tablespoons tamarind juice
1 teaspoon palm sugar or
   brown sugar

Mrs. Tien Kumoro invited me one afternoon to her home in Jakarta to share a typical Indonesian lunch. It included chicken sate and this vegetable dish, which my hostess says she fixes almost daily. Her recipe comes from an Indonesian cookbook but Mrs. Kumoro has made a few changes in the recipe, such as omitting cooked quail eggs. This recipe makes 8 to 10 servings. (Recipe: Mrs. Kumoro/Indonesian Dishes and Desserts, Gaya Favorit Press)

1

Place the beef roast, salt, and enough water to cover in a large saucepan and bring to a boil. Lower the heat and simmer the meat for about 15 minutes. Drain the meat, reserving the cooking liquid. When the meat is cool enough to handle, cut it into 1-inch cubes.

2

Heat the oil in a wok or skillet over medium heat. Fry the shallots, garlic, chilies, galangal, and bay leaves until fragrant, about 10 minutes. Then add the beans and stir-fry them until crisp-tender, about 5 minutes.

3

Place the meat, 1 cup of the reserved cooking liquid, and the stir-fried beans in a saucepan and bring to a gentle boil over medium heat. When the beans are tender, about 4 to 5 minutes, add the remaining ingredients and simmer for another 5 minutes. Serve immediately.

Note:

Star fruit are small yellowish fruits that when sliced through the middle show a star pattern in cross section. These are often available in supermarkets.

Indonesian Fried Rice

4 tablespoons vegetable oil
½ pound lean ground beef
7 cloves garlic, peeled and
  chopped
1 to 3 tablespoons chili sauce or
  sambal (see page 145)
3 tablespoons tomato sauce or
  ketchup
½ pound raw large shrimp, peeled,
  deveined, and sliced in half
  lengthwise
6 cups cooked and cooled
  long-grain rice
Salt and freshly ground black
  pepper to taste
1½ tablespoons soy sauce
1½ tablespoons oyster sauce
1 cup Chinese cabbage, sliced
2 tablespoons diced shallots
1 cup sliced leeks
6 large eggs
Garnish
3 tablespoons fried garlic
6 chicken drumsticks, fried
12 shrimp crackers, fried

Nasi goreng, *a staple of the Indonesian diet, is a good accompaniment for a barbecued meat, but it can really be a meal in itself. For the meat, you can use chicken, beef, or pork, and regardless of which you choose, you should allow 1 fried drumstick per person. Pass chopped chilies and both regular and sweet soy sauces as condiments. (Recipe: Chefs Hubert Lorenz and Nen-jah Sujartha, Bali Hyatt)*

1

Heat the oil in a skillet and add the meat, breaking it up with a fork to cook evenly. Add the garlic and stir-fry for 3 to 4 minutes.

2

Stir in the chili sauce, tomato sauce, shrimp, and rice and continue to stir-fry. After 5 minutes of cooking, add the salt and pepper, soy sauce, oyster sauce, cabbage, shallots, and leeks. Cook for another 2 or 3 minutes and spoon out to a serving platter. Fry the eggs to your liking and, when they are cooked, place them on top of the rice. Garnish with the fried garlic and drumsticks and poke the shrimp crackers into the rice around the edges.

Mrs. Tatie Wawo-Runtu's Gado-Gado

½ *pound green or long beans, rinsed and trimmed*
½ *head white cabbage, rinsed and shredded*
¼ *pound bean sprouts*
½ *pound watercress, rinsed and trimmed*
½ *pound tofu*
½ *pound tempeh (see Note)*
2 *tablespoons vegetable oil*

Peanut Sauce
1 *pound roasted peanuts*
2 *cloves garlic, peeled*
1 *large onion, sliced*
1 *fresh red chili*
1 *teaspoon sugar, or more to taste*
1 *teaspoon salt, optional*
1 *teaspoon vinegar*
Enough water to puree the ingredients into a pourable sauce

Garnish
4 *hard-boiled eggs, quartered*
4 *shallots, peeled and thinly sliced*
Fried shrimp crackers

Gado-Gado is a beloved Indonesian dish of cooked and cooled vegetables served like a salad. Its components can vary according to taste and what's fresh in the market. You may pour the sauce, or dressing, over the salad before serving, or pass it separately. Shrimp crackers are always served as a garnish. (Recipe: Mrs. Tatie Wawo-Runtu, Tandjung Sari Hotel)

1
Blanch the vegetables in boiling water, starting with the beans, then adding the cabbage, and finally the bean sprouts. Cook no longer than 5 minutes total, or just until the vegetables are crisp-tender. Plunge into ice water immediately, and drain them thoroughly. Arrange them on the platter with the watercress.

2
Cube the tofu and tempeh and soak them in cold water for about 5 minutes with added salt and crushed garlic —this seasoning gives them a better taste. Drain and stir-fry the tofu and tempeh in the vegetable oil until they become crisp and golden, about 10 minutes. Remove from the skillet or wok and drain on paper towels.

3
Put the sauce ingredients in the container of a blender or food processor and puree. You may need to add some water to help process. Top the vegetables with the peanut sauce, and garnish with the hard-boiled eggs, shallots, and shrimp crackers.

Note:
Tempeh is a fermented vegetable protein usually made from compressed and cultured soybeans, but sometimes from other foods. It is available both at Asian markets and at many health-food stores. Tempeh should be stored in the refrigerator but it may also be safely frozen.

DESSERTS

Black Rice Pudding

3 cups raw black rice
1 cup raw sticky, or glutinous,
   white rice
6 cups water for cooking the rice
2 cups palm sugar or brown sugar
3 tablespoons pandan extract, or
   5 pandan leaves
One 13½-ounce can coconut milk
Pinch salt

The black rice cooks and softens into an almost custardlike consistency—this is a superlative dessert. You may use regular granulated sugar instead of the palm or brown sugars. You may also omit the sticky white rice if you cannot find it in the market, but it is readily available in most Asian groceries. (Recipe: Mrs. Tatie Wawo-Runtu, Tandjung Sari Hotel)

1

Soak both rices in water to cover for 1 hour. Drain the rice. Pour the 6 cups of water into a large saucepan and bring to a boil. Add the drained rice, bring to a boil again, lower the heat to medium and cook, uncovered, until the water is absorbed and the rice is tender, porridgelike, and soft. Check the consistency after 40 minutes and continue cooking until all water is absorbed. Stir occasionally to prevent sticking.

2

Stir in the sugar and the pandan extract, mixing well. Remove from the heat.

3

Pour the coconut milk and salt into a saucepan and heat until bubbly. Remove from the heat. Spoon the rice into a large serving bowl or into individual bowls and top with the coconut milk. Serve immediately.

Sweet Potatoes with Brown Sugar

4 sweet potatoes, peeled
½ to 1 cup grated young coconut
½ cup grated palm sugar or
   brown sugar
Pinch salt

Coconut Milk Pudding

2 tablespoons butter
¾ cup brown sugar
4 tablespoons flour
¼ teaspoon ground cinnamon
6 egg yolks
1½ cups coconut milk
Pinch salt
6 egg whites, stiffly beaten

A favorite West Sumatran dessert. (Recipe: Aminah Lanif)

Steam the sweet potatoes and, when tender, mash the flesh. Stir in the coconut, sugar, and salt and serve at once.

This dessert has an excellent flavor that is enhanced with a splash of chilled coconut milk. (Recipe: Embassy of the Republic of Indonesia, Washington, D.C.)

1
Preheat the oven to 350°.
2
Cream the butter and gradually add the sugar. Combine the flour with the cinnamon and add to the butter mixture.
3
Beat in the egg yolks one at a time, until the mixture is light and fluffy.
4
Gradually add the coconut milk and salt. Fold the egg whites into the mixture. Pour into a buttered 2-quart baking dish and set in a shallow pan of water. Bake in the preheated oven for 45 minutes, or until set. Chill and serve cold.

Balinese Pancakes

Filling
1 teaspoon ground cinnamon
3 teaspoons cocoa powder
1¾ cups chopped dry-roasted
  cashews
1 cup sugar

Batter
1 quart milk
5 large eggs
1¼ cups sugar
3½ cups unbleached white flour
4 tablespoons baking powder
¾ cup butter, melted
Vegetable oil for brushing
  the griddle
Palm sugar or maple syrup
  for topping

On Bali, these delicate pancakes are filled with a mixture of nuts and sugar—delicious. This recipe serves 8 to 10. (Recipe: Chefs Hubert Lorenz and Nenjah Sujartha, Bali Hyatt)

1
Combine the filling ingredients in a small bowl and set aside.

2
Combine the milk, eggs, and sugar and beat well. Sift together the flour and baking powder and stir into the milk mixture. Stir in the butter.

3
Heat a lightly greased griddle or skillet. Add 4 tablespoons of pancake mixture and cook it on one side until golden. Sprinkle some filling mixture on top and fold the pancake over in half. Flip it over and continue cooking until golden. Continue until all the batter and filling are used up. Serve with palm sugar or maple syrup.

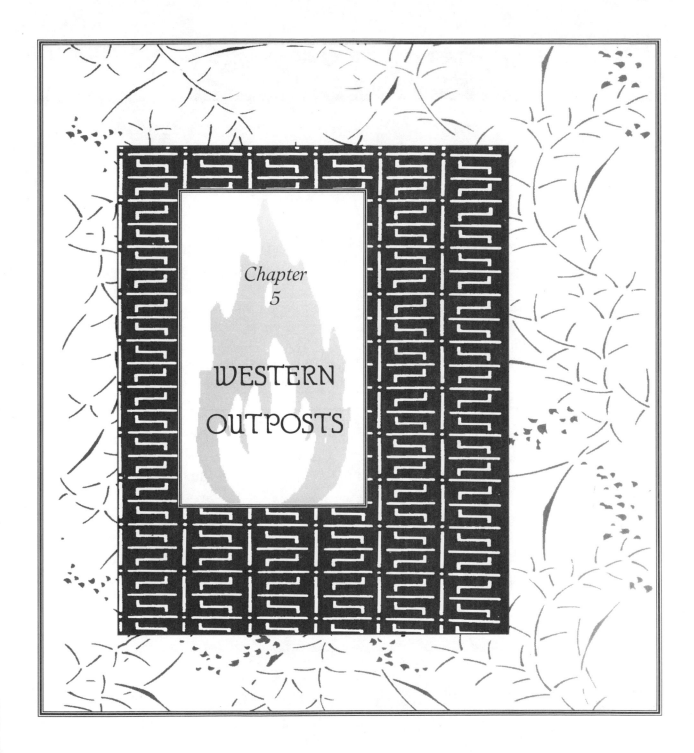

Chapter
5

WESTERN

OUTPOSTS

A TRIO OF ASIAN COUNTRIES—HONG KONG, THE PHILIPPINES, AND Macau—make strange bedfellows. Despite their Asian roots, they have little in common. Hong Kong—the "Borrowed Place, Borrowed Time" land (as the late British journalist Richard Hughes described it in his book)—is Asia's capitalist boom town with an uncertain economic future, which is, for the time being, governed by the British. The Philippines, despite political turmoil and wanton beauty, is Asia's Latin Lover. And Macau, the smallest of all Asian ports, looks like a sleepy Portuguese village with strong Chinese overtones. But all three do share one characteristic: their strong Western influence and presence.

The sun has almost set on the Western empires in Asia. Hong Kong and Macau return to the Chinese fold at the end of this century. And already independent, the Philippines struggle with its Asian-Latin identity, possibly trying to shed the latter. Meanwhile, Asia watchers wonder: What next for these former Western outposts?

Hong Kong

IN THE MID-1970S, WE LANDED IN HONG KONG ON THE HEELS OF A typhoon. And in those days, Hong Kong was an amazing blend of old East and new West: British gentry lived on the Peak and looked down, often through wisps and clouds of fog, to the city—Central—below, where rickshaw men still pulled Chinese businessmen and shoppers, and local Chinese practiced *tai chi* at dawn. In Central, Sundays were best for browsing along Cat Street for antiques or shopping in the Chinese Emporium with its quirky merchandise or taking the Star Ferry across the harbor for a day in Kowloon. From Central, people could catch doubledecker buses that took them down to Repulse Bay for lunch on the verandah at the old hotel, which, before its owners tore it down to build a new high-rise, commanded a majestic view of the South China Sea. Or to Stanley, then a quaint fishing village, for buying flowers and for looking at crows pickled in rice wine. Further around the island, where the fishing junks anchored in Aberdeen, vendors reportedly offered the rare wild beast or live snake for a winter stewpot. There were rumors that if you looked carefully in Western District, you could still see a few tottery old Chinese women with bound feet. China was still shut and the closest anyone could get to the Mainland was a hilltop point in the New Territories, the agricultural lands of Hong Kong where Hakka farmers still lived in walled villages and the women still wore their black outfits and black-fringed straw hats. To most foreigners, all this seemed unimaginably exotic and improbable, especially since Hong Kong was a lively, sophisticated, and by all accounts, totally modern city.

To me, however, food was the most riveting aspect of Hong Kong. For diversity, excellence, and abundance, eating in Hong Kong had no rival. Its sprawling public markets offered everything from "thousand-year-old" eggs and unplucked chickens to live turtles, fresh tomatoes, and seasonal lotus pods. Local *dim sum* eateries, restaurants, and teahouses served the best in traditional Chinese regional (particularly Cantonese) and Asian foods. Night-market stalls did a lively business with peasanty stir-fries. Cooking junks in the typhoon shelter vied to offer the freshest seafood delicacies. Tiny restaurants

on outlying islands lured customers with their local specialties while fancy Western-style restaurants earned praise for their creative menus. Everyone had a favorite place for shark's fin soup, roast pigeon, and stir-fried crabs with black beans. And that was just the catalog of Cantonese foods. Finally, the aroma of freshly brewed teas; the daily sight of mahogany-hued roast ducks, strips of grilled pork ribs, and curls of barbecued innards hanging in windows; and the endless clatter of chopsticks became an indelible part of my Hong Kong memories.

Friend and mentor, Hong Kong's ultimate gastronome William Mark, helped me make sense of this diversity and taught me some of the finer points of Chinese eating: for starters, how to swallow "dancing" (live) prawns, a Shanghainese special; which dishes to buy at Shatin's pigeon restaurants; and what to order at the Luk Yu Tea House for early-morning *dim sum*. He also taught me about the splendors of Cantonese cooking—which does not resemble anything served by most American Chinese restaurants—and I decided a particular banquet of his, that included Cantonese roast duck; chunks of Swatow (or Shantou) lobster in a sauce with black beans, ginger, and red chilies; a gingery mutton stew; and cups of wine that tasted like gardenias, would be my choice for a last supper.

Today, after a frantic building boom and urbanization, Hong Kong has a greatly altered skyline and intensified consumerism. It is a different place, even if traces of Old China and Old Hong Kong remain. But food—fine dining and splendid cooking—still plays a definitive role in local life. Eating out, observed one friend, is the major pastime here since there are few other diversions. So the food has to be good: Competition is stiff and it's easy enough for patrons to go elsewhere. Apparently many older Chinese chefs have left Hong Kong—either to teach cooking in China or to find a sanctuary in the West —but younger Chinese chefs are taking over and demonstrating their own style.

"Gastronomy, like any other art," says Mr. Mark, "is a living thing and you cannot just confine yourself to what you are. You have to be enriched by outside influences." Often innovation works: Some chefs have picked up seasoning techniques from various Chinese regional styles or from other Asian cuisines and achieved some pleasant results. But others have gone too far in mimicking Western creativity and have forgotten some of the traditional rules of their own kitchen. They spend too much time on presentation and garnishing, and not enough on the seasoning, the timing, and the cooking, says Mr. Mark. "Food is food. It is not *ikebana* (Japanese flower arranging)."

Nevertheless, many of Hong Kong's chefs can still outcook other Asians, and in one way, Hong Kong has come into its own. Once considered the melting pot of China and the bastion of traditional Chinese cooking, Hong Kong has developed an international reputation for having its own distinctive cooking style. Just exactly what that is, even Mr. Mark can't quite pinpoint, except to say that modern Hong Kong cooking combines the traditional Chinese with Western techniques, equipment, and ingredients—and that Hong Kong–style dishes cost more in restaurants. Even in their rush to be on the culinary cutting edge, maybe enough young chefs will still want to keep the flames of traditional cooking burning bright, and will not forget how to roast a goose to succulent perfection, or to hand-stretch elastic noodle dough, or to select the liveliest fish from the holding tank.

Very simply speaking, Chinese cooking—and probably every style is represented somewhere in Hong Kong—evolved along rough geographic boundaries: Wheat eaters live in the North, rice eaters in the South, fish eaters in the East, and chili-pepper eaters in the West. Further, this ancient cuisine has been shaped by several universal principles: frugality (every edible animal or plant part is used); seasonality (foods are eaten fresh whenever possible, and thus are eaten seasonally); and sensuality (a proper Chinese meal is balanced for contrasting tastes, colors, aromas, and textures). The Chinese cook relies on a standard repertoire of preparation techniques—chopping, slicing, and mincing, to name a very few. And he relies on numerous cooking techniques—commonly stir-frying, boiling, braising, and steaming, or a combination of several. Grilling was once more popular and widespread throughout China than it is today. Even in Hong Kong, with its Westernized cooking, grilling is scarce, practiced by only a handful of restaurants or other establishments that still use charcoal or wood for cooking fuel. Grilling is probably never done in a Chinese home.

According to many Sinophiles, the Cultural Revolution nearly terminated a majestic cooking tradition. As one wag has noted about Mainland policy, "During the Cultural Revolution, they [the leaders] associated good living with political impropriety. That's the first time ever that eating out has become a political crime." Reportedly, life may be looking brighter for Mainland chefs. There have been more raw ingredients available to work with, proper training provided by Chinese chefs from Hong Kong, and more incentives to cook well.

What all this means to Hong Kong's cuisine after 1997 is anyone's guess. But if the Chinese are as wise as Confucius, they will let well enough alone.

THE·GRILLS

Beggar's Chicken

One 5- to 7-pound roasting chicken
3 lotus leaves (see Note)
Disposable foil roasting pan
Kitchen string
2 tablespoons soy sauce
¼ pound salt pork, thinly sliced
Wax paper for wrapping
Clay (see Note)
Marinade
1 cup Chinese rice wine (also known
   as Chinese cooking wine)
2 tablespoons soy sauce
3 tablespoons minced onion
3 tablespoons minced fresh ginger
1½ teaspoons salt
Pinch freshly ground white pepper
2 tablespoons sugar

If you have ever eaten the authentic Chinese classic Beggar's Chicken, you are not likely to forget it. Quite apart from its dramatic presentation—a waiter brings the chicken, still wrapped in clay, to the table and whacks the covering off with a mallet—its multiple seasonings leave a haunting memory on your palate. And the tales of its creation are as colorful. The most familiar variation: A Ching Dynasty beggar, a poor and hungry man, stole a chicken, and to hide his theft, as well as to cook the chicken, he wrapped it, feathers and all, in pond mud and buried it in a pit on live coals. After several hours, he dug up his treasure, cracked open the baked mud, and found that his chicken had become an aromatic meal. Future cooks improved on this primitive technique, filling the cavity with savory ingredients, scenting the chicken with rice wine, and wrapping it in lotus leaves and then a thick coating of clay—thus creating a dish fit for an emperor. Residents of several cities, including Hangzhou and Suzhou, claim that the dish is theirs. Suzhou resident Mrs. Chen Yu-ping goes on to explain that the dish no longer has the same name, since China no longer has beggars. Anyone can re-create this dish and do so without pond mud. The chicken makes a filling entrée, since the stuffing mixture gets eaten as well. (Recipe: Mrs. Chen Yu-ping, adapted)

1

Put the chicken in a large mixing bowl. Combine all the marinade ingredients and pour them over the chicken. Cover the chicken with foil or plastic wrap and refrigerate it for at least 3 hours, turning several times to be sure the mixture coats all the surfaces well. Meanwhile, soak the lotus leaves in warm water.

Stuffing Mixture

1½ teaspoons fresh or dried jasmine
   flowers (see Note)

2 teaspoons fried sesame seeds

3 tablespoons dried shrimp

4 tablespoons coarsely chopped
   dried Chinese mushrooms,
   presoaked for 20 minutes

½ cup chopped bamboo shoots

2 tablespoons dried scallops or
   dried oysters (see Note)

1 bunch scallions, cleaned and
   trimmed

2 tablespoons minced fresh ginger

⅓ pound Chinese ham, or American
   country-style ham, julienned

2

Remove the chicken from the marinade and set it into a small roasting pan, breast side up. Combine the stuffing mixture ingredients in a large bowl and spoon the stuffing into the cavity of the chicken. Truss the chicken with the string. Spread the 2 tablespoons of soy sauce over the surface of the chicken. Place the thin slices of salt pork over the chicken breast. Wrap the entire chicken with a lotus leaf and then with a sheet of wax paper. Repeat the wrapping process 2 more times.

3

Wrap the entire chicken in a 1-inch thick layer of clay and place the chicken back in the roasting pan. Place the pan on the rack of a covered barbecue and grill the chicken by the direct method (page xxix) but with the lid on, over medium-hot coals. The chicken must cook slowly for at least 3 hours, and you will have to replenish the coals as needed several times during the cooking process. (The directions for one version of this dish, sent to me by a student in Beijing, call for the following: To roast, make a fire of pine wood and place the chicken on the fire for about 15 minutes. Then cover the chicken with burning pine wood and roast it for another 30 minutes. Turn the chicken over and roast for 30 minutes. Then bury the chicken in the hot ashes for about 2 hours.)

4

Remove the chicken from the fire and put it on a baking sheet. Knock off the clay with a hammer or mallet, and peel off the layers of wax paper, lotus leaves, and fat. For a dramatic effect, you may want to do this at the table. Transfer the chicken to a platter. When you slice it for serving, scoop out the stuffing mixture to pass with the meat. Serve immediately.

Note:
Lotus leaves are very large and several can easily wrap this chicken. They are readily available dried at most Asian markets and because they are fragile, should be moistened or soaked in warm water before use. They last indefinitely if stored in an airtight container.

Use gray ceramic pottery clay—the kind that can be fired—as the outer covering for the chicken. Be sure to buy a brand that is nontoxic and to allow at least 1½ pounds of clay for each pound of chicken. Some Chinese-American restaurants use a flour-water paste instead of clay. One cook suggested putting the lotus-wrapped chicken (tie leaves in place) in a covered clay casserole, but then you would probably have to bake it in an oven rather than cook it over hot coals.

Dried jasmine flowers are not as esoteric as they sound—you will find them at well-stocked natural-foods stores. Dried scallops, also known as *conpoy,* are not readily available even in Chinese markets and are also extremely expensive. You can substitute dried oysters— more available and less expensive—with satisfactory results.

Chinese Barbecued Pork Spareribs

5 pounds lean spareribs
Marinade
4 tablespoons hoisin sauce
4 tablespoons sugar
4 tablespoons wine
2 cloves garlic, peeled and minced
2 tablespoons grated fresh ginger
2 teaspoons salt
1 tablespoon soy sauce
2 tablespoons black beans
2 tablespoons minced tofu
½ teaspoon five-spice powder

This is a guaranteed rib-lover's feast. Use the leanest ribs you can find and be sure to marinate them the full length of time. (Recipe: Chef Joyce Piotrowski, Epicurean Events)

1
Trim the ribs into chunks of 3 or 4 bones. Bring a large pot of water to a boil. Put the ribs in the water and boil for about 15 minutes. Remove from the heat and put the ribs in a large baking dish. Drain off any excess water.

2
Combine the marinade ingredients and pour over the ribs. Cover with foil or plastic wrap and marinate for about 4 hours at room temperature. Turn the ribs occasionally to make sure they are covered with the marinade.

3
Grill the ribs by the indirect method (page xxix) over hot coals for 15 minutes, or until done. At this time, brush them with the marinade and if you wish, pour the remaining marinade into the drip pan to produce a flavorful sauce. Grill for another 5 minutes, or until completely cooked through. Remove from the fire and serve immediately.

Barbecued Whole Suckling Pig

One 12-pound suckling pig
2 quarts boiling water
3 tablespoons maltose (see Note)
3 tablespoons vinegar
12 scallions, cut into 2-inch lengths
3 fresh red chilies, cut into 12 circles
12 Peking Pancakes (see page 185)

Seasoning Mixture
1 tablespoon sweet bean paste
2 tablespoons red bean curd (see Note)
1 tablespoon salt
2 teaspoons sugar

Dipping Sauce
4 tablespoons sugar
4 tablespoons sweet bean paste
½ cup water
2 tablespoons sesame oil

Traditionally, the pig roasts—often hand turned—on a spit over very hot coals. One description indicates that a suckling pig was also hung upside down over a blazing fire in the old-style cone-shaped Chinese ovens. This is a celebratory dish not prepared at home, but you can achieve somewhat the same results by using a large covered barbecue and a hot fire—although this chef assures me the pig will never taste exactly the same. The customary way to eat the sliced pig is on a thick, small pancake, about 2 inches in diameter, that has been smeared with sweet bean paste and garnished with scallions and sliced chilies. People who like their pig meat sweeter can sprinkle sugar on the "sandwich." This particular recipe is a specialty of the Shang Palace Restaurant, Kowloon Shangri-La in Hong Kong. Because the fires he uses are so intense, this chef can cook his pig in half an hour. He holds the pig over the fire and turns it constantly to make the skin crispy. Home cooks will certainly need 3 to 4 hours, depending on pig size and fire heat. (Recipe: Chef Cheung Hoi Cheung, Kowloon Shangri-La, adapted)

1
Preheat the oven to 300°.

2
Rinse the pig in cold water, draining it well. Pour 1 quart of boiling water over the pig, then repeat with a second quart. Combine the maltose and vinegar in a small mixing bowl, and when the maltose has dissolved, pour this mixture slowly over the pig, being sure to cover all surfaces.

3
Place the pig on a large shallow roasting pan and put the pan in the preheated oven for about 10 minutes, or until the pig dries off.

4

Meanwhile, combine the seasoning ingredients. When the dried pig has cooled enough for easy handling, smear the surface of the pig with the seasoning mixture and let the pig marinate for at least 10 minutes, preferably longer.

5

Prepare the dipping sauce by combining the sugar with the sweet bean paste and water. Heat a wok and add the sesame oil. When the oil is hot, add the sugar mixture and stir until the sugar is completely dissolved. Set the dipping mixture aside.

6

Using a long metal skewer, spear the pig from head to tail for barbecuing. Or grill the pig by the indirect method (page xxix) over medium-hot coals. Turn frequently so that the skin crisps evenly—it will turn a slightly reddish color so do not be alarmed. Cook the pig for 3 or 4 hours, or until the joints move easily. Remove from the fire and place on a cutting board.

7

Slice off the skin and the meat into bite-sized pieces and arrange these on a serving platter. Garnish the meat with the scallions and red chilies. Pass the suckling pig with the pancakes and dipping sauce. Serve immediately.

Note:

Maltose is a sweetener from fermented barley and is commonly used in the Chinese kitchen. If you cannot find it at an Asian market, you can substitute honey. Red bean curd is a fermented tofu colored with red rice. It is available at Asian markets.

Barbecued Peking Duck

One 5- to 6-pound duck
Salt
½ teaspoon ground ginger
1 teaspoon star anise
2 teaspoons five-spice powder
2 teaspoons sugar
¼ teaspoon ground cinnamon
2 tablespoons honey
½ cup white vinegar
2 slices lemon
2 quarts boiling water
1 cup vegetable oil, heated
Accompaniments
Sliced leeks
Hoisin sauce
Peking Pancakes (see page 185)

In his book Peking Cooking, *Kenneth Lo wrote that a certain type of duck must be specially raised for this dish. Caramel-colored crispy skin puffs away from the juicy flesh so that the chef can make a showy presentation of slicing the skin and the meat separately. But achieving that exceptionally crisp, nonfatty skin is a task. Drying the duck properly is one part of the process —in a traditional kitchen the chef would hang the duck upside down out of the sunlight for several hours. Some chefs would also use such mechanical devices as bicycle pumps or bellows to plump up the skin. According to Chef Joyce Piotrowski, home cooks can hang the duck in a refrigerator for several days or use a convection oven at the lowest heat to blow the duck dry. According to Chef Leung Kit, a modern method is to "roast" it in a 200°F oven until the carcass feels dry to the touch. My oven apparently was not cool enough because all this did was to melt the fat under the skin into a greasy smear on the duck's surface. On the second try, I let the duck air dry overnight and that was much more successful. The chef has provided a recipe for using up any leftover duck meat (see page 182). (Recipe: Chef Leung Kit, Lee Gardens Hotel)*

1

Rinse and dry the duck and its cavity, removing any excess fat and gizzards. Mix together the salt, ginger, star anise, five-spice powder, sugar, and cinnamon and smear this mixture in the duck's cavity.

2

Insert a sharp-pointed bamboo skewer into the duck, from breast to backbone, starting midway down the breastbone. This helps the duck cavity to keep its shape.

3

Combine the honey, vinegar, and lemon slices in a saucepan and bring to a simmer. Continue cooking until this mixture caramelizes. Keep it hot while you douse the duck in the boiling water.

4

Using tongs or a long-handled fork to prop the duck on its end, neck end down, pour the boiling water slowly over the duck, being sure to cover all outer surfaces. This scalds the duck and helps keep the skin crisp when serving.

5

With the duck still propped up on end, slowly pour the caramelized mixture over the hot carcass, making sure to cover all outer surfaces. Dry the duck out by whichever method you choose, as described above.

6

When the duck feels dry, hold it with tongs or a fork over a large pan, and pour the hot vegetable oil over it, repeating this procedure for about 10 minutes. Reuse the same oil by catching it in the pan and spooning it over the carcass. Then skewer the duck for cooking on a rotisserie or place it on the rack of a barbecue. Grill the duck by the indirect method (page xxix) over medium-hot coals for about 40 minutes. (The chef says if you have used the modern drying method, the duck will be about 80 percent cooked before you start to grill it.) To test for doneness, poke a metal skewer into the thigh—if the juices run clear, the duck is ready to eat.

7

Remove the duck from the fire and place it on a large serving platter. Use a very sharp carving knife to slice off the skin and the meat into thin pieces for wrapping. Pass the duck with the sliced leeks, hoisin sauce, and Peking Pancakes.

Barbecued Pork Filet

5 pounds fresh boneless pork,
   preferably pork butt or collars

Marinade

1 tablespoon salt

1 cup sugar

2 teaspoons sesame paste

¼ cup oyster sauce

1 cup soy sauce

2 teaspoons five-spice powder

½ cup rosé wine

¼ cup soybean paste

¼ cup honey

Sweetening Mixture

2 cups soy sauce

3 cups sugar

2 cups water

Orange or red food coloring

Dipping Sauce (optional)

¼ cup vegetable oil

4 cloves garlic

½ large onion

2 tablespoons minced fresh ginger

1 tablespoon oyster sauce

1 tablespoon sesame paste

Dash of sesame oil

3 tablespoons soy sauce

Pinch salt

Also known as char siu, these popular pork snacks can be used as an appetizer or served with other dishes for a main course. The chef calls for using meat that has a high (33 percent) ratio of fat, otherwise this will be too dry. He also skewers and hangs the pork to dry. (Recipe: Chef Alan Chan, Foreign Correspondents' Club, adapted)

1

Trim all excess fat from the pork and slice it into 4-inch long x 1-inch wide x ¼-inch-thick strips. Place the strips in a baking dish and set aside.

2

Combine the marinade ingredients in the container of a food processor or blender, and process until smooth. Pour the marinade over the meat, cover the baking dish with aluminum foil or plastic wrap, and refrigerate for 3 to 4 hours or overnight.

3

Meanwhile, stir together the sweetening mixture and pour it into a long pan. To make the dipping sauce, combine the vegetable oil, garlic, onion, and ginger and simmer for 30 minutes. Strain and mix the flavored oil with the oyster sauce, sesame paste, sesame oil, soy sauce, and salt. Bring the mixture to a boil and cook for about 5 minutes. Set aside.

4

Grill the meat slices by the indirect method (page xxix) over medium-hot coals for about 20 minutes. The meat cooks slowly. Remove the meat from the fire, dip it into the sweetening mixture, hang on a rack or place in a pan, and allow it to air-dry for about 1 hour. Serve the meat at room temperature with the dipping sauce to spoon over the meat, if desired.

Mongolian Lamb

1 pound boneless lean lamb
1 pound of scallions, julienned
Marinade
4 tablespoons vegetable oil
2 tablespoons soy sauce
1 teaspoon salt
2 tablespoons rice wine
1 teaspoon Szechuan peppercorns
Seasoning Sauce
6 cloves garlic, peeled and minced
2 tablespoons soy sauce
2 tablespoons white vinegar
2 tablespoons sesame oil

A simple barbecue dish, this resembles the lamb from a Mongolian Barbecue, except that here the meat marinates in one mixture and is then tossed in a sauce with another combination of flavors. Finally, the cooked meat is served with rice, not stuffed into a bun. You can also stir-fry the lamb in a wok with oil and the seasoning ingredients. (Recipe: Chef Joyce Piotrowski, Epicurean Events)

1

The lamb should be partially frozen and sliced very thin. Combine the marinade ingredients in a shallow baking dish and put in the lamb slices. Marinate the meat for at least 30 minutes.

2

Meanwhile, combine the ingredients for the seasoning sauce and set aside.

3

Grill the meat with its marinade and the scallions by the direct method over hot coals (as you do in the Mongolian Barbecue), turning once, for 2 or 3 minutes. Remove from the fire and place them on a serving platter. Pour the seasoning sauce over the top and serve immediately.

Roast Goose

One 8- to 10-pound goose
2 tablespoons sugar
2 tablespoons honey
½ cup rice wine vinegar or white
    vinegar
3 cups vegetable oil, heated until
    bubbly
Stuffing Mixture
1 teaspoon salt
1 teaspoon sugar
Pinch MSG (optional)
2 tablespoons hoisin sauce
1 tablespoon sesame paste
1 teaspoon soybean paste
1 teaspoon mashed sour plum (see
    Note)
1 tablespoon Chinese wine or a dry
    rosé wine
1 teaspoon ground ginger
1 teaspoon ground cinnamon
1 teaspoon oyster sauce
1 teaspoon dried tangerine powder
    or dried orange peel

Very early recipes for roasting goose called for cooking it in large clay or ceramic pots over burning straw or lumps of charcoal. However, the geese are now hung in large ovens, fired at the Yung Kee Restaurant by the traditional charcoal method, and cooked elsewhere by the more modern heat source, gas. Although many Cantonese restaurants serve roast goose, the Yung Kee Restaurant, which has been serving this specialty for over 50 years, may well be the most famous, and it is the last of its kind in Hong Kong permitted to use charcoal for cooking. Credit for its fame goes to the chef Master Tang Hin Wa, who may be the genius of roast goose. His geese are specially raised, selected, and fed, and when they weigh 4 or 5 catties (about 6 pounds) they are ready for cooking. The geese are the most succulent in the fall, but Master Tang roasts about 200 geese a day all year round, except during the Mid-Autumn Festival, when he roasts up to 400 a day. He uses a special kind of charcoal from Singapore. Hong Kong home cooks would not have the equipment or space to prepare this dish, but it can be more easily reproduced in a Western kitchen. Master Tang does not follow any written recipe for the stuffing mixture, relying instead on tasting as he mixes. As a result, the quantities here are only approximate. The seasonings will work for a duck or chicken as well. He recommends serving roast goose with steamed fish and fried broccoli with scallops, or steamed prawns, soup, and rice. He served us clear mushroom soup, fried and braised tofu, and young leaves of the pear tree with crab sauce. (Recipe: Master Tang Hin Wa, Yung Kee Restaurant)

1
Remove any innards and excess fat from the goose. Rinse and wipe it dry with paper towels and set aside.

2

Fill a stockpot with water and bring it to a boil. Meanwhile, combine all the stuffing mixture ingredients in the container of a food processor or blender and puree. Spoon this mixture into the cavity of the goose and skewer the neck and tail openings closed. When the water is boiling, either pour it over the goose or dunk the goose into the boiling water for about 30 seconds. Set the goose aside.

3

Combine the sugar, honey, and vinegar in a saucepan and heat until the sugar has dissolved. Brush this mixture evenly over the skin of the goose. Hang the goose upside down to "wind" dry it—this helps the skin become crispy during grilling—or place it on a roasting pan rack in a warm place for about 2 hours. The flavor from the seasonings should be absorbed by that time. Drain out the stuffing paste and reserve it for making a gravy, if desired.

4

Grill the goose by the indirect method (page xxix) over medium-hot coals for about 45 minutes. You must use a drip pan when roasting the goose—it is very fatty and its fat needs to drip into a container, not on the coals. If the fat splatters into the fire, it will cause flare-ups when lifting the lid. These scorch the goose skin and give it a burnt taste. Remove from the fire and pour bubbly oil over the entire surface to crisp the skin. Serve immediately.

Note:

These are actually salted, dried plums sold almost everywhere in Hong Kong and popular there as something to suck, much like a hard candy would be. These are readily available in Asian markets. Because they are dried and hard, they will need soaking prior to use.

Mongolian Barbecue

1 pound boneless lamb shoulder
1 pound beef tenderloin or New
 York strip steak
1 pound boneless, skinless chicken
 breasts
1 pound pork tenderloin
Baked Sesame Seed Buns (page 174)

Accompaniments

5 cups thinly sliced scallions
4 cups julienned green bell peppers
4 cups thinly sliced cabbage
4 cups shredded carrots
4 cups bean sprouts
4 cups sliced mushrooms
2 cups whole coriander leaves
2 cups sliced celery
2 cups quartered tomatoes

Chef Joyce Piotrowski talked about having eaten Mongolian Barbecue in Taiwan several years ago. It was an inexpensive and popular way to dine, and the favorite spot was at a Chinese house down by the river where grills and tables were set out under the trees. Patrons picked up their bowls and selected what they wanted from a display of paper-thin meat slices, vegetables, and flavorful seasoning sauces that usually included light soy sauce, rice wine, ginger water, garlic water, and shrimp oil. Patrons personalized their selection by choosing their own combination of meat and sauce. (Chef Piotrowski to this day favors the lamb, green onions, coriander, sesame oil, and garlic combination.) After filling up their bowls, they carried them to the cook at the fire. The cook dumped the bowlful onto a large rack made of slotted carbon steel (the slots let the smoke of the wood flavor the food) set over burning coals or logs. With long chopsticks, he quickly stirred the mixture and scooped it back into the bowl. The shao ping sesame buns for stuffing with the cooked meats were set out on the dining tables. Chef Piotrowski only regrets that she did not try the wild boar with coriander. You can use any kind of meat you wish—venison, wild boar, duck breast, bear, and turkey are some of the more unusual choices—but commonly the selection includes lamb, pork, chicken, beef, and shrimp. You can substitute pita bread for the sesame buns, if you wish. To approximate the authentic carbon-steel grill top for the Mongolian Barbecue, Chef Piotrowski suggests substituting the upper portion of a stove-top grill, the square basket section of the grill-top wok, or a sheet of expanded aluminum that you slash and stretch. You can also find a steel or enamel-coated "mesh" rack for the top of a barbecue grill for sale with barbecuing tools and equipment; this may also be a

Flavoring Sauces

1 quart soy sauce

2 cups rice wine

*2 cups sugar water (2 cups water
    mixed with ½ cup sugar)*

*1 cup shrimp oil (heat ½ cup
    vegetable oil with ½ cup dried
    shrimp and 2 tablespoons
    cayenne)*

*2 cups ginger water (2 cups water
    mixed with 3 tablespoons grated
    fresh ginger, stirred together and
    strained)*

1 cup hot chili oil

*1 cup garlic oil (1 cup minced garlic
    in vegetable oil to cover)*

1 cup hot bean paste (see Note)

1 cup sesame oil

good substitute. This recipe serves 8 to 10 people. (Recipe: Chef Joyce Piotrowski, Epicurean Events)

1

All the meats should be partially frozen and shaved into very thin slices. These should be wrapped in wax paper or foil and stored in the freezer until serving time. All the vegetables should be prepared and set aside in separate serving containers. All the sauces should be prepared and set aside in separate serving containers.

2

Ask guests to fill a bowl with any combination of meat and/or vegetable and to sprinkle on top any one or more of the flavoring sauces. Grill the meat-vegetable-sauce mixture by the direct method (page xxix) over hot coals. Use very long chopsticks or tongs or a spatula for stirring and removing the food from the fire. Serve immediately with the sesame buns.

Note:

This paste is made with hot chilies and fermented black beans. It is sold at most Asian markets.

Baked Sesame Seed Buns (Shao Ping)

5 cups flour
1½ teaspoons salt
1½ cups boiling water
⅔ cup cold water
Special mix: 1 cup flour and ⅔ cup
    vegetable oil
⅓ cup sesame seeds

1

Preheat the oven to 450°.

2

Place the flour and salt in a mixing bowl and add the boiling water. Mix for 3 minutes by hand or with an electric beater. Add the cold water and mix for 5 minutes more. Let the dough rest for 20 minutes or longer. Meanwhile, combine the flour and oil for the special mix and set it aside.

3

Knead the dough in the bowl and roll it out into a thin rectangle. Spread the special oil and flour mixture evenly over the dough. Roll up like a jelly roll—that is, start with one of the long sides and roll the dough firmly over to the other side to form one long roll. Cut into 20 pieces.

4

Working with one piece at a time, place the dough in front of you, and, with your rolling pin, roll from the center of the piece toward you. Fold the unrolled part toward you and roll again. Repeat the process. Turn the dough sideways and repeat the above steps. Dip one end into the sesame seeds, roll the dough out to a 5-inch x 2-inch rectangle, and place on a baking sheet. Repeat this procedure with the remaining pieces of dough.

5

Bake in the preheated oven for 5 minutes. Turn the rolls over with a spatula and bake for another 5 minutes. Remove from the oven, cool slightly, and serve.

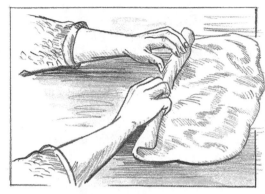

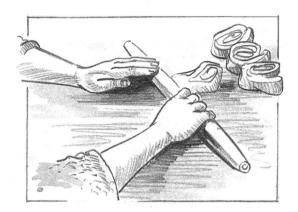

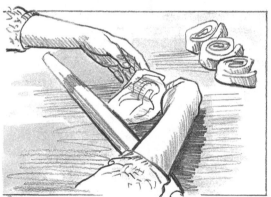

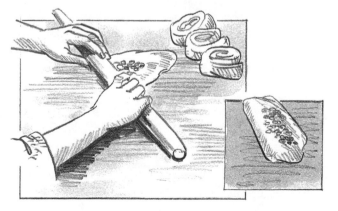

Szechuan Camphor and Tea-Smoked Duck

Seasoning Rub
3 tablespoons salt
2 tablespoons Szechuan
   peppercorns (see Note)
1 star anise

One 4- to 5-pound duck
1 cup water
2 dish towels
2 cups vegetable oil

Steaming Ingredients
2 cups wood shavings or small twigs
¼ teaspoon camphor oil or spirits
   (see Note)
2 tangerine peels, or about 3
   tablespoons dried orange peels
½ cup black tea leaves (see Note)
2 tablespoons sugar
1 small flat rock

Dipping Sauce
2 tablespoons vegetable oil
2 tablespoons hoisin sauce
2 tablespoons sugar
2 tablespoons Chinese rice wine

This duck is tricky, but it is worth every preparation moment. My sister says it is the best duck she has ever eaten. (Recipe: Chef Joyce Piotrowski, Epicurean Events)

1
Put the salt, peppercorns, and star anise in a saucepan and heat until they become fragrant. Rub the duck inside and out with this seasoning. Place the duck in a baking dish and put it in the refrigerator for 6 hours, uncovered, to dry out.

2
Start a fire in your barbecue.

3
Rinse the duck cavity with the 1 cup of water and brush off any excess salt from the skin. Put a steamer rack in the center of a large wok and set the duck on top of it. Add about 1 inch of water to the wok, put the cover on, and steam the duck over medium heat for about 45 minutes. Check the water level often and replenish the water as needed.

4
After steaming the duck, discard the water and line the bottom of the wok with a double thickness of foil. Combine the steaming ingredients (except the rock) and put them on the foil. Weigh them down with the rock. Heat the wok over high heat and when the mixture begins to smoke, put the duck on its back on the steamer tray above the rock. Cover the wok with the lid and seal in the smoke with wet dish towels.

5
Put the wok directly onto the coals in the barbecue and smoke the duck for 10 minutes. Remove the wok lid, turn the duck over, replace the lid, and smoke for an-

other 10 minutes. When the shavings have burnt away, the duck has finished smoking.

6

Meanwhile, make the dipping sauce. Heat the oil in a saucepan. Add the remaining ingredients, remove from the heat, and set aside.

7

Remove the duck from the fire. Heat the 2 cups of vegetable oil in a deep, wide saucepan—a wok would be fine, but it can tip easily, so be careful. When the oil is bubbly, very carefully fry the duck on both sides to crisp the skin. Fry for a total of 15 minutes. Remove from the oil, drain off the excess fat, and serve immediately with the dipping sauce.

Note:

Szechuan peppercorns are not pepper but are seeds from a tree native to the province of Szechuan. These are sold at well-stocked supermarkets and Asian markets.

According to several pharmacists, camphor oil is no longer sold over the counter, but you can find camphor spirits, also called spirits of camphor. This is available at some pharmacies, but call ahead to make sure it is in stock. The camphor imparts a distinctive flavor to the duck.

Use the dark Chinese or Indian tea leaves.

Cantonese Roast Pigeons

▤▤▤▤▤▤▤▤

4 pigeons, cleaned and plucked
2 cups white vinegar
2 cups water
½ cup sugar syrup, made from ¼
  cup water and ¼ cup sugar
1½ tablespoon salt
1 tablespoon sugar
1 teaspoon five-spice powder
Stuffing
1 tablespoon salt
1 tablespoon sugar
1 teaspoon five-spice powder
4 cloves garlic, peeled
One 1-inch piece fresh ginger, cut
  into 4 pieces
2 scallions, peeled and minced
4 shallots, peeled
4 star anise
1 teaspoon bean paste

If you can find pigeons, you may want to try this very typical Cantonese dish. Pigeons, also known as squab, may be available frozen from a gourmet food shop, but they may be rather costly. The chef suspends, or "hang-roasts," the pigeons during cooking; if your barbecue cooker is large enough, you may want to try this. (Recipe: Chef Alan Chan, Foreign Correspondents' Club, adapted)

1
Bring a pot of water to a boil and dip the pigeons in it for about 30 seconds. Remove and set aside.

2
Combine 1 tablespoon salt, sugar, and five-spice powder and rub with your finger on the inside of each pigeon. Crush or bruise the stuffing ingredients and combine them in a mixing bowl. Divide the mixture equally and spoon into the cavity of each piegon. Skewer the pigeons closed.

3
Combine the vinegar, water, sugar syrup, and salt and brush on the skins.

4
Grill the pigeons by the indirect method (page xxix) over medium-hot coals for about 15 minutes, brushing the skins with the vinegar mixture several times. Discard the stuffing mixture and serve immediately.

ACCOMPANIMENTS

Corn and Crab Meat Soup

One 17-ounce can creamed corn
1 cup chicken broth
½ pound crab meat, picked clean of
    shell and cartilage
2 tablespoons soy sauce
1 tablespoon grated fresh ginger
Dash of sesame oil

This modern version of an old classic is simplicity itself. My friend often uses evaporated milk to make the soup creamier. (Recipe: Katie McDonald)

Combine all the ingredients in a large saucepan. Bring to a boil, lower the heat, and simmer for 10 minutes. Serve immediately.

Vegetable Noodle Soup

4 ounces bean thread noodles
1 tablespoon vegetable oil
½ onion, peeled and chopped
1 clove garlic, peeled and slivered
1 stalk celery, chopped
2 quarts chicken stock or water
1 cup cubed cooked chicken breast
    meat
5 black mushrooms, presoaked and
    sliced
1 cup bamboo shoots
Salt to taste
Pinch MSG (optional)

This is a simple, fast, and generic Chinese soup that is full of flavor. (Recipe: Vasouthep Sananikone)

1
Break the bean thread noodles into shorter lengths—hold them over a sink or pot when you do this to catch the brittle noodles. Soak them in warm water for 15 minutes.
2
Meanwhile, pour the oil into a heavy skillet and heat until bubbly. Add the onion, garlic, and celery and sauté for 3 to 5 minutes, or until golden.
3
Put the stock or water into a large saucepan and add all the ingredients. Bring the soup to a simmer and cook for about 15 minutes. Serve immediately.

Won Ton Soup

¼ pound boneless pork loin, diced
  and cooked
2 ounces raw shrimp meat, diced
½ tablespoon cornstarch
½ tablespoon light soy sauce
¼ teaspoon sesame oil
Salt and freshly ground black
  pepper to taste
1 tablespoon beaten egg
18 to 24 won ton wrappers
  (see Note)
3 cups chicken stock
Salt to taste
Sesame oil to taste
¼ pound spinach or carrots,
  trimmed into 4-inch pieces and
  blanched
¼ cup chopped chives

Lucy Lo is a familiar figure in Hong Kong's food world because for years she has been teaching generations of local women—Chinese and Western—the secrets of the Chinese kitchen. This light and delicate offering is one of her dishes. Food writer Kenneth Lo (no relation, I don't think) once wrote that won tons should "float in the soup like so many 'floating clouds.' " You may wish to increase the amount of soup liquid. You can make the won tons ahead of time. (Recipe: Lucy Lo)

1

Put the pork and shrimp into a large mixing bowl and stir in the cornstarch, soy sauce, sesame oil, salt and pepper, and the tablespoon of beaten egg. Set aside to marinate for 30 minutes.

2

Fill a saucepan with water and bring to a boil. Meanwhile, put 1 teaspoonful of filling mixture into the center of a won ton wrapper and fold it over to seal the wrapper shut. (Follow the package directions for wrapper use.) Repeat the procedure until all the filling is used. With a slotted spoon, put the won tons into the boiling water, 3 or 4 at a time, and cook for 1 to 2 minutes. Remove from the water and set aside to drain.

3

Meanwhile, heat the chicken stock to a boil. Season the stock with salt and sesame oil to taste. Add the won tons, vegetables, and chives and serve immediately.

Note:

Won ton wrappers are sold in the produce section of most supermarkets. Follow package directions for folding.

Honeyed Chicken Wings

2 pounds (about 8 large) chicken
   wings, tip joints removed
Seasoning
¼ teaspoon freshly ground black
   pepper
1 teaspoon sesame oil
2 tablespoons rice wine
2 tablespoons minced fresh ginger
3 teaspoons oyster sauce
⅓ cup soy sauce
¼ cup honey

You can serve these as an appetizer or with the main meal. (Recipe: David Quang)

Put all the seasoning ingredients into a 2-quart saucepan. Bring the mixture to a boil and add the chicken. Cover the pan and cook for 3 to 5 minutes. Using tongs, turn the pieces over, cover the pan again, and lower the heat. Simmer for 3 to 5 minutes. Repeat the turning and cooking step again. To thicken the sauce, remove the lid and turn the heat up high. Cook for 3 to 5 minutes more and remove from the heat. Serve hot or at room temperature.

Sautéed Minced Duck Meat Wrapped with Waffle Papers

½ cup vegetable oil
1 cup minced cooked duck meat
½ cup pine nuts
¼ pound mushrooms, diced
½ cup diced carrots
1 package waffle papers (see Note)

This is a good way to use up leftover duck meat. Serves 2. (Recipe: Chef Leung Kit, Lee Gardens Hotel)

1

Heat 1 tablespoon of the oil in a heavy skillet or wok and add the duck, pine nuts, mushrooms, and carrots. Sauté until all the ingredients are cooked through, about 5 minutes. Set aside to cool slightly.

2

Put 1 tablespoon of cooled filling in the center of each waffle paper and wrap up into rolls, like wrapping a spring roll.

3

Heat the remaining oil in the skillet and fry the rolls until golden and crisp. Remove from the pan and drain on paper towels. Serve while still hot.

Note:

"Waffle" papers are the rice-and-flour wrappers Vietnamese cooks use for wrapping their spring rolls, or *cha gio*. Soften them by dipping the stiff sheets of paper in warm water and lay them on a flat surface to dry slightly. These papers are readily available at Asian markets.

Pan-fried Scallops with Pine Nuts and Greens

2 tablespoons vegetable oil
2 ounces pine nuts
½ pound bay scallops
3 stalks fresh asparagus, diced
1 tablespoon cornstarch
1 teaspoon salt
2 tablespoons water
6 scallions, trimmed, shredded
   lengthwise, and sliced into 2-inch
   pieces
6 thin slices carrot

This recipe might feed 6 people if you are serving many other courses. But if your meal consists of only a grill, a soup, and this dish, increase the quantities of this recipe. (Recipe: Chef Cheung Hoi Cheung, Kowloon Shangri-La)

1
Heat a wok, add the oil, and when it is very hot, reduce the heat slightly. Add the pine nuts and fry until golden. Remove and drain.

2
Add the scallops carefully to avoid splattering and stir-fry until golden, about 20 seconds. Remove and drain.

3
Add the asparagus and stir-fry for about 10 seconds. Remove and drain and discard most of the oil. Combine the cornstarch, salt, and water in a small bowl and set aside.

4
Reheat the oil remaining in the wok, and over high heat, add the scallions and carrot and stir-fry for 5 or 6 seconds. Return the pine nuts, scallops, and asparagus to the wok and stir-fry for about 10 seconds more. Pour in the cornstarch mixture and bring to a boil, cooking and stirring until the sauce thickens and becomes clear. Serve immediately.

Cantonese Ginger-Flavored Beef Cubes

12 ounces sirloin steak, trimmed of
     fat and cut into ¾-inch cubes
2 cups plus 1 tablespoon oil,
     preferably peanut
6 thin slices fresh ginger
3 scallions, cut into 2-inch lengths

Marinade
1 egg white
1 tablespoon Chinese yellow wine,
     or Shaoshing wine (see Note)
1 teaspoon sesame oil
1 tablespoon light soy sauce
1 tablespoon cornstarch

Seasoning Sauce
1 tablespoon oyster sauce
2 teaspoons light soy sauce
1 teaspoon dark soy sauce
6 tablespoons chicken stock
2 teaspoons cornstarch

This is one of William Mark's specialties. This recipe makes 2 to 4 servings. (Recipe: William Mark)

1

Put the steak cubes in a shallow baking dish. Combine the marinade ingredients and pour over the meat. Set aside for 10 minutes.

2

Pour 2 cups of the oil into a wok or skillet and heat. Add the beef, stirring to prevent the cubes from sticking together. Cook for 40 seconds over high heat and drain. Set the beef aside.

3

Pour the remaining tablespoon of oil into the wok or skillet and heat. Add the ginger and scallions and sauté until fragrant. Return the beef to the wok and stir-fry over high heat for 30 seconds. Remove from the heat.

4

Combine the seasoning sauce ingredients and pour them over the beef. Return to the heat, and keep stirring. Bring the sauce to a boil. Remove from the heat. Serve immediately.

Note:

Chinese yellow wine, or Shaoshing wine, is made by fermenting glutinous rice and millet, which produces a full-bodied flavor that enhances food. This is sold at most Asian markets. Chef Joyce Piotrowski suggests a good dry sherry as a substitute.

Peking Pancakes

2½ cups unsifted all-purpose flour
½ teaspoon salt
1 cup boiling water
Sesame oil for brushing

These pancakes may be made ahead and refrigerated or frozen. To soften, steam them at serving time. These are suitable for any wrapped Chinese foods. They are available frozen as dan bing *(or pancakes), and as* moo shu *wrappers or pancakes, at many Asian markets. Don't be surprised if you find them difficult to make the first few times, until you get the hang of it. (Recipe: Chef Joyce Piotrowski, Epicurean Events)*

1

Place the flour and salt in a mixing bowl and add the boiling water, stirring it in with a fork. When cool enough to handle, knead until the dough is soft, pliable, and not sticky—the dough should be silky. Form the dough into a long log and let it rest for 20 minutes—this is important. Cut it into 24 equal portions.

2

Lightly flour a flat surface and place 2 portions of the dough on the surface. Press each into 3-inch-round circles, ¼ inch thick. Brush the top of each circle with sesame oil and stack one circle on top of the other, placing the oiled surfaces together.

3

Roll this circle into a thin pancake—about 7 inches in diameter—with a lightly floured rolling pin. Roll from the center to the edges and turn the pancake over several times to be certain both sides are the same size and the edges are even. Repeat with the remaining pancakes. Heat an ungreased skillet and cook each pancake for 2 to 3 minutes on each side. The tops will bubble slightly during cooking. Remove from the skillet and before the pancake cools, gently pull the 2 layers apart so that you have 2 pancakes. Repeat with the remaining pancakes.

Fragrant Cabbage

2 tablespoons dried shrimp
1 cup water
2 tablespoons peanut oil
1 teaspoon salt
1 teaspoon sugar
1 teaspoon vinegar
1 pound Chinese cabbage, rinsed
  and shredded
1 teaspoon white wine
2 sprigs coriander, coarsely
  chopped

This side dish is a simple, straightforward cabbage preparation that comes together quickly. (Recipe: William Mark)

1
Wash and dry the shrimp and soak them in the 1 cup of water for 10 minutes. Heat the oil in a wok or skillet and add the salt, sugar, and vinegar. Add the cabbage and stir-fry over high heat.

2
Add the shrimp with their soaking water, stir well, and cover the wok. Steam for 3 minutes. Splash in the wine, stirring well, and sprinkle with coriander just before serving.

Stir-fried Chinese Kale

4 tablespoons vegetable oil
1 teaspoon salt
1 teaspoon chopped garlic
1½ pounds Chinese kale (kailaam),
  rinsed and trimmed (see Note)
3 tablespoons water
2 teaspoons sugar
1 tablespoon ginger juice (see Note)
1 tablespoon rice wine

(Recipe: William Mark)

1
Place the oil in a wok and heat. Add the salt and garlic.

2
Add the kale and, over very high heat, stir-fry for 30 seconds. Add the water and sugar and stir-fry for another 30 seconds. Add the ginger juice and rice wine, stirring well. Remove from the heat and serve immediately.

Note:
If Chinese kale is not available, substitute Western kale.

Ginger juice is made by grating fresh ginger, wringing out the juice from the fresh shreds, and diluting the juice with water so that the concentration is about 6 parts ginger juice to 2 parts water.

DESSERTS

Toffee Apple and Banana

⅞ cup all-purpose flour
2 apples, peeled and cut into
  wedges
2 bananas, peeled and cut
  into 1-inch rounds
3 cups peanut oil
¾ cup sugar
½ cup water for sugar syrup
1 tablespoon sesame seeds

Apples or bananas coated in molten caramel, then cooled, is a classic Chinese dessert. These come to the table very hot and must be cooled before eating by a quick dunk in ice water. (Recipe: William Mark)

1
In a mixing bowl combine the flour with about ½ cup water—just to form a medium-thick paste or batter. Coat each apple and banana piece well.

2
Heat 2½ cups of the oil in a skillet and, when bubbly, fry the apple and banana pieces until slightly browned, about 2 to 3 minutes. Remove from the pan and set aside.

3
Heat the remaining ½ cup of oil and add the sugar and ½ cup water. Stir constantly to dissolve the sugar and to prevent its scorching. When the sugar is dissolved, add the fruit to the syrup, coating each piece well. Sprinkle with sesame seeds. Remove from the heat and transfer to a serving dish.

4
Serve with a bowl of ice water chilled with ice cubes. Use chopsticks to pick up each piece and dip it into the water to cool and harden the sugar.

Date-Paste Pancake

1¼ cups all-purpose flour
1 large egg
1 cup water
2 tablespoons vegetable oil, plus
   additional for frying
Water and flour (1 to 1 ratio)
   combined to make a paste, to seal
   pancake

Filling
1¾ cups Chinese red dates
   (see Note)
2 tablespoons vegetable oil
3 tablespoons sugar

This makes one very large pancake that is ample for 4 people. (Recipe: William Mark)

1
Sift the flour into a mixing bowl. Make a hole in the center of the flour and add the egg. Mix the egg with the flour and add the water, a little at a time, to form a smooth batter.

2
Place the dates in a saucepan and add enough water to cover by 2 inches. Cook until very soft, about 45 minutes. When cool enough to handle, mash the dates through a sieve and discard the skins. Add enough water to the dates to make a thick paste. Heat the oil in a skillet, add the sugar, and cook until it dissolves. Add the date paste and combine well. Set aside.

3
Heat a lightly greased 10-inch skillet and ladle in the batter to make a thin pancake. Flip once and, when lightly browned on both sides, remove from the heat and cool.

4
Place a tablespoon of date mixture into the middle of the pancake and fold it into a rectangular casing. Seal the edges with the water-and-flour paste.

5
Heat about 2 tablespoons more oil, and fry the pancake on both sides until browned and crispy. Remove from the heat and, when cool enough to handle, slice into small pieces for serving. Serve immediately.

Note:
Unlike the familiar Western brown dates, these Chinese dates—known as jujubes—are tiny dried red fruits, which apparently are not dates at all. These are available in packets at most Asian markets.

Empress Dowager Cakes

2.5 catties white flour
10 catties cornstarch
37.5 catties sugar
37.5 catties walnut meat
18.5 catties honey
2.5 catties preserved cassia flowers
  or blossoms (see Note)
Vegetable oil for frying

These pastries were probably created for the last empress of China. Today they are local delicacies in Beijing. This unedited recipe comes from the chef at the Embassy of the People's Republic of China, Washington, D.C., courtesy of Mrs. Chen Yu-ping and Second Secretary Li Jian. You might want to plan this for a special occasion banquet—it serves 1,200 people. Incidentally, 1 catty equals 1¼ pounds. For quantities to serve 10, see Note.

1

Mix the flour and cornstarch together. Mix with enough water to make a stiff dough. Set aside.

2

Mix the sugar, walnut meat, honey, and cassia flowers to make a thick paste to use as a filling. Set aside.

3

Put some oil in a skillet and heat. By spoonfuls, pour batter into the hot oil and swirl it around to make it flat like a crêpe, about 4 to 6 inches round. Cook for about 30 seconds until browned. Remove from the heat. Spread this with some filling mixture. Cook a second spoonful of batter and place on top of the first. They will stick together and may be eaten right away. Repeat with the remaining batter and filling mixture.

Note:

Yellow cassia flowers or blossoms, if you can find them at all, come from the cassia tree, which also produces sticks of curled bark that are used as a seasoning substitute for cinnamon. Look for these flowers at Chinese or gourmet specialty food stores. If you do find them, and want to try the recipe, here are the quantities to make 10 servings: ½ cup flour, 2 cups cornstarch, 2½ cups sugar, 3½ to 4 cups walnut meat, 2 cups honey, ½ ounce cassia flowers.

The Philippines

SHOES, SHOES, AND MORE SHOES. THE MARCOSES HAVE IMMORTAL-
ized the Philippines, but not for the right reasons. Many Filipinos and old Asia hands
must have a cleaner image of this verdant Asian country whose many islands curl through
the South China Sea like so many pebbles tossed into a pond. They might reminisce about
the friendly Filipinos chattering in Tagalog, about the dramatic landscapes and sculptured
rice terraces, and about the beautiful Filipina women, the countless beaches, the free-
wheeling lifestyle, the American presence, and of course, typhoons and the damp Filipino
heat.

I would talk instead of *buko* pie. *Buko,* or very young coconut meat, is custard-soft
and barely sweet. It is also the key ingredient of an ultra-rich, dense, buttery pastry that
used to be sold (and maybe still is) at countless roadside stands along country highways.
Driving back to Manila once from the International Rice Research Institute, two of us
stopped to buy a pie—and in true local custom, we enjoyed an afternoon snack, or
merienda. But instead of a light repast, we ate the whole thing (see recipe, page 201).

For nearly four centuries, the Philippines was under a tight Spanish rule—with a
subsequent, brief American hiatus before Filipino independence—that has left a permanent mark. Because there is such a Latin beat to its life, language, architecture, and food,
the casual visitor can be fooled into thinking momentarily that he has landed in Puerto
Rico or is passing through an ethnic neighborhood in Manhattan. But a drive through
Manila, past the garbage dump that may still be home to many squatters, past the Mala-
cañang Palace where the Marcoses once lived, through Chinatown and Quiapo and into
the tourist, commercial, and residential areas—and eating a full-scale Filipino meal—
would convince anyone that the Philippines may have a Latin shell but is Asian to the
core.

Imagine, for example, a Spanish cook adding soy and oyster sauces, sugar, and
Chinese noodles to her meal of simmered pork, onions, tomatoes, garlic, and vinegar. A
Filipino cook does, and creates an earthy, Asian-Iberian cuisine of stews and soups and

chowders and stir-fries, sweetened with sugar and soured with vinegar or with tamarind, *kalamansi* lime, or starfruit. Unlike other Asian foods, however, surprisingly few Filipino dishes call for chilies, giving the cuisine a reputation for mildness. "Ours is a salty, vinegary, and sweet food," says Shirley Janairo Roth, a professional cook and cooking teacher—and a Filipina. "It is not the bursting of flavor like in Thai cooking." She explains that Filipino food is a mixture of Chinese and Malay (for ingredients and flavors) and Spanish (for cooking techniques). But the meals local cooks prepare have a distinct Filipino character.

Breakfasts, for example, typically consist of leftover rice fried in garlic and salt, and garnished with fried eggs, sardines, garlic, onions, tomatoes, soy sauce, and chopped green onions. And always, each meal includes a dry course and a soupy or stew course, for a contrast of textures and flavors.

Stir-frying, frying, sautéing, and steaming are basic cooking methods, but grilling is reserved mainly for special occasions or for roadside vendors who have only in modern times introduced barbecued pork or beef take-out snacks. Festival meals might feature grilled goat, or grilled stuffed fish, or barbecued suckling pig *(lechon),* and would certainly include stews; noodles; steamed rice; platters of stir-fried taro root, potatoes, green beans, and/or chayotes; fresh papayas, pineapples, mangoes, jackfruit, or *guabano;* and an array of coconut-based sweets.

Mrs. Roth has assembled a booklet of Filipino recipes (giving me permission to use some) that makes educational, and disarming, reading. The recipes' names are often in Spanish, but the ingredients are often pure Southeast Asia.

THE GRILLS

Roast Suckling Pig

1 whole suckling pig (10 to 12
  pounds), ready for grilling
1 pound lemongrass stalks or
  tamarind leaves

Lechon Liver Sauce
2 tablespoons vegetable oil
8 large cloves garlic, peeled and
  crushed
2 tablespoons finely chopped onion
Whole pig's liver, grilled and
  pureed, or two 4½-ounce cans
  liver paste
Salt and freshly ground black
  pepper to taste
½ cup water
¼ cup white vinegar
¼ cup sugar
¼ cup unseasoned bread crumbs

Filipinos love to celebrate, and any occasion will do to gather for a magnificent spread. Lechon—the famed Filipino roast suckling pig—is usually the featured dish, and is a real delicacy. My Filipina friend Shirley Janairo Roth says that the villagers where she lived would first grill, then pound the pig's liver to make the rich sauce, a key part of this celebratory meal. Suckling pigs are often hard to find in the United States or weigh more than the 10- to 12-pound limit. To re-create this popular dish here, says Mrs. Roth, Filipinos buy an 8- to 9-pound fresh ham butt or a whole fresh pork leg and grill it at home. Or if they can find a moderate-sized suckling pig, they ask a restaurant to prepare it for them—because chances are it will have outgrown any domestic oven or barbecue. Then they make the sauce by using canned liver paste and seasoning it in the typical manner. It's the sauce and the crackling skin that make this dish. (Recipe: Chef Paul Amado, The Manila Restaurant)

1

Stuff the pig's cavity with the lemongrass or tamarind leaves and sew up the cavity with soft wire, or use a skewer closure.

2

Insert a bamboo pole or metal spit through the pig, from tail to head. Place both ends of the pole on supports secured to the ground, or set the metal spit into a rotisserie stand and start grilling the pig. You can also use a covered barbecue, provided it is large enough for the pig to fit, and cook the pig by the indirect method (page xxix) over medium-hot coals. In any case, you must regularly brush the skin with water to make the skin crisp. The cooking will take several hours—3 to 4 probably—

and you may need to replenish the coals during the cooking.

3

While the pig is cooking, heat the oil in a saucepan. Add the garlic and sauté until brown. Then add the onion and cook for 1 minute more. Add the liver paste, combining well. Season with salt and pepper to taste. Gradually add the water and stir well.

4

Add the vinegar and sugar and let the mixture come to a boil without stirring. Then add the bread crumbs and cook, stirring until thick, about 15 minutes.

5

Remove the pig from the fire and put it on a large serving platter. Slice the suckling pig into individual portions and serve with the sauce.

Grilled Garlicked Fish

1 pound fish fillets
Vegetable oil for brushing the grill
Marinade
4 cloves garlic, peeled and minced
Salt and freshly ground black
  pepper to taste
¼ cup coconut vinegar (see Note)

This is a simple grilled dish for which you can use any firm-fleshed fish fillets. (Recipe: Joey Bogambal)

1

Put the fish in a shallow baking dish. Combine the marinade ingredients and pour over the fish. Cover with foil or plastic wrap and set aside for at least 30 minutes.

2

Brush the grill rack with oil, or use the special wire basket for grilling and brush it with oil. This prevents the fish from sticking. Grill the fish by the direct method (page xxix) over medium-hot coals for 4 to 5 minutes, turning once and brushing with the marinade.

3

Remove from the fire and serve immediately.

Note:

This is a vinegar that has a coconut flavor—the cook suggests using the Sukang Paombong brand, which is available in some Asian markets.

Barbecued Pork Cutlets

1 pound boneless pork loin roast,
  thinly sliced
Marinade
3 to 4 cloves garlic, peeled and
  mashed
Salt to taste
White vinegar to cover

This is a simple family dish that is delicious with mashed potatoes or rice. (Recipe: Shirley Janairo Roth)

1

Put the pork slices in a large baking dish. Sprinkle with the garlic and salt and pour on enough vinegar to cover the meat. Cover with foil or plastic wrap and set aside for 30 minutes.

2

Grill the pork by the direct method (page xxix) over medium-hot coals for 5 to 7 minutes, turning once. Remove from the fire and serve immediately.

Lemon Barbecued Chicken

8 *whole chicken breasts, split in half*
Marinade
⅓ *cup fresh lemon juice*
⅓ *cup soy sauce*
6 *cloves garlic, peeled and crushed*
⅓ *cup vegetable oil*
½ *teaspoon sugar*

This Filipina cook says you can substitute pork chops for chicken, if you wish. (Recipe: Lenor Basto)

1
Put the chicken breasts in a large glass baking dish. Combine the marinade ingredients and pour over the chicken. Cover the dish with foil or plastic wrap and refrigerate overnight.

2
Remove the chicken from the refrigerator 30 minutes before cooking. Grill the chicken by the direct method (page xxix) over hot coals for 10 to 12 minutes, turning the pieces and basting them often as they cook. Remove from the fire and serve immediately.

Fish Stuffed with Tomatoes and Onions

One 3- to 4-pound whole firm-fleshed white fish, such as snapper or sea bass, boned
Salt and freshly ground black pepper to taste
Juice of ½ lemon
Melted butter for basting
Banana leaves or foil for wrapping
Vegetable oil for brushing

Stuffing
2 tablespoons vegetable oil
2 cloves garlic, peeled and crushed
1 large onion, peeled and chopped
2 large tomatoes, chopped
Salt and freshly ground black pepper to taste

(Recipe: Shirley Janairo Roth)

1
Ask your fishmonger to clean, scale, and bone the fish. Otherwise, clean it by slitting open the stomach and pulling out the intestines. Scale it by scraping a sharp knife carefully across the surface of the skin against the natural lie of the scales. Bone it by using a very sharp paring knife to make a slit directly below the head along the top of the spine to the tail. Cut along one side of the spine, as close to the bone as you can, and pull the meat slowly away from the bone. Repeat this on the other side. Use scissors to cut and remove the bones, leaving the head and tail intact.

2
Lay the fish on a flat surface and sprinkle with salt, pepper, and lemon juice. Set aside.

3
To make the stuffing, pour the oil into a skillet and heat. Fry the garlic until golden brown. Add the onion and cook until transparent. Add the tomatoes and stir-fry for about 5 minutes over medium heat. Add salt and pepper, remove from the heat, and cool slightly.

4
With metal skewers, close the stomach opening of the fish. Spoon the stuffing mixture into the opening along the spine, packing it in gently. With metal skewers, close the spine opening to keep the stuffing inside. Brush the fish with the butter and wrap. If you are using banana leaves, soften them according to the directions in the Glossary. Put the fish in the center of several layers of leaves and fold the sides to the center to cover the fish. Secure both ends with toothpicks. If using foil, crimp the ends closed. Brush the banana-leaf packet with oil, if desired.

5

Grill the fish by the indirect method (page xxix) for about 30 minutes, turning once. Serve immediately.

Barbecued Pork Loin

1 pound boneless pork loin roast, cubed
Bamboo skewers
Marinade
5 cloves garlic, peeled and crushed
⅓ cup lemon juice sweetened with sugar to taste
1½ tablespoons annatto oil (see Note)
1 tablespoon sugar
1 tablespoon hot pepper sauce
1 tablespoon ketchup
2 tablespoons soy sauce
⅛ teaspoon salt
1 to 2 fresh red chilies, chopped

This dish is about the closest the Filipinos get to serving a satay. *The sweetness in the marinade comes from sweetened lemon juice. Mrs. Roth swears you can get the same effect from using an equal amount of 7-Up. (Recipe: Shirley Janairo Roth)*

1

Put the pork cubes in a large baking dish. Combine the marinade ingredients and pour them over the meat. Mix well to coat the pork. Cover with foil or plastic wrap and set aside for at least 30 minutes. For best results, refrigerate and marinate the meat overnight. Take the meat out of the refrigerator at least 30 minutes before cooking.

2

Thread the pork on skewers and grill by the direct method (page xxix) over medium-hot coals until thoroughly cooked, about 5 minutes on each side. Remove from the fire and serve immediately.

Note:

The small annatto seeds produce a reddish color that is popular in many Filipino dishes. To make the oil, combine ½ cup vegetable oil with 1½ tablespoons annatto seeds in a skillet and cook over low heat until the oil turns red. Discard the seeds and save the oil. Store it in a bottle in the refrigerator. If annatto seeds are unavailable, use equal portions of turmeric and paprika—⅛ teaspoon each for each teaspoon of annatto seeds. Annatto is also known by Latin cooks as achiote.

ACCOMPANIMENTS

Pork Noodle Soup

1 pound boneless lean pork
2 pounds pork neck bones
1¾ quarts water
4 tablespoons vegetable oil
2 large eggs, beaten
One 8-ounce package fresh or dried
    Chinese egg noodles
2 tablespoons sesame oil
1½ quarts pork or chicken stock
1 medium onion, peeled and diced
1½ teaspoons salt, plus extra to taste
1 teaspoon MSG (optional)
1 dried red chili, crumbled
    (optional)
1½ cups shredded cabbage
5 scallions, thinly sliced, for garnish
Soy sauce for seasoning

The recipe for this popular Filipino soup may look complicated, but it is actually simple to put together. (Recipe: Shirley Janairo Roth)

1
Put the pork and pork neck bones in a deep stockpot. Add the water and bring to a boil, cooking until the pork is tender, about 45 minutes. Skim off the scum. Remove the meat from the stock and, when cool enough to handle, dice the meat and scrape any meat off the neck bones. Reserve the stock. Heat a wok or skillet and add 1 tablespoon of the oil; stir-fry the cubed pork and neck meat until golden. Remove from the heat, and set the meat aside.

2
Put 1 more tablespoon of oil in the skillet or wok and heat until the oil is bubbly. Pour in the beaten eggs and make into a thin, flat omelet. When cooked, remove from the skillet, shred, and set aside.

3
Fill a large saucepan with water and bring to a boil. Add the noodles and cook for 3 to 5 minutes, stirring frequently to separate the strands. Remove from the heat and drain the noodles in a colander, rinsing them with cold water to stop the cooking. Heat the remaining 2 tablespoons of oil in a skillet and stir-fry the noodles for 2 minutes. During cooking, sprinkle the noodles with the sesame oil.

4
Bring the stock to a boil, adding water if needed to make 6 cups. Add the onion, seasonings, and cabbage and boil for 5 minutes.

5
Spoon the noodles into individual bowls or into a soup tureen. Pour in the soup and garnish with the pork,

shredded omelet, and scallions. Serve immediately and offer soy sauce for seasoning on the side.

Chicken Adobo

One 2½- to 3-pound frying chicken, cut into serving pieces
Flour for dusting
¼ to ½ cup vegetable oil for browning
1 large onion, peeled and diced
3 or more cloves garlic, peeled and minced
1 bay leaf
About 10 whole peppercorns, or to taste
⅓ cup soy sauce
¼ cup white vinegar
1 tablespoon sugar
¾ cup water

This chicken casserole combines the sour and sweet flavors Filipinos love so much, and it is so popular that it could be a national dish. This would be a fine accompaniment to a festive barbecue party featuring the suckling pig. My children ate the adobo *often when we lived in Hong Kong, and have carried their love for this dish into adult life. I double the recipe when I make it for them. (Recipe: Ildefonsa Pabros)*

1
Dust the chicken pieces with flour. Heat the oil in a large skillet and brown the pieces on both sides. Remove them to a large saucepan or stockpot.

2
Add all the remaining ingredients and cover the pot with a lid. Simmer for 1 to 1½ hours. You can prepare this dish a day ahead and refrigerate and reheat it, if you wish.

String Beans with Ground Pork

2 tablespoons vegetable oil
2 cloves garlic, peeled and minced
1 medium onion, peeled and diced
1 medium tomato, chopped
½ pound ground pork
1 teaspoon salt
Freshly ground black pepper to taste
½ cup chicken stock or water
1 pound green beans, strings removed, trimmed into 1-inch pieces
1 dried red chili (optional)

(Recipe: Shirley Janairo Roth)

Heat the oil in a saucepan. Add the garlic and cook until golden brown, stirring often. Add the onion and cook for 1 minute. Add the tomato and cook for 1 more minute. Add the ground pork and stir-fry for 5 minutes. Add the salt, pepper, and broth or water. Simmer for 15 minutes. Add the beans and simmer for 10 minutes, or until the beans are crisp-tender. Crumble the chili and sprinkle it over the beans. Serve immediately.

DESSERTS

Buko Pie

1 cup sugar
¼ cup cornstarch
5 eggs, beaten
½ teaspoon salt
1½ cups evaporated milk
2 tablespoons sweet butter
2 tablespoons vanilla extract
Two 1-pound packages frozen buko, drained, or 10 ounces shredded coconut (see Note)
One 10-inch pie shell

Both Lenor Basto and Shirley Janairo Roth gave me recipes for this wonderful sweet, which is actually a glorified coconut cream pie. I took liberties with both recipes, combining them to come up with the custardy flavor and texture I remember from that drive down a Filipino highway.

1

Preheat the oven to 350°.

2

In a saucepan, over medium heat, stir together the sugar, cornstarch, beaten eggs, and salt. Slowly stir in the milk, and continue cooking over medium heat until the mixture begins to thicken and comes to a boil. Lower the heat and simmer until the mixture is thick.

3

Remove from the heat and blend in the butter and vanilla. Add the *buko* and pour the mixture into the pie shell. Bake at 350° for 30 minutes, or until the pie is firm and the crust is golden. Remove and refrigerate, chilling thoroughly before slicing.

Note:

Buko, or young coconut, is available canned or frozen at many Asian markets. My grocer says that the frozen product produces better results than the canned, but I didn't try the canned. If you cannot find *buko,* use shredded, dried coconut instead. It won't give the same texture, but it is better than nothing.

Halo Halo

Jackfruit (see Note)
Red mung beans
Palm nut, or palmyra fruit (see Note)
Prepared sweetened gelatin
    pudding, cut into cubes
Jalea ube (see Note)
Macapuno (see Note)
Evaporated milk
Shaved ice
Scoop of vanilla ice cream

Halo Halo is a do-what-you-want refreshment that is eaten or drunk as a cooling snack. You add the ingredients you like in the quantities you want and top them off with shaved ice and a scoop of vanilla ice cream. A typical assortment includes the following ingredients. (Recipe: Joey Bogambal)

Combine all but the last 2 ingredients in a large bowl or soda glass, top off with the ice and ice cream, and serve with a spoon and straw.

Note:
Jackfruit, palm nut (palm nut, or *baong* in the Philippines, has a nutlike covering and a white, semitranslucent, soft, edible, and sweet inside) *jalea ube* (yam), and *macapuno* (coconut product) are all available canned at most Asian markets.

Bibingka Royal

3 eggs
¾ cup sugar
2 cups all-purpose flour
4 teaspoons baking powder
1½ cups coconut milk
4 tablespoons butter, melted
Sugar for sprinkling
Freshly grated meat from 2 whole
    coconuts, or about 3 cups dried
    shredded coconut

This Philippine cake is enriched with plenty of coconut and needs no frosting. The 2 layers are served separately and resemble 2 very thick pancakes. (Recipe: Shirley Janairo Roth)

1
Preheat the oven to 350°. Grease two 9-inch round cake pans and set aside.

2
Put the eggs in a large mixing bowl and beat them well. Gradually add the sugar, a few spoonfuls at a time, beating well after each addition. Sift and stir in the flour and baking powder, adding them alternately with the coconut milk. Beat well. Add 2 tablespoons of the melted butter.

3
Divide the cake batter evenly between the 2 pans. Bake in the preheated oven for 30 minutes—during baking, brush or sprinkle some of the remaining melted butter twice on the surface of the batter. When the cake is firm in the center, remove it from the oven and brush the surface of each layer with more melted butter and sprinkle sugar on top. Cool before serving, slice into wedges, and pass the cake with a bowl of grated coconut.

Macau

IF CHINA WERE A FACE, THEN THE TINY PORTUGUESE COLONY OF Macau (Macao) would be a dimple somewhere along the jawline. Washed on one side by the South China Sea and on the other by the Pearl River, the peninsula and islands of Macau are all but invisible on any grand-scale map. But it is not a forgotten spot: Tourists love it. Gamblers love it. And China has its eye on it. Until the borders opened in the late 1970s, Chinese gunboats steamed up and down the Pearl River in full view of the Macanese, keeping people both in and out of the mainland.

In those days, Macau seemed oddly exotic, a strange Portuguese backwash in Asia, locked away in a Mediterranean time-warp with its pink colonial buildings, fraying European-style churches, and cobbled streets. The leading Macanese personality and historian at the time, Father Manuel Teixiera, S.J., in his long white robes, delighted in showing off his homeland, leading visitors through back streets to meet his parishioners, and displaying his dusty archives in the Seminario de San Jose. Afterwards, perhaps a Portuguese or Macanese lunch and a quick drive over the bridges to the two outer islands, Taipa and Colôane, were in order.

Today, like every place else, Macau has changed. Father Teixiera may still welcome visitors, but gone are the town's cluttered back alleys full of genuine treasures and curios. Instead, smart new hotels, casinos, shops, racetracks, and restaurants give Macau a resort atmosphere. Sight-seeing daytime tourists from Hong Kong arrive by early-morning jetfoil, hire a taxi or pedicab, and make a slow swing through the narrow streets and along the waterfront before catching the return boat home. By night—according to Macauphile Harry Rolnick, Hong Kong's writer-about-town—yuppies from Hong Kong head to Macau for gambling and dining.

Macau may have gone upscale, but many local restaurants still offer the grilled and stewed Portuguese-Macanese dishes of a less glittery era. I remember the bracing lunches of steamy *caldo verde* soup, grilled African chicken, baskets of fresh hot rolls with scoops of sweet butter, a thick caramel flan for dessert, and glasses of the chilled Portuguese Faisca sparkling wine.

THE GRILLS

African Chicken

2 frying chickens, about 2½ pounds
   each, halved lengthwise

Marinade

4 tablespoons grated coconut, fresh
   or dried
1 tablespoon paprika
1 large onion, peeled and finely
   chopped
6 shallots, peeled and finely
   chopped
6 cloves garlic, peeled and crushed
1 teaspoon salt
4 dried red chilies, crushed
1 teaspoon cayenne
1 tablespoon MSG (optional)
¾ cup olive oil

Sauce

1 tablespoon butter
Grated rind of 1 lemon
Juice of ½ a lemon
Pinch salt
Dash of Tabasco sauce
Dash of MSG (optional)

According to Harry Rolnick, the original recipe for this dish was brought to Macau by Portuguese soldiers via Mozambique. But nobody seems to know why African Chicken is so popular in Macau. There are many versions—some stewed, others grilled, and all spicy. This dish is marvelous when served with mashed or country-fried potatoes, a side of codfish cakes, and cooked green beans. (Recipe: Harry Rolnick/Macau Tourist Information Board)

1

Remove the chicken skin and chop it fine. Set aside for use in the marinade. Flatten the chicken halves so they grill evenly and set them aside in a shallow baking dish.

2

Combine all the marinade ingredients, including the chicken skin, in a saucepan and bring to a boil. Lower the heat and simmer uncovered for about 10 minutes. Remove from the heat and cool.

3

When the marinade is cool, pour it over the chicken, being sure that all surfaces are covered. Wrap the dish in foil or plastic wrap and refrigerate for at least 2 hours, turning the chicken frequently.

4

Grill the chicken by the indirect method (page xxix) over medium-hot coals for 15 or 20 minutes, basting it with the marinade and turning it frequently until all the sides are evenly browned. Meanwhile, prepare the sauce by melting the butter in a saucepan and adding the other ingredients. Simmer for several minutes.

5

Remove the chicken from the fire. Place each half on an individual serving dish and pour the sauce over the chicken before serving.

ACCOMPANIMENTS

Fried Codfish Cakes

One 6½-ounce piece bacalao, moist-packed (see Note)
1 pound potatoes, peeled
1 large onion, peeled and finely chopped
1 tablespoon olive oil
1 tablespoon chopped parsley
1 large egg, beaten
Salt and freshly ground black pepper to taste
2 tablespoons milk
¼ pound rice vermicelli, broken up, soaked in hot water, and drained
Vegetable oil for frying

(Recipe: Mandarin Oriental Hotel)

1

Soak the bacalao for 2 days in a large bowl of water if you use the dried pieces. Otherwise soak the fish overnight or at least several hours. Remove the fish from the water and put it in a saucepan with the potatoes. Cover with water and bring to a boil. Reduce the heat and simmer uncovered until the potatoes are cooked and the fish is softened, about 30 minutes.

2

Meanwhile, sauté the onion in the olive oil until the onion is translucent. Drain off the oil. Carefully remove the fish from the water and drain the potatoes well. Remove the bones and skin from the fish and put the flesh in the container of a food processor (use plastic blades; metal blades will make the flesh mushy). Process the fish until the fibers are separated and the flesh is feathery.

3

Mash the potatoes and add to the fish. Combine the onion, parsley, egg, and salt and pepper with the fish mixture and mix everything together with your hands. Add 1 tablespoon of the milk—the mixture should not be too moist or the cakes will lose their shape. Add more of the milk if necessary. Drain the vermicelli and chop the pieces very small. Combine the vermicelli with the fish mixture. Scoop out ¼ cupful of the mixture and shape it into a patty. Continue until all the mixture is used up.

4

Pour enough oil into a deep skillet to cover the cakes and place them gently, a few at a time, into the hot oil. Fry them, turning to brown and crisp evenly. Remove

them from the skillet with a slotted spatula and drain well on paper towels. Serve at once.

Note:

Bacalao, or salted codfish, is sometimes available in dried slabs, a form that some people prefer. But because it is so salty, it needs presoaking for many hours to get rid of the saltiness. Bacalao is also sold in moist chunks wrapped in plastic and stored in the refrigerator case. This form needs only minimal soaking before use. You can find bacalao in some Asian markets or in Latin markets.

Portuguese Green Vegetable Soup

4 whole potatoes, peeled and cubed
2 large onions, peeled and cubed
2 quarts water
2 tablespoons olive oil
Salt and freshly ground black
    pepper to taste
½ pound spinach, rinsed, trimmed,
    and chopped
½ pound kale, rinsed, trimmed, and
    chopped
Portuguese sausage, sliced, for
    garnish (see Note)

Known as caldo verde, this steamy soup, as a one-dish meal or as a first course, will ward off winter chills. (Recipe: Harry Rolnick/Macau Tourist Information Board)

1

Combine the potatoes and onions with the water in a large saucepan. Bring the water to a boil and cook the vegetables uncovered until tender, about 20 minutes. Add the olive oil, salt, and pepper.

2

Add the chopped spinach and kale and cook briefly. Adjust the seasonings. Serve the soup immediately, garnishing each serving with slices of sausage.

Note:

Portuguese sausage, also known as linguiça, is a mild, garlicky sausage often available at specialty food stores, at some Asian markets, and in Latin and Spanish markets. Mexican chorizo sausage is a reasonable substitute.

DESSERT

Rice Pudding

½ cup raw long-grain rice
2 tablespoons sugar or to taste
3 to 4 cups milk
2 tablespoons sweet butter
Fresh fruit or fruit syrup for topping

(Recipe: Harry Rolnick/Macau Tourist Information Board)

1

Drain and rinse the rice and place it in the top section of a double boiler. Stir in the sugar, milk, and butter. Fill the bottom section of the double boiler with water, but do not allow the water to touch the top section. Cover the pot with a lid and cook the rice over boiling water until it is soft, about 2 hours. Check occasionally that the water has not boiled away; if so, add more water and continue cooking.

2

Serve hot, with fresh fruit or a fruit syrup, such as a pineapple or mango puree, if desired.

Chapter
6

ANCIENT

KINGDOMS

TRAVEL WRITER CARL PARKES IN HIS SOUTHEAST ASIAN GUIDEBOOK
describes Indochina (French Indochina)—Vietnam, Cambodia, and Laos—as "Asia's
final frontier." These three countries fit like elongated jagged jigsaw pieces into an area
known as the Golden Peninsula, bound on one side by the South China Sea and on the
others by China and Thailand. I think of these timeless exotic lands as ancient kingdoms
with a history as fascinating as that of any country in Europe.

But to this group I would add Burma (Myanmar), which borders Thailand, the
northern tip of Laos, and China, India, and Bangladesh. While they are not contiguous
lands and do not share the same culture, language, or recent political history, these four
countries bear several striking similarities: Their founding stocks came from Tibet, China,
or India, or some combination of the three. All four have cultures strongly influenced by
China or India. All are tropical lands with bands of mountain ranges that slice through the
country. Many of their inhabitants are fervent Buddhists. All four countries have had
highly developed and sophisticated cultures. All four countries have had ruling royalty.
All four countries have been under European rule. All four countries have been governed
by Communist, pro-Communist, or totalitarian rulers. All have been virtually closed to the
outside world for a period of time in the past several decades.

As for food, the Burmese, Vietnamese, Lao, and Cambodians link food with hospitality, and sharing a meal is a way to honor friends and strangers. The dishes themselves
—which in each country bear Chinese and Indian influences—use many similar ingredients and seasonings, though with very different results. And rice is the foundation of each
of their cuisines.

Burma

FIRST IMPRESSIONS OFTEN BEAR NO RELATION TO REALITY, AND THAT is certainly true for me with Burma. My childhood knowledge of Burma came from the "Burma Shave" signs posted along California highways. Burma, my parents said, was a very far distant—and somewhat mysterious—country in Asia. Decades later, Burma still is a remote land, but I know a little more about this essentially closed society. (At this writing, foreigner visitors are allowed no more than two weeks in Burma.) In fact, Burma —to the consternation of the Burmans I have met—is no longer Burma but Myanmar, and its capital city is no longer Rangoon but Yangon, names that do not conjure up the same romantic images of Kipling-style derring-do. The name changes have also affected the nomenclature of the citizens: Burmese are now Myanmar, but I gather that the term "Burmans" is still used to describe the largest ethnic group.

Yvonne Khin and her husband U Khin, retired from the diplomatic service of the Union of Burma, now live in Maryland, and speak with great passion of the Burma they knew as children—a lush country teeming with wildlife, blanketed with Buddhist temples, and stocked with gentle people who were bolstered by the assurance that everything works for the best. I would guess, judging from their reports of Burma's climate, that people also move through life with the ease and grace of those weighed down by dense tropical heat. No one hurries when temperatures range between 90 and 110° Fahrenheit.

Burmese cooking, influenced by China and India and the immigrants from neighboring Asian countries, has developed in its own unique way with obvious Chinese and Indian overtones. But it quite obviously is neither Chinese nor Indian. It is better than either, says Yvonne Khin, who explains that Burmese cooking is a "happy medium between the highly spiced foods of India and the mild sweetish food of China." The Burmese spice shelf includes the basics of turmeric, ginger, salt, sugar, garlic, and onion, and the less commonly used galangal and lemongrass. "And, of course, a lot of chilies," says Mrs. Khin. "Our food can be as hot as Malaysian food." In her cookbook, Burmese Mi Mi Khaing describes the Burmese litany of flavors: sour, sweet (sugar-sweet and rice-

sweet), salty, peppery hot, gingery hot, vaguely hot, aromatic, nutty, bitter, barely bitter, full-bodied, light, tangy, and surfeiting.

Without access to refrigerators, freezers, or packaged foods, traditional Burmese eat according to the calendar, but there is one year-round constant: rice, rice, and more rice (Burma used to be a major rice-growing country), accompanied by seafood and meat, plain or made into a curry, and accompanied by soups, vegetables, and pickles. "We eat all kinds of meat," explains Mrs. Khin, "including pork, fish, and chicken. We do not eat monkeys, dogs, frogs, or snakes." A typical day's eating would start with cold leftover rice very early in the morning followed by a large midmorning meal about 10 A.M., before the real heat of the day. A second similar, and final, meal would be served in late afternoon when things had cooled down a bit.

Despite the fact that traditional Burmese kitchens use wood- and charcoal-burning stoves and braziers, there are surprisingly few Burmese grilled dishes. "We hardly grill," says Burman Mrs. Eleanor Law-Yone. "But when we do, it is seafood." Mrs. Khin explains why: "It's so hot. In such a tropical country, we can get intestinal problems with eating things raw and kept out for a while. We buy meat in the morning and the maggots come out by evening."

Burmese cook by taste and tradition without consulting written recipes. To help Westerners and to document a national cuisine, the Khins have compiled in book form an exhaustive collection of typical recipes, and they have generously allowed me access to their manuscript.

THE GRILLS

Barbecued Shrimp

2 pounds large shrimp, shelled and
  deveined
Bamboo skewers soaked in water
Marinade
½ cup soy sauce
¼ cup sugar
1 teaspoon grated fresh ginger
1 teaspoon red wine

A simple seafood dish, this is typically served with boiled rice, but it is a fine accompaniment for noodles and a light salad. (Recipe: Yvonne and U Khin)

1
With a sharp knife, slice along the length of the curved back of the shrimp, cutting almost through the body. Open the shrimp out flat, then place them in a large mixing bowl. Combine the marinade ingredients and pour over the shrimp. Cover the bowl with aluminum foil or plastic wrap and refrigerate for 30 minutes.
2
Thread the shrimp, 3 to a skewer, on bamboo skewers. Grill by the direct method (page xxix) over low to medium-hot coals, turning once, for about 7 to 10 minutes. Remove from the fire and serve immediately.

Roasted Duck on Sugarcane

One 3- to 5-pound duck
1 teaspoon salt
2 tablespoons soy sauce
½ pound ground pork
3 large onions, peeled and sliced
8 cloves garlic, peeled and sliced
½ ounce dried Chinese mushrooms,
    soaked in hot water and sliced
2 stalks celery, sliced into 1-inch
    pieces
1 large egg
1 teaspoon freshly ground black
    pepper
1 cup vegetable oil
1 foot-long stalk fresh sugarcane,
    trimmed into 3-inch pieces, or
    canned sugarcane
Disposable foil pan, 10 x 14 inches

This recipe comes from a Burmese cookbook published by the Woman's Society of Christian Service of the Methodist English Church in Rangoon in 1956. The contributor of this recipe—"Mrs. Kyi Win, wife of U Kyi Win, Chief Engineer, Burma Railways"—described a cooking method that sounds something like grilling by the indirect method in a covered barbecue— using live charcoal on the lid of a cooking utensil. A renowned local cook at the time, she called this one of her most "delectable" dishes. (Recipe: Mrs. Kyi Win, adapted)

1

Rinse and pat the duck dry. Mix ½ teaspoon of the salt and 1 tablespoon of the soy sauce and rub on the inside and the skin of the duck. Set aside.

2

Combine in a large mixing bowl the pork, remaining salt, remaining soy sauce, the onions, 4 cloves of garlic, the mushrooms, celery, egg, ½ teaspoon of the pepper, and ¼ cup of the oil and mix together well. Stuff this in the cavity of the duck. Skewer the cavity closed. Put the remaining ¼ cup of oil in a saucepan and heat. Add the remaining 4 cloves of garlic and ½ teaspoon of pepper and cook briefly. Remove from the heat and set aside to use for basting during cooking.

3

Arrange a layer of sugarcane on the bottom of the pan. Place the duck on top of these and set the pan on a rack inside a covered barbecue. Grill the duck by the indirect method (page xxix) for 1½ hours over medium-hot coals, brushing it occasionally with the basting mixture. Remove from the heat and place the duck on a platter. Scoop out the stuffing mixture to serve on the side.

ACCOMPANIMENTS

Fried Burmese Fish Cakes

1 pound catfish fillets
1 pound potatoes
2 large eggs, beaten
2 cups of vegetable oil
1 teaspoon freshly ground black pepper
1 teaspoon salt
½ cup all-purpose flour

(Yvonne and U Khin, adapted)

1
Boil the catfish in 1 quart of water for about 10 minutes. Drain and set aside.

2
Boil the potatoes in 1 quart of water until tender. Remove from the water, peel, and mash.

3
Combine the fish and potatoes in the container of a food processor or blender and puree. Add the eggs, 1 tablespoon of the oil, and pepper and salt.

4
Heat the remaining oil in a 10-inch skillet. When bubbly, dust hands with flour and shape ¼ cup of the fish mixture into a patty. Fry the cakes in the skillet, 3 or 4 at a time. Turn to brown on both sides. Remove from the oil and drain on paper towels. Set aside until ready to use.

Burmese Rice Vermicelli

2 pounds fish fillets, such as flounder
1½ cups vegetable oil
1½ cups dried yellow split peas
2 quarts water
3 tablespoons fish paste
1 teaspoon salt
4 large onions, peeled and
    quartered
2 cups banana shoots, optional (see
    Note)
1 cup coconut milk
1½ pounds thick rice vermicelli

Seasoning Mixture
4 large onions, peeled and chopped
4 cloves garlic, peeled and
    chopped
1 tablespoon crushed red chilies
One 1-inch piece fresh ginger,
    grated
4 stalks lemongrass, very thinly
    sliced and crushed
1 teaspoon ground turmeric

Accompaniments
1 cup thinly sliced scallions
12 cloves garlic, peeled, sliced, and
    fried in oil until golden
4 medium onions, peeled, sliced,
    and fried in oil until golden
1 cup finely chopped coriander
    leaves

My Burman resources, Mr. and Mrs. Khin, describe this as the "most popular dish in Burma," really its national dish. Known as mon hinga, *this potent fish curry may be eaten morning, noon, and night—the Khins remember it being sold in Burma by street hawkers and served in more conventional restaurants. It makes an ideal party dish, suited to buffets and other casual get-togethers. Although this recipe serves 6, Mrs. Khin notes that you can increase the ingredients proportionately to serve larger crowds. (Recipe: Yvonne and U Khin)*

1
Put the fish fillets into a large saucepan and add enough water to cover. Bring to a boil, lower the heat, and simmer uncovered until the fish is cooked and the water evaporates. Meanwhile, combine the seasoning mixture ingredients in a bowl.

2
When the fish is cooked, add the vegetable oil and seasoning mixture and continue to cook uncovered over low heat, stirring often.

3
Meanwhile, combine the yellow split peas with the 2 quarts water in a large saucepan and bring to a boil. Continue to cook until the peas are very soft and mushy, about 30 minutes. Add the peas and their liquid to the fish curry along with the fish paste, salt, the quartered onions, and the banana shoots, if using them. Continue simmering the fish curry for 15 minutes more and add the coconut milk. Reduce the heat to the lowest possible setting until you are ready to serve.

4
Meanwhile, put the vermicelli in boiling water and cook for 7 to 10 minutes or until tender, and drain. Put the

6 *large eggs, hard-boiled,*
quartered
Fried fish cakes (see Note)
2 *tablespoons crushed red chilies*
Juice of 6 limes or lemons

accompaniments in separate dishes. When you are ready to serve, assemble the dish by putting ¾ cup of vermicelli into an individual soup bowl. Pour over it 1 cup or more of the fish curry, and put some of each accompaniment over the top.

Note:
The original recipe calls for using as garnish fried fish cakes (page 215) or squash, zucchini, or gourd, fried crisp. The recipe also calls for 2 cups sliced banana shoots—you may use these fresh or canned. You can find them at most Asian markets.

Burmese Pickles

2 *pounds apples, peels intact, cut*
into 1-inch squares
1 *cup vegetable oil*
2 *large pickling jars with lids*
Curry Mixture
4 *tablespoons red chili powder*
2 *tablespoons garlic powder*
2 *tablespoons ground ginger*
2 *tablespoons ground cumin*
2 *tablespoons mustard powder*
6 *bay leaves, crushed*

Burmese cooks Mr. and Mrs. Khin explain that Burmese dishes are rather rich and lend themselves to an accompaniment of pickles to offset the richness. Burmese cooks make three categories of pickle: sour, oily, and sweet-sour. The following recipe is for an "oil pickle." The original recipe calls for partially drying the apples in the sun—you may dry them in a 200° oven instead. (Recipe: Yvonne and U Khin)

1
Layer the apple squares on a clean baking sheet and bake them in a 200° oven for several hours, or until they are partially dried out.

2
Meanwhile, combine the ingredients for the curry mixture in a large mixing bowl. Heat the oil in a skillet until it is smoking, then lower the temperature. Add the curry mixture and the apples and cook for about 15 minutes, stirring often and mixing well. Remove from the heat and cool. Pour into sterile glass jars and seal. Store in the refrigerator and use as needed.

Watercress Salad

2 bunches watercress, rinsed and
    trimmed into 1-inch lengths
Dressing
4 tablespoons vegetable oil
1 medium onion, peeled and sliced
2 cloves garlic, peeled and sliced
1½ tablespoons sesame seeds
2 scallions, including green tops,
    thinly sliced
1 teaspoon ground red chilies
2 tablespoons soy sauce
1½ tablespoons sugar
Salt to taste
2 tablespoons white vinegar
½ teaspoon freshly ground black
    pepper
1 teaspoon MSG (optional)

This light salad provides a peppery taste that serves as a foil for rich and heavy meat dishes. (Recipe: Yvonne and U Khin)

1

Pour the oil for the dressing into a skillet and heat. Sauté the onion and garlic until golden brown. Toast the sesame seeds in a dry skillet, stirring to keep them from burning. Remove from the heat and set aside.

2

Combine the remaining dressing ingredients in a bowl. Add the onion and garlic and watercress to the bowl and toss until the leaves are well-coated. Sprinkle the sesame seeds on top.

DESSERTS

Burmese Sweet Cakes

3 large eggs
1 pound sugar
1 pound uncooked regular cream of
   wheat
3 quarts coconut milk
1 teaspoon salt
½ cup sliced almonds
½ cup raisins
1 tablespoon poppy seeds

Despite an abundance of fresh, seasonal fruit, Burmese also love an abundance of pastries, cakes, and puddings. These sensational cakes may be served as dessert, but I am tempted to snack on them all day long, or even to have a portion for breakfast—to blazes with the cholesterol. The mixture may look as if it will never thicken, but it eventually does. (Recipe: Yvonne and U Khin)

1
Preheat the oven to 350°. Grease a 10- x 14-inch baking pan.

2
Beat the eggs and sugar together until light, adding the cream of wheat while still mixing. Pour in the coconut milk gradually. Cook over medium heat, stirring constantly, until the batter thickens, about 30 minutes. Add the salt.

3
Pour the thick mixture into the baking pan and sprinkle on the almonds, raisins, and poppy seeds. Bake in the preheated oven for 15 to 20 minutes, or until evenly browned. Cool thoroughly before slicing into diamond-shaped pieces.

Cambodia

WHEN I SPEAK TO A CAMBODIAN, I CAN'T HELP WONDERING, "HOW were you able to survive?" Whenever I hear that certain bit of Puccini's opera *Turandot*—played as background music midway through the movie *The Killing Fields*—my blood chills. And when I eat Cambodian food, I wonder what is left of the cuisine there now, a little over a decade after the Pol Pot regime almost destroyed the country and its people. Brutalized and plundered by mad politicians, ancient Cambodia, nonetheless, exists in the memories of the refugees who escaped the bloodbath. Their quiet voices describe a simple cuisine of country people who lived by freshwater ponds and lakes, fished daily for the shrimp, crabs, and fish that made up their fare, and who picked water lilies and cut bamboo stalks to augment their diet. Without contrivances, cloying sauces, and complex seasonings, Cambodian foods are basic, flavorful, and wholesome. Rice is a staple—"Cambodians revere rice," explains one refugee—and basic seasonings include lemongrass, citrus leaves, garlic, galangal, cumin, turmeric, salt, pepper, and coconut milk. The use of chilies in cooking is limited, and as a result, Cambodian food is quite mild. However, says Cambodian Yann Ker, his countrymen are fond of using sliced chilies as a table condiment, and that is where the heat comes in. Mrs. Pheng Chu adds that one variety of Cambodian chili is so hot that its name, *mateh khamang,* means "enemy." Yann Ker speculates that this and the Thai "rat dropping" chili are really the same.

Breakfasts usually consist of rice porridge topped with dried fish or meat, or possibly barbecued pork, salty egg, and pickles. Lunches and dinners are very similar and consist of rice, of course, a soup, a grilled or fried meat or fish, maybe a stir-fry, and fresh vegetables. Snack and street foods include grilled bananas and tubes of bamboo, stuffed with sweetened rice flour and sprinkled with coconut.

There is a strong tradition of grilling, says Ms. Teng Kim Soeun, owner of the Angkor Wat Cambodian restaurant in Northern Virginia, and meats are usually skewered rather than placed directly on a grill.

THE GRILLS

Grilled Fish

4 whole fish, about 1 pound each, cleaned, head and tail intact
4 bamboo poles, each 2 feet long and split halfway down the middle, or 4 metal skewers
4 stalks lemongrass, soaked in water for 30 minutes to prevent burning
Kitchen twine, soaked in water for 30 minutes to prevent burning

Seasoning Sauce
3 tablespoons tamarind pulp diluted in ½ cup water
2 cloves garlic, peeled
2 or more green chilies
1 teaspoon salt
1½ teaspoons sugar
1½ teaspoons fish sauce

A large percent of the Cambodian diet is comprised of seafood, says Cambodian Teng Kim Soeun. And most rural Cambodians—without the amenities of microwaves or gas or electric ovens—grill their fish bound between lengths of bamboo slit down the middle: the fish and lemongrass are slid down the opening. The tension of the bamboo and the thong binding the top of the stick sandwiches the ingredients in place and keeps them from dropping into the fire. You can use a metal skewer instead, or cook the fish in a metal barbecue basket. (Recipe: Teng Kim Soeun, Angkor Wat Restaurant)

1

Place the fish between the split parts of the bamboo poles. Or use the metal skewers and tie the lemongrass to the fish with the twine. (Alternatively, you can place the fish in a well-oiled wire grill basket with the stalks of lemongrass and close the basket tightly.) Set aside.

2

Combine the ingredients for the seasoning sauce in the container of a food processor or blender and puree. Add a little water if the sauce needs thinning.

3

Brush the fish with the seasoning sauce and grill it on one side by the direct method (page xxix) over medium-hot coals for 3 to 4 minutes. Turn once and brush it again on the other side. Grill for another 3 to 4 minutes, or until the fish is crispy. Remove from the fire and pour the remaining sauce over the fish before serving.

Seasoned Chicken Legs

6 chicken legs (thighs and
  drumsticks), deboned
Marinade
6 stalks lemongrass, finely chopped
1 clove garlic, peeled and minced
3 shallots, peeled and chopped
One ½-inch piece galangal
2 lime leaves, shredded
½ teaspoon salt
½ teaspoon sugar
3 tablespoons soy sauce
½ to 1 teaspoon ground turmeric

This is good with steamed or fried rice. (Recipe: Chef Sareth Kim, The Cambodian Restaurant)

1
Place the chicken legs in a shallow baking dish. Combine the marinade ingredients in the container of a food processor or blender and puree. Pour the marinade mixture over the chicken. Cover the dish with foil or plastic wrap and refrigerate for 3 to 4 hours.

2
Grill the legs by the direct method (page xxix) over medium-hot coals for about 10 to 12 minutes, turning once to brown evenly. Remove from the fire and serve immediately.

Grilled Chicken

One 3-pound fryer, cut into
  serving pieces
Seasoning Paste
1 stalk lemongrass, thinly sliced
4 cloves garlic, peeled
One 2-inch piece galangal
3 citrus leaves
1 teaspoon ground turmeric
Salt and pepper to taste

Serve this chicken with rice and pickled vegetables. (Recipe: Sivong Chea)

1
Put the chicken pieces in a shallow baking dish. Combine the seasoning paste ingredients in the container of a food processor or blender and puree. Add some water or oil to help process. Pour the seasoning paste over the chicken, stirring to coat well. Cover with foil or plastic wrap and refrigerate for 3 to 4 hours.

2
Grill the chicken by the direct method (page xxix) over medium-hot coals for about 15 minutes, turning once to

brown evenly. Remove from the fire and serve immediately.

Grilled Beef

Marinade

One 3-inch piece fresh ginger, thinly
  sliced
One 3-inch piece galangal, thinly
  sliced
½ to ¾ cup rum
Salt and freshly ground black
  pepper to taste

1 to 1½ pounds top round steak
Bamboo skewers

The cook suggests serving this skewered beef as an appetizer or first course. (Recipe: Sivong Chea)

1
To make the marinade, put the ginger and galangal in the container of a food processor or blender and add the rum. Process to make a paste. Add the salt and pepper.

2
Slice the steak into thin strips about 2 inches long. Put them in a shallow baking dish and pour the marinade over the top. Cover with foil or plastic wrap and refrigerate for 3 to 4 hours.

3
Thread the steak on the skewers and grill the meat by the direct method (page xxix) over medium-hot coals for 7 to 10 minutes, turning once to brown evenly. Remove from the fire and serve immediately.

Grilled Beef Anchovy

One 1½-pound sirloin steak
Lettuce leaves
1 large tomato, thinly sliced
1 cucumber, thinly sliced
Dipping Sauce
2 teaspoons of prahok, or other fish
   paste, or use 1 whole tin of flat
   Western anchovies (see Note)
1 tablespoon water
2 tablespoons Thai fish sauce
Juice of 1 lime
Pinch MSG (optional), or
   ½ teaspoon sugar
1 small round Thai eggplant, split in
   half and thinly sliced
⅛ to ¼ red bell pepper, chopped
½ to ¾ stalk lemongrass, thinly
   sliced
Few leaves fresh basil or mint,
   chopped

This is a simple and delicious beef meal. The Cambodian way to eat this is to wrap a piece of meat and a piece of tomato and/or cucumber in lettuce and dunk this packet in the sauce. (Recipe: Chef Sareth Kim, The Cambodian Restaurant)

1

To make the dipping sauce, put the anchovies and water into a saucepan and heat, cooking to extract the juice from the fish. Reduce the heat, simmer, and stir until the mixture becomes like a sauce, about 2 minutes. Remove from the heat and cool for 5 minutes or more. Stir in the fish sauce, lime juice, and MSG or sugar, and adjust the seasonings to taste. Add the remaining sauce ingredients and set aside.

2

Grill the steak by the direct method (page xxix) over hot coals for 10 minutes, or according to the degree of doneness you prefer. Turn once. Remove from the fire and slice the beef thinly across the grain. Arrange the lettuce leaves on one side of a serving platter, and layer the tomato and cucumber in overlapping slices on top. Arrange the beef slices next to the lettuce and save space on the platter for a small serving bowl filled with the dipping sauce.

Note:

The Cambodian fermented fish *prahok* is available in jars at Asian markets. The fish most often used for pickling is mudfish because it contains few bones, but gourami is also popular.

Pork Brochette

1 to 1½ pounds pork, cubed or cut
  into thin 3-inch-long slices
Bamboo skewers
Marinade
2 stalks lemongrass, thinly sliced
1 lime leaf, thinly sliced
1 clove garlic, peeled
3 shallots, peeled
One 1-inch slice galangal
1 tablespoon ground turmeric
2 fresh red chilies
1 tablespoon roasted peanuts
1 tablespoon fish sauce
2 tablespoons coconut milk
2 tablespoons honey

You can use pork chops or pork roast to make a Cambodian version of satay *for this versatile recipe. Start this dish the night before or early the day you wish to serve it; this gives the meat enough time to absorb the flavors of the marinade. Adjust the quantities of pork and marinade to suit the number of servings you are making. These quantities will serve 4 to 6. This is delicious served with rice noodles and a simple salad of mint, coriander, and scallions. (Recipe: Teng Kim Soeun, Angkor Wat Restaurant)*

1
Put the pork cubes or slices in a baking dish.
2
Combine the marinade ingredients in the container of a food processor or blender and process to make a smooth paste. Pour this over the meat, cover the baking dish with foil or plastic wrap, and refrigerate overnight or until serving time.
3
Thread the meat on the skewers and grill the pork by the direct method (page xxix) over medium-hot coals, brushing and basting with the remaining marinade mixture, for about 8 to 10 minutes. Turn often to brown evenly. Remove from the fire and serve immediately.

ACCOMPANIMENTS

"Salt and Pepper"

2 to 3 tablespoons Thai fish sauce
1 to 2 chilies, chopped, or a
    generous amount to taste
Juice of ½ fresh lime
Chopped garlic to taste (optional)

"We put this on the table, and whoever needs it, digs in," says Yann Ker, manager of The Cambodian Restaurant. In other words, this is the Cambodian equivalent of Western salt and pepper. As a rule of thumb, for every portion of juice from about half a lime, use 3 tablespoons of fish sauce. The rest goes in according to your taste. (Recipe: Yann Ker, The Cambodian Restaurant)

Combine all ingredients and adjust seasonings to taste.

Fried Bread Stuffing

1 pound ground pork
3 ounces crab meat, picked clean
½ cup cooked green peas
½ cup chopped onion
½ cup chopped coriander
1 large egg
1 teaspoon salt
1 teaspoon pepper
1 teaspoon sugar
1 tablespoon fish sauce
1 loaf French bread, sliced into
    ½-inch-thick pieces
About 2 cups vegetable oil

The wife of the owner of Apsara, my local Cambodian grocery store, is a wonderful home cook and generously teaches Westerners how to prepare Cambodian food. She says that this dish may be eaten as a snack or first course. (Recipe: Bora Chu)

1
Combine the pork, crab, peas, onion, coriander, egg, salt, pepper, sugar, and fish sauce. Mound 1 or 2 tablespoons of this mixture on each slice of bread and spread it out to flatten and adhere to the bread.
2
Heat the oil in a large skillet. When it is bubbly, fry each slice of bread on both sides, about 5 minutes on each side. When brown, remove from the skillet and drain on paper towels. Serve immediately.

Pickled Vegetables

2 quarts water
3 cucumbers, peeled and sliced
2 carrots, peeled and sliced
2 cups cauliflower flowerettes
½ pineapple, rind removed, cut into cubes
2 tablespoons minced fresh ginger
Salt, sugar, and vinegar to taste

A favorite accompaniment for meat at the main meal of the day, pickles provide a light vegetable course—and pickling preserves vegetables that might otherwise rot in the heavy heat. If you prefer a more piquant flavor, adjust the seasonings to suit your taste. (Recipe: Sivong Chea)

Bring the water to a boil. Put the vegetables and pineapple in a large heatproof dish and pour in enough boiling water to cover. Stir in the ginger, salt, sugar, and vinegar. Let the vegetables marinate at least half a day, but they are better if they "pickle" overnight at room temperature. These should be stored in the refrigerator.

Lemongrass Soup

1 quart chicken stock
1 stalk lemongrass, crushed
¼ onion, peeled and thinly sliced
1 tablespoon fish sauce
1 cup cubed raw dark chicken meat
Fresh lime juice to taste
Thai basil leaves for garnish

A very basic soup, this light offering comes together quickly and would be a good beginning for a hearty meal. (Recipe: Chef Sareth Kim, The Cambodian Restaurant)

1
Put the chicken stock in a large saucepan and bring to a boil. Add the crushed lemongrass and bring to a boil again. Add the onion and fish sauce, and simmer for 2 or 3 minutes. Add the chicken and boil for another 3 minutes.

2
Remove from the heat, squeeze in the lime juice, and garnish with basil leaves. Serve immediately.

Spicy Beef Soup

This first-course soup is often served with rice. (Recipe: Teng Kim Soeun, Angkor Wat Restaurant)

Seasoning Mixture
2 stalks lemongrass, thinly sliced
1 lime leaf, thinly sliced
1 clove garlic, peeled
3 shallots, peeled
One 1-inch slice galangal
1 tablespoon ground turmeric
2 fresh red chilies
1 tablespoon roasted peanuts

3 tablespoons vegetable oil
One 1½-pound beef roast, such as a
 rump roast cut into cubes
1 tablespoon fish sauce
Salt and freshly ground pepper to
 taste
4 stalks celery, sliced
4 to 5 cups water

1
Put all the seasoning mixture ingredients into the container of a food processor or blender and puree. Add some water to help process. Set aside.

2
Heat the vegetable oil in a skillet. Add the meat cubes and brown them lightly. Add the seasoning mixture, fish sauce, and salt and pepper and sauté, stirring often, for about 10 minutes. Spoon this mixture into a large saucepan and add the celery and water. Bring to a simmer and cook for 30 minutes or so.

Chicken Ginger

This recipe makes 1 serving. (Recipe: Chef Sareth Kim, The Cambodian Restaurant)

1 to 2 tablespoons vegetable oil for
 frying
½ cup shredded fresh ginger
2 cups raw dark chicken meat,
 cubed
1 tablespoon sugar
1 tablespoon oyster sauce
1½ teaspoons fish sauce

Heat the oil in a wok. Add the ginger and stir-fry briefly. Add the chicken meat and stir-fry for 4 or 5 minutes. Add the remaining ingredients and cook for 2 or 3 minutes more. Remove from the heat and serve immediately.

Cambodian Special Shrimp

8 *large raw shrimp in their shells*
4 *to 5 cups vegetable oil for frying*
Marinade
1 cup ginger juice (see Note)
3 scallions, thinly sliced
1 teaspoon sugar
Salt and freshly ground black
    pepper to taste
Seasoning Mixture
1 tablespoon vegetable oil
1 clove garlic, peeled and chopped
¼ teaspoon salt
¼ teaspoon freshly ground black
    pepper
¼ teaspoon sugar
1 scallion, slit down the middle and
    sliced into 1-inch lengths

This recipe serves 1. (Recipe: Chef Sareth Kim, The Cambodian Restaurant)

1
Cutting along the curve of the shell, split the shrimp nearly in half. Devein but leave shells intact. Put shrimp in a mixing bowl.

2
Combine marinade ingredients and pour over the shrimp. Cover with foil or plastic wrap and set aside for about 30 minutes.

3
Put 4 or 5 cups of vegetable oil into a saucepan or deep fryer and heat. Remove the shrimp from the marinade and dry them slightly so the water does not splatter when you put the shrimp into the oil. Fry the shrimp for 2 minutes, or until the shells crisp. Remove from the oil and place the shrimp in a colander to drain.

4
To make the seasoning mixture, heat the oil in a 10-inch skillet. Add the garlic and sauté until golden, stirring constantly. Add the reserved shrimp. Add the salt, pepper, and sugar individually, stirring well after each addition. Turn the heat off and add the scallions, stirring well. Serve immediately.

Note:
Ginger juice is made by grating fresh ginger, wringing out the juice from the fresh shreds, and diluting the juice with water so that the concentration is about 6 parts ginger juice to 2 parts water. You can make a reasonable facsimile for this recipe by combining 1 teaspoon of ground (powdered) ginger with 1 cup water.

DESSERTS

Banana and Coconut Milk Pudding

2 to 3 cups water
5 tablespoons small sago
6 bananas, peeled and sliced in half
   lengthwise
1 cup sugar
1 cup coconut milk
Sesame seeds for garnish (optional)

Very much a typical native dessert, this pudding may be eaten by itself or spooned over a serving of sticky, or glutinous, rice. (Recipe: Teng Kim Soeun, Angkor Wat Restaurant)

Combine the water and sago in a large saucepan and bring to a boil. Lower the heat and simmer for about 15 minutes, stirring often, or until the sago swells and becomes translucent. Add the bananas and sugar and simmer uncovered for another 5 minutes. Stir in the coconut milk just before serving. Serve this hot or cold. Garnish with a sprinkle of sesame seeds, if desired.

Rice Flour Pudding

2 quarts plus 1½ cups water
One 4-ounce bag pandan leaves
2 cups rice flour
2 cups tapioca flour
1 teaspoon borax (see Note)
2 tablespoons vegetable oil
Few drops of green food coloring
½ cup Thai palm sugar or brown
   sugar
½ cup coconut milk
4 tablespoons black sesame seeds
⅓ teaspoon salt

This popular Cambodian dessert requires constant stirring and vigilance for about 45 minutes, but the cook insists it is worth the effort, and it is. She warned me several times about how difficult this stirring becomes. What I didn't understand from her is that after 20 minutes or so, the mixture becomes a very stiff, cohesive mass that slightly resembles a melted volley ball. Keep stirring, or turning the mixture over and over, until it begins to become somewhat translucent and easier to stir. This should have the texture of a firm gelatin. (Recipe: Bora Chu)

1

Combine half the water and all the pandan leaves in the container of a food processor and puree. Strain the water into a large saucepan and discard the pandan pulp. Add the remaining water, both flours, borax, vegetable oil and food coloring. Stir together and bring to a boil. Lower the heat to medium and stir constantly for about 1 hour, or until the mixture becomes very thick.

2

Scoop the mixture into a large rectangular baking dish and let it cool. If you are using brown sugar, dissolve it in enough water to make it liquid. When the mixture is cool, pour on the sugar and the coconut milk and sprinkle the top with the sesame seeds and salt. Slice and serve.

Note:

Borax powder is not soap powder, says Mrs. Chu. But it is a chemical that, while necessary to give this dessert body, should not be used to excess. The Hàr The brand is sold in small plastic packages at Asian markets.

Vietnam

AS WITH MANY AMERICANS, MY FIRST SERIOUS EXPOSURE TO VIET-
nam came during the war. I was living in Puerto Rico at the time, and I had dinner the
night before my daughter was born with a friend who had just learned her brother was the
174th or 175th American casualty. Many years later, Vietnam again became an issue for
me when living in Hong Kong I came to learn about the skills of Vietnamese chefs. At the
time, a dingy grocery on Hong Kong's Lantao island was one of the better-kept dining
secrets of the area. Run by a Vietnamese immigrant, the place had no name, was open for
served meals only on weekends, and consisted of four or five formica-topped tables set
out by the dusty roadside. Hopeful patrons called in advance to reserve the owner's time
and space, and planned well ahead for the hour-long ferry ride to the island. The food—
French or Vietnamese, depending on your choice—was sensational, and the chef willingly
talked about his rigorous classic culinary training.

Even more years later, my Chinese-Vietnamese friend David Quang talked at great
length about his native cuisine over a lavish six-course Vietnamese meal. He talked about
the Chinese domination of Vietnam for many centuries, and about how the Chinese rulers
treated the Vietnamese like the "little brother." He explained how Chinese and French
influences have played a role in shaping the national cuisine, and he spoke of regional
cooking styles and multiple seasonings—chilies, lime juice, lemongrass, coriander, shallots, mint, garlic, and ginger are basic to most Vietnamese kitchens—that characterize the
food.

He talked also of his early days living at a Vietnamese fish sauce–making factory on
the island of Phu Quoc—of all the coastal areas where fish sauce is made, the product
from Phu Quoc is considered the best. As a newcomer, he had found the harsh pungence
of the raw sauce repulsive. But after living there for a few weeks, he came to appreciate
and enjoy its fishy fragrance. He also watched the way the masters composed the sauce
by fermenting fresh anchovies in large barrels for several months, and then decanting the
first, prized liquid, always reserved for the best customers, or mixing that with the second,

third, and even fourth "pressings" that end up as the commercial seasoning, *nuoc mam,* that every Vietnamese treasures. This salty-fishy seasoning is a requisite component in most indigenous dishes and is the basis for making *nuoc cham,* a blend of chilies and other ingredients used as a table seasoning as freely as Westerners use salt and pepper.

Mr. Quang remembers an earlier Vietnam, when a typical breakfast might be a bowl of hot congee (Chinese rice porridge) or a fish- or beef-noodle soup sprinkled with onions and roasted peanuts, or a piece of fried chicken wrapped in a banana leaf that children could buy on the way to school. As a change of pace, the Vietnamese might prefer corn sliced into a cup or made creamy and boiled with sugar, peanuts, and coconut milk. Or a bowl of sticky (glutinous) rice sweetened with sugar and coconut and garnished with roasted peanuts.

Lunches and dinners, he recalls, were meals of several courses that usually centered on a huge portion of rice—a Vietnamese staple—or rice noodles, garnished with fish and pork stewed with fresh coconut milk or with grilled strips of pork or beef, and accompanied by fresh, usually raw, vegetables. He also remembers how often his family enjoyed the *cha gio*—that is, the Vietnamese spring rolls—and the popular grilled shrimp paste on sugarcane, a homemade or street-food snack that is a light, sweet national favorite. Everywhere and at all times, he remembers, food was plentiful and affordable even for the poorest villager.

Vietnamese politics and society have certainly changed the country since Mr. Quang left, but he says the marvelous foods and flavors endure. And so do traditional cooking techniques: Like their Chinese brethren, the Vietnamese boil and stir-fry, and like their Indochinese neighbors, the Vietnamese love to barbecue. The ubiquitous, multipurpose charcoal stove heats rooms, warms hands, and grills food.

ASIAN GRILLS

THE GRILLS

Shrimp on Sugarcane

3 pounds raw shrimp, shelled and
   deveined
3 teaspoons sugar
½ pound pork fat, minced
1 teaspoon salt
1 teaspoon MSG (optional)
1 teaspoon ground white pepper
5 teaspoons cornstarch
Vegetable oil for hands
About thirty 4-inch pieces sugarcane

Accompaniments
Leaf lettuce leaves
Scallions, trimmed into 3-inch pieces
Fresh mint leaves
Rice paper wrappers, moistened
   and softened for use
Cooked thin rice vermicelli
Bowl of nuoc cham (see page 240)

If there are any two Vietnamese dishes that Americans know well, they are Vietnamese spring rolls (cha gio) *and grilled shrimp paste on sugarcane. There are many versions of the latter, some more heavily seasoned than others, but some requiring that the shrimp be pounded with mortar and pestle for a very different texture. But you can make this light and delicate offering by pureeing the shrimp in the food processor. You can use fresh sugarcane, which requires peeling, or canned, which is readily available, and also ready to use. The chef says that if you want the cooked shrimp to look white, you can precook it on the cane by steaming for 10 to 15 minutes or by putting it in a microwave oven for 3 minutes. After that, grill the shrimp-wrapped cane for 2 or 3 minutes. This dish is traditionally served with lettuce leaves, trimmed scallions, mint leaves, a prepared fish sauce* (nuoc cham) *for dipping, and moistened rice papers for wrapping up selected items. To eat, remove the shrimp from the sugarcane and break the shrimp paste covering in half. Hold a wrapper in your hand and place a piece of shrimp and any other of the accompaniments in the wrapper. Fold it over and dunk it into the sauce. You may also suck or chew on the sugarcane. (Recipe: Chef Tô-Ly, Viet Royale Restaurant)*

1
Put the shrimp, sugar, pork fat, salt, MSG if using it, and pepper in the container of a food processor. Process the mixture for 5 to 8 minutes, slowly adding the cornstarch. Rub your hands lightly with oil. Scoop out the paste by hand, about 2 tablespoons at a time, and wrap it around the sugarcane, making a smooth covering and leaving about 2 inches of cane uncovered that you can

use as a handle. Repeat the process until all the paste is used up. Always keep your hands lightly oiled.

2

Grill the cane by the direct method (page xxix) over a medium-hot fire, for 8 to 10 minutes, turning often. Remove from the fire and serve immediately with the accompaniments.

Offer a bowl of the fish sauce nuoc cham *with the cooked pork. (Recipe: Chef Tô-Ly, Viet Royale Restaurant)*

Grilled Meatballs

2½ tablespoons sugar
1½ tablespoons nuoc mam
1 teaspoon white pepper
1 carrot, peeled and shredded
2½ pounds boneless pork with some
    fat remaining, thinly sliced, or 2½
    pounds lean ground pork
½ tablespoon MSG (optional)
1 or 2 cloves garlic, peeled
Vegetable oil for hands
Bamboo skewers

1

Put the sugar and *nuoc mam* in a saucepan and heat slowly. Cool and add the pepper, carrot, and pork. Mix together well and refrigerate for 4 hours.

2

If using the sliced pork, put the mixture into the container of a food processor and puree. Add the MSG, garlic and enough oil to make the mixture stick together and to help process. If using the ground pork, combine with the MSG and the garlic. Rub your hands lightly with oil. Scoop up the pork, about 2 tablespoons at a time, and wrap it around a skewer. You may make the balls any size you wish, and allow 3 to 4 per skewer. Repeat the process until all the pork is used up.

3

You may precook the meatballs by steaming or cooking them in the microwave (see recipe for Shrimp Paste on Sugarcane above). Alternatively, you may grill the pork by the direct method (page xxix) over medium-hot coals for 8 to 10 minutes or more, turning often. Remove from the fire and serve immediately, preferably with rice or rice noodles and *nuoc cham*.

Grilled Ground Beef with Grape Leaf

Meat Mixture
½ pound ground lean beef
1 teaspoon oyster sauce
1½ tablespoons soy sauce
1½ tablespoons sugar
2 teaspoons finely minced garlic
1 teaspoon freshly ground black pepper
¼ teaspoon MSG (optional)
1 leek, finely chopped

Seasoning Mixture
3 tablespoons vegetable oil
2 tablespoons finely chopped scallions, including the green tops
1 tablespoon chopped roasted peanuts

8 to 10 grape leaves (see Note)
Bamboo skewers

In Vietnam, cooks use a leaf called lot, *but it is generally unavailable here. Grape leaves are an acceptable alternative. If you use pickled grape leaves, treat them carefully because they are very fragile and tear easily. Always put the underside up and put the filling at the stem end, which is the strongest point, before rolling. You may serve this as an appetizer or main course. This recipe makes 2 servings, or about 10 pieces. (Recipe: Lan's Vietnamese Restaurant)*

1
Combine all the meat-mixture ingredients in a large bowl and use your hands to mix everything together well. Set aside.

2
Combine the ingredients for the seasoning mixture in another bowl and set aside.

3
Lay 1 grape leaf flat, with its veined underside up, on a smooth surface. Place 1 to 2 tablespoons of the meat mixture on the stem end of the grape leaf where the large vein is prominent. Fold the pointed end of the leaf up over the filling. Fold the two sides in over the filling. Fold the top edge of the leaf over, tucking in the first three folds tightly to form a packet and securing it closed with the stem. Thread the stuffed leaf on a bamboo skewer, starting at the stem end of the leaf and going through the center of the leaf out the opposite end. This helps seal the packet closed.

4
Grill the packets by the direct method (page xxix) over medium-hot coals for about 4 to 5 minutes on each side. Brush each jacket with the seasoning mixture. Remove from the heat and serve immediately.

Note:
Popular in Middle Eastern cooking, fresh grape leaves are pickled and packed in cans or jars. Alternatively, you may use fresh leaves, if available. Rinse canned leaves before using and store any leftovers in a plastic, sealed container in the refrigerator. Grape leaves are sold at Middle Eastern markets and some well-stocked supermarkets.

Grilled Lemongrass Beef

1 pound top round or sirloin steak, cut into thin, 3-inch-long strips
Bamboo skewers
Marinade
1 stalk lemongrass, thinly sliced
6 cloves garlic, peeled and crushed
2 tablespoons sugar
3 shallots, peeled and thinly sliced
1 to 2 tablespoons nuoc mam

Use top-quality beef for this dish. You may also substitute prawns for the beef. Serve it on skewers with a portion of rice or rice noodles, plain or garnished with chopped mint, shredded lettuce, diced cucumbers, 1/2 cup crushed peanuts, and several tablespoons of scallion oil (see Grilled Pork Strips on Rice Vermicelli, page 238). Alternatively, you can take the meat off the skewers and layer it on top of the noodles. (Recipe: Chef Tô-Ly, Viet Royale Restaurant)

1
Place the meat in a shallow baking dish. Combine the marinade ingredients, mixing well, and add to the meat. Toss to be sure all the meat is well seasoned. Cover with foil or plastic wrap and set aside for at least 1 hour.

2
Thread the meat on bamboo skewers, and grill by the direct method (page xxix) over hot coals for 7 to 10 minutes, turning once. Remove from the fire and serve immediately.

Grilled Pork Strips on Rice Vermicelli

1 pound lean pork, cut into ⅛-inch-
   thick slices
One 10½-ounce package dried rice
   vermicelli
1 tablespoon potato starch
   (see Note)
Nuoc cham (see page 240) for
   dipping

Marinade
2 tablespoons soy sauce
2 tablespoons hoisin sauce
4 tablespoons sugar
2 stalks lemongrass
1½ tablespoons finely minced garlic
2 tablespoons vegetable oil
¼ teaspoon MSG (optional)

Scallion Oil
3 tablespoons vegetable oil
2 tablespoons finely chopped
   scallions, including the green tops
1 tablespoon chopped roasted
   peanuts

Garnish
Fresh coriander leaves
8 or 9 lettuce leaves
½ onion, peeled and thinly sliced

You must serve this delicious pork dish with the nuoc cham. (Recipe: Lan's Vietnamese Restaurant)

1
Place the pork in a baking dish. Combine the marinade ingredients, mixing well, and pour over the meat. Turn the pork slices several times to cover them well, and set aside for about 30 minutes.

2
Combine the ingredients of the scallion oil in a small mixing bowl and set aside.

3
Prepare the rice noodles by placing them in a large saucepan and pouring boiling water over the top to cover the noodles. Let them soften for about 2 minutes, then place them in a colander and let them drain well. Sprinkle the potato starch on top of the noodles and mix it in with your hands. The starch helps the noodles stick together to form a flat "pancake" on which the grilled pork strips will rest. Take a handful of noodles from the colander—enough to form a 5-inch round pancake—and pat them down to form a ⅛-inch-thick disc. Repeat this process until you have formed 4 to 6 pancakes. Cover each one with a moistened paper towel and set them on a glass or plastic plate. Cook in a microwave for 1 to 2 minutes or in a conventional oven for 4 to 6 minutes. Place each softened pancake on a dinner plate or serving dish. Brush the surface of each pancake with the scallion oil and fold them in half.

4
Grill the pork by the direct method (page xxix) over hot coals for 3 to 4 minutes, turning once. Remove from the fire and slice the meat into ½-inch-wide strips. Divide the grilled pork equally among the pancakes and sprinkle the meat with coriander leaves. Garnish each plate

or the serving platter with lettuce leaves and sliced onions and pass a bowl of the *nuoc cham* sauce. Serve immediately.

Note:

Potato starch is a thickening agent used by some Asian chefs. It is sold at most supermarkets.

Grilled Lime Chicken

3 *whole chicken breasts, skinned, deboned, and cubed*

Marinade

Rind of 3 limes, minced

Juice of 1 or 2 limes

6 *tablespoons* nuoc mam

4 *tablespoons sugar*

1 *tablespoon black soy sauce*

(Recipe: Chef Tô-Ly, Viet Royale Restaurant)

1

Place the chicken in a shallow baking dish. Combine the marinade ingredients, and add to the chicken, mixing well. Cover with foil or plastic wrap and refrigerate for at least 1 hour.

2

Thread the chicken on bamboo skewers and grill by the direct method (page xxix) over hot coals for 7 to 10 minutes, turning once. Remove from the fire, and serve immediately.

ACCOMPANIMENTS

Nuoc Cham (Fish Sauce)

2 to 3 tablespoons sugar
1 tablespoon white vinegar
2 to 3 tablespoons boiling water
2 tablespoons nuoc mam
1½ tablespoons finely minced garlic
½ tablespoon chili paste
¼ tablespoon lemon juice

One or another variation of this sauce is used at the table to season virtually everything. (Nuoc mam, on the other hand, is used as a seasoning only during cooking.) Usually the family or restaurant cook makes this up in quantities because it stores well and because people use it as a condiment at almost every meal. It's very versatile, one cook explained, and can be modified to suit anyone's taste. Want it sweeter? Add more sugar. Saltier? More nuoc mam, the briny fish sauce. Milder? More hot water. It's that simple. If you prefer to cut the fishy taste of the fish sauce, use proportionately more lemon juice and less vinegar. Just let the sauce age or ripen slightly, at least several hours, before using it. This recipe makes enough for 4 small portions, so if you like it and want some on hand, simply increase the quantities. Store the sauce in a covered container in the refrigerator (Recipe: Lan's Vietnamese Restaurant)

Combine all the ingredients in mixing bowl and stir until the sugar dissolves.

Fish Sour Soup

1 quart water
2 stalks lemongrass
2 tablespoons tamarind paste
2 tablespoons nuoc mam
2 tablespoons sugar
Salt and pepper to taste
¼ pound raw shrimp, shelled and
    deveined
½ pound fish fillets
1 large tomato, cubed
½ pound okra
⅓ pound bean sprouts
Fried shallots for garnish (see
    instructions in Glossary)

(Recipe: Chef Tô-Ly, Viet Royale Restaurant)

1

Put the water and lemongrass into a saucepan and bring to a boil. Remove the lemongrass once it has imparted its flavor to the water—you can tell that once the water begins to smell good. Add the tamarind paste, *nuoc mam,* sugar, and salt and pepper, stirring well.

2

Add the shrimp, fish, tomato, and okra and simmer uncovered for about 10 minutes. Meanwhile, put the bean sprouts into a soup tureen or into individual bowls. When the soup is ready, ladle it over the bean sprouts. Garnish with the shallots. For those who like a spicier dish, offer sliced chilies or chili paste on the side.

Caramel Shrimp

½ pound shrimp, peeled and
    deveined
Caramel Sauce
1 cup water
5 to 7 tablespoons nuoc mam
5 to 7 tablespoons sugar
2 tablespoons very finely chopped
    lemongrass
1 tablespoon minced garlic

These shrimp make a sweet offering in a multicourse meal. You may substitute ¹/₂ pound spareribs per person, but the ribs must be precooked by boiling until almost done. This recipe makes 1 or 2 servings. (Recipe: Chef Tô-Ly, Viet Royale Restaurant)

Combine the sauce ingredients in a saucepan and bring to a boil. Lower the heat and simmer for about 30 minutes, or until the sauce reduces and gets very thick. Stir in the shrimp and cook for 5 minutes more. Serve immediately with rice.

Shrimp and Pork Salad

¼ pound boneless pork butt or roast
¼ pound large raw shrimp
1 cucumber, peeled and shredded
2 carrots, peeled and shredded
1 cup shredded daikon
¼ cup chopped fresh mint
1 stalk celery, trimmed and diced
⅛ cup jellyfish shreds, cut into short
  pieces
¼ cup white vinegar
1 tablespoon sugar
1 tablespoon nuoc mam
Garnish
Shrimp crackers
*2 or more tablespoons crushed
  peanuts*

This favorite salad is dressed with white vinegar, which removes the fishy aroma and "cooks" the vegetables slightly. It also makes jellyfish crisper. You should have a total of about 12 ounces of salad mixture when you have combined the cucumber, carrots, daikon, mint leaves, celery, and jellyfish. Use this as an accompaniment to grilled dishes and rice or noodles. Vietnamese call this "jellyfish salad." (Recipe: Chef Tô-Ly, Viet Royale Restaurant)

1

Put the pork in a saucepan with water to cover and bring to a boil. After half an hour, when the pork is cooked through, remove it from the water, set aside, and cool before slicing it into thin, 3-inch-long strips. Add the shrimp to the water and cook for about 3 minutes, or until the shrimp turn slightly pink. Drain the shrimp and set them aside until cool enough to peel, clean, and slice in half lengthwise. Put the pork and shrimp in a container, cover with foil or plastic wrap, and refrigerate until ready to use.

2

Combine the cucumber, carrots, daikon, mint, celery, and jellyfish in a large mixing bowl. Add the vinegar, sugar, and *nuoc mam* and mix with your hands—this method combines the ingredients better than using spoons or forks. Cover with foil or plastic wrap and refrigerate for at least 30 minutes.

3

At serving time, add the shrimp and pork to the salad mixture. Stir once again with your hands, scoop into a serving bowl, and garnish with crisp shrimp crackers and peanuts.

DESSERTS

Mung Bean and Coconut Milk Parfait

1 pound dried mung beans
2 quarts water
1 cup sugar, or to taste
One 13½-ounce can coconut milk

(Recipe: Chef Tô-Ly, Viet Royale Restaurant)

1
In a saucepan, put the mung beans in the water, bring to a boil, and cook until the beans are soft, about 40 minutes. Add the sugar and stir until dissolved.

2
When you are ready to serve, add the coconut milk, bring the beans to a boil, again, and serve hot.

3 cups water
1 cup raw sticky, or glutinous, rice
3 firm bananas, peeled
Sugar to taste
One 13½-ounce can coconut milk

According to my Vietnamese friend David Quang, this is a true family dessert that can be served hot or cold. But for the most intense coconut flavor, eat it cold. (Recipe: David Quang)

1
Combine the water and rice in a large saucepan and bring to a boil. Cover the pan, lower the heat, and simmer until the mixture becomes thick and glutinous like a porridge, about 20 minutes.

2
Cube the bananas and stir them gently into the rice mixture. Continue cooking, but do not overcook the bananas —they should retain their shape and not turn mushy. After 10 minutes, remove from the heat.

3
Stir in the sugar and add the coconut milk. Serve warm or cold.

Laos

THE STILL AIR AND THE SHIMMERY HEAT OF A SUMMER DAY SEND THE festive Lao to a stand of trees in the parched meadow. Under the sheltering leaves, long-skirted Lao ladies have spread out on ground mats an array of celebratory dishes in traditional hammered-silver bowls. Meanwhile, saffron-robed monks and the devout carry towering fringed parasols as they parade through the tall grasses. The chanting and gongs of a Buddhist ceremony fill the air. Hawkers display and sell fresh produce and grilled meats along a dusty footpath. And late arrivals, pressing their palms together in the traditional greeting, rush to their places. This was my introduction to a Laotian adventure, and it began in a Northern Virginia pasture—not in an Asian countryside.

I have learned many things since about this fairy-tale kingdom—known historically as *Lan Xang,* or Land of a Million Elephants—and about its gentle, cordial, and welcoming people. I have learned many things since about stoicism, bravery, and kindness from the Lao refugees whom I have met. I have also learned, from my Lao friend and mentor Bounsou Sananikone, that many dishes Westerners think of as Thai (particularly Northern Thai)—barbecued whole chicken, green papaya salad, "sticky" rice pudding, and *lap,* to name a few—are Laotian as well, with a different spin.

But one quickly sees that despite the overlappings of some dishes and of some seasonings—chilies, lemongrass, lime leaves, galangal, fish sauce, and garlic, for example—the Lao have developed a singular cuisine different from that of Thailand, and of neighboring Cambodia and Vietnam. Lao cooking is based on a love of chilies, sour flavors, and the raw ingredients at hand—these may include frogs, any number of exotic freshwater river fish, snails, and eel; deer; water buffalo; pigs; and a forest-, field-, or pond-full of vegetation unfamiliar to Westerners. And unlike any other Southeast Asian peoples, all of whom eat firm, long-grain rice, the Lao prefer sticky (glutinous) rice, which when steamy hot, compresses into a sticky wad for convenient eating. It also packs easily for transport in special woven baskets with long loop handles, reports one woman who carried it with her on the long jet flight from Vientiane to America. Some of Mrs. Sanani-

kone's first words to me were: "This is our Lao proverb—'he who belongs to the Lao race lives in a house up from the ground [house on stilts], plays the melodious *khene* [a hand-held wind instrument of bamboo strips] music, and eats sticky rice.' "

Former British Ambassador to Laos Alan Davidson has written the two seminal books on Lao cooking, one of which contains the translations of the recipes of Phia Sing, a former chef in the royal Lao Palace in Luang Prabang. As one gathers from Mr. Davidson's books, the Lao traditions of hospitality, use of seasonings and "significant" foods, assortments of cooking equipment and methods, and the creation of beautiful serving pieces of clay or woven bamboo, defy any quick description.

As to grilling, the Lao do so often, particularly grilling whole bodies of fish, or deer, or pig, or cows, and they stuff these creatures with seasonings, such as mint leaves and lemongrass. "We play a lot with charcoal," says Mrs. Sananikone. "It was our only heat source. . . . I have seen many times in the village people put the food directly into the charcoal, or hot ash, like the dry meat ["Meat from Heaven," see page 248] and snails and fish." Even in more modern Laos, with access to electricity and gas stoves, many cooks still prefer old-fashioned techniques: Mrs. Sananikone talked about her visits to the former royal family at their palace, and how the mother of one of the princes still liked to cook with charcoal and wood because of the good flavor imparted to the food.

But the words of Mrs. Sananikone best describe her native foods: "Almost one thousand years ago, the Lao people resettled in the valley of the Mekong River and its tributaries. The rivers, the lakes, and the interior of the plains offer to the Lao good and delicious fish and animals. Laotian food is generally simple. The delicious taste will come from the perfume of banana leaves, the variety of mints, the mode of cooking, and the degree of heat from the charcoal, the ash, or the fire itself.

"But how much more delicate and precious are the food and the dishes when one can have occasion to eat in the real Lao family house. The food will be served on the elegant plates of bamboo or rattan and the smelling of these lets the mind feel you have found the real Lao food."

Grilled Lao Sausages

1 stalk lemongrass, trimmed,
    preferably fresh
2 pounds ground pork
½ cup finely chopped garlic (about
    8 to 10 medium cloves)
¾ cup minced onions
5 to 6 fresh green chilies, split
    lengthwise, seeded, and minced
¾ cup raw long-grain rice
¾ cup packed coriander leaves and
    tender stalks, finely chopped
1 tablespoon or more fish sauce
½ teaspoon salt
Freshly ground black pepper
5 yards of pork sausage casing,
    1 inch in diameter, soaked
    overnight in water and
    refrigerated (see Note)

Known to the Lao as say oua Lao, *these popular sausages are ideal for picnics and buffets. They may be served hot or cold, as desired, and are usually accompanied by red chili paste and sticky rice, the staple foods of the Lao. You can make the sausages ahead of time. Any unused meat can be stored in a container and frozen. (Recipe: Princess Moun Souvanna-Phouma)*

1

Slice the lemongrass paper-thin and set aside.

2

Put the meat into a large bowl and add the garlic and onions. Mix well with your hands. Add the lemongrass and mix again. Add the chopped chilies.

3

Put the rice in an ungreased skillet and "dry-fry" it, stirring and cooking until it is fragrant and golden, about 10 minutes. Put the rice into the container of a blender and pulverize it. Sift this powder through a sieve and add to the meat mixture. Add the coriander, fish sauce, and salt and pepper. To determine the taste, fry a small piece of the meat mixture and adjust the seasonings as desired.

4

Prepare the casing by cutting it into 1-yard lengths. Slip one end of each casing piece over the nozzle of a faucet and rinse out with cold water. Tie each casing piece closed at one end.

5

Using the nozzle of a sausage stuffer or a pastry tube, pull open the untied end of the casing and slide it over the nozzle until you reach the other end of the casing. Force the meat into the casing to make a 3- or 4-inch-long sausage. Tie off the casing by twisting the casing

several times in the same direction or by tying it with a string. This makes a long string of sausage links. Repeat this process until all the sausage mixture is used up.

6

Prick the sausages with the tines of a fork to prevent them from bursting during cooking. Grill them by the direct method (page xxix) over medium-hot coals for 5 minutes. Turn them over and grill for 5 minutes more, or until they are golden brown and slightly crisp. Remove from the fire. (Alternatively, preheat the oven to 450°. Prick the sausages with the tines of a fork. When the oven is hot, place the sausages on a broiling pan about 5 inches from the heat source and cook for about 5 minutes on each side, or until golden brown and slightly crisp.) Slice the sausages diagonally into ⅛-inch-thick pieces, place on a bed of fresh coriander leaves or other greens, and serve.

Note:

Sausage casings are available at specialty meat markets, gourmet-food stores, and many supermarkets—ask the butcher. Leftover natural casings should be stored in cold, salty water in the refrigerator.

"Meat from Heaven"

2½ pounds boneless rump roast
Marinade
2 to 3 tablespoons sugar
1½ teaspoons salt
Freshly ground pepper
1 tablespoon crushed coriander
   seeds
1 to 2 tablespoons sesame seed oil
2 cloves garlic, peeled and crushed
2 tablespoons vegetable oil
   (optional)

Westerners might recognize this as beef jerky, and in many ways, the two are similar. But the Lao version has different seasonings—some versions of the marinade also include minced lemongrass, ginger, fish sauce, and soy sauce. And Lao cooks insist that the meat dry out in the sun—one very old recipe describes how the beef strips are hung out on a piece of bamboo string to dry for at least 1 day—not in an oven (although in cloudy climates the Lao grudgingly use a gas, not an electric, oven with only the pilot light as a heat source to dry the meat). The Lao lady who gave me this recipe says she has dried her beef in the family car and in a sunny dining-room window. Then the strips of dried beef receive a final cooking: They are either deep-fried, broiled, or, preferably, they are grilled. This meat is almost daily fare—even for breakfast—and is eaten with sticky rice, papaya salad, and a chilied dipping sauce. (Recipe: Bounheng Inversin)

1
Slice the meat along the grain in strips about ⅛ inch thick.

2
Mix the meat with all the marinade ingredients in a large bowl, and, using your hands, make sure that each piece of meat is well coated. Cover the bowl with foil or plastic wrap and leave it at room temperature for 3 to 5 hours, or overnight in the refrigerator.

3
Spread the strips of meat on metal racks, leaving enough room between each piece for air to circulate. Let the meat dry for about 10 hours, either in a gas oven or in direct sunlight. If the meat is sun dried, turn the pieces over halfway through the process.

4

When all strips are dry and hard, store the meat in an airtight container, where it keeps well for 3 weeks at room temperature. Grill, deep-fry, or broil the meat before serving.

Roasted Pig

One 15-pound suckling pig
Seasoning Mixture
Fish sauce [3 to 4 tablespoons]
Sugar [1 tablespoon]
Salt [to taste]
Lemongrass [3 or 4 stalks, thinly
    sliced]
Onion [2 to 3, peeled and
    quartered]
Garlic [3 to 4 cloves, peeled and
    sliced]
Lime leaves [4 or 5]
Sugarcane leaves, [optional]
Basting Sauce
Vegetable oil [½ cup]
Salt [to taste]
Fish sauce [½ cup]

This recipe is from a family that came from Muong Thene, the "Immortal Place of Paradise," in the north of Laos near China. My Lao friend Bounsou Sananikone explained that native cooks never measured ingredients exactly, so she could not give me any proportions. I have put suggested amounts in brackets next to each ingredient. (Recipe: Bounsou Sananikone)

1

Combine all the seasoning mixture ingredients except the sugarcane leaves in the container of a food process or blender and puree. Crush the sugarcane leaves by hand and add to the other ingredients.

2

In a bowl combine the basing sauce ingredients and set aside.

3

Fill the cavity of the pig with the seasoning mixture, put the pig on a long, metal spit, and let it roast over an open fire. Alternatively, put the pig in a covered barbecue and grill it by the indirect method (page xxix). In either case, cook for about 3 or 4 hours, brushing it often with the basting sauce.

Grilled Chicken Legs

12 to 14 chicken drumsticks (about 3 to 4 pounds)

Marinade
1 stalk lemongrass, minced
1 tablespoon salt
2 tablespoons soy sauce
½ teaspoon freshly ground black pepper
2 cloves garlic, peeled and crushed

(Recipe: Nom Viponsanarath)

1
Place the drumsticks in a shallow baking dish. Combine the marinade ingredients, stirring to combine well, and pour the marinade over the chicken. Let the chicken marinate for at least 30 minutes in the refrigerator before cooking.

2
Grill the drumsticks by the direct method (page xxix) over medium-hot coals for 15 to 20 minutes, turning once. Remove from the fire and serve immediately.

ACCOMPANIMENTS

Nuoc Cham (Fish Sauce)

2 to 3 tablespoons sugar
1 tablespoon white vinegar
2 to 3 tablespoons boiling water
2 tablespoons nuoc mam
1½ tablespoons finely minced garlic
½ tablespoon chili paste
¼ tablespoon lemon juice

One or another variation of this sauce is used at the table to season virtually everything. (Nuoc mam, on the other hand, is used as a seasoning only during cooking.) Usually the family or restaurant cook makes this up in quantities because it stores well and because people use it as a condiment at almost every meal. It's very versatile, one cook explained, and can be modified to suit anyone's taste. Want it sweeter? Add more sugar. Saltier? More nuoc mam, the briny fish sauce. Milder? More hot water. It's that simple. If you prefer to cut the fishy taste of the fish sauce, use proportionately more lemon juice and less vinegar. Just let the sauce age or ripen slightly, at least several hours, before using it. This recipe makes enough for 4 small portions, so if you like it and want some on hand, simply increase the quantities. Store the sauce in a covered container in the refrigerator (Recipe: Lan's Vietnamese Restaurant)

Combine all the ingredients in mixing bowl and stir until the sugar dissolves.

Cha Gio

½ head medium green cabbage, finely shredded and cut into short pieces
¼ pound ground pork
2 scallions, thinly sliced
¼ pound rice vermicelli, soaked until soft, then cut into 1-inch lengths
¼ cup minced black dried Chinese mushrooms soaked to soften
1 tablespoon dried shrimp
¼ cup shredded jicama
3 shallots, peeled and minced
3 large eggs, beaten
Salt and pepper to taste
1 package rice wrapping papers
½ cup vegetable oil

Dipping Sauce
1 clove garlic, peeled and minced
2 green chilies
2 tablespoons sugar
2 tablespoons nuoc mam
¼ cup shredded carrots
1 to 2 tablespoons lime juice

These spring rolls look like the Vietnamese version. But they become Lao with the addition of mushrooms, dried shrimp, shredded jicama, and shallots, says Mrs. Sananikone. The Lao use no bean sprouts or onions because these make the spring rolls too soggy. Ordinarily, the cook would use the round rice papers to make spring rolls, but this lady uses the triangular-shaped papers, also used to wrap foods at the table. Makes about 20 spring rolls. (Recipe: Tanh Sykhammountry/ Bounsou Sananikone)

1
Combine the cabbage, pork, scallions, rice vermicelli, mushrooms, shrimp, jicama, and shallots in a large bowl. Mix together well and add the beaten eggs and salt and pepper. This is best mixed together by hand.

2
Dip the wrapping papers in water and lay them on a flat surface until softened. Put 1 tablespoon of filling in the center of the wrapper and roll from the wide end to the point, folding in the sides as you roll. Make the packet tight so it holds together.

3
Heat the oil in a skillet and fry the spring rolls, 2 or 3 at a time, until crisp and brown. Turn often so these brown evenly. Remove from the pan and drain on paper towels. Set aside.

4
Combine the ingredients for the dipping sauce and put in a serving bowl. Eat the spring rolls while they are still hot, dipping them in the sauce.

Steamed Sticky Rice

my Lao friend Bounsou Sananikone told how the Lao cook their staple, sticky rice: Start to soak the raw sticky (glutinous) rice before you go to bed at night. How much you soak depends on the size of your family. (Soak 2 or more cups of sticky rice in water for at least 2 hours, but preferably overnight. Before cooking, drain and rinse the rice until the water runs clear. Soaking the rice in hot water can shorten the soaking time to 1 hour.) Get up early in the morning to cook it so you can offer it to the monks when they pass by your house at 6:30 or 7 A.M. Place the rice in the houad, the traditional bamboo steamer, and set this into the maw nung, *the lower pot (usually made of metal or clay) used for the boiling water to steam the rice. This should be half-filled with water. Turn on the heat and let the rice steam, covered, over the boiling water. After about 20 minutes, remove the bamboo steamer, bang its bottom on a firm surface to loosen the clumped rice, and flip the rice over so that the top layer gets some steam. Turn the heat down. Remove from the heat after 5 minutes. Spread the rice out on a flat surface (the Lao use a special platter called* souay khao *just for that purpose) and toss it with your hands. This cools the rice grains enough so that they do not stick to your fingers when you eat. Put the rice into a bamboo basket (or serving bowl), and eat. (Recipe: Bounsou Sananikone)*

In his translation of Phia Sing's recipes, Alan Davidson points out that cooks can also use the Chinese stacking bamboo steaming baskets, which Western cooks may find more readily available. I haven't tried it, but a small-meshed Western vegetable steamer may work as well for cooking this rice.

Sticky Rice in Bamboo

3 *pieces bamboo tube, each about 12 inches long*
6 *cups sticky, or glutinous, rice*
6 *tablespoons grated taro root (see Note)*
3 *teaspoons salt*
4½ *cups coconut milk*
Coconut husks (or banana leaves)

(Recipe: Bella Flor Natividad, Lao Foods)

1
Cut bamboo tubes so that each section has an enclosed end and an open end. Soak the rice in water overnight, or for at least 3 to 4 hours.

2
Mix together the rice, the taro root, and salt. Divide this mixture into 3 equal portions. Spoon each portion into a bamboo tube and pour into each 1½ cups of coconut milk. Cover the open end with coconut husks (or banana leaves). Place the bamboo tubes near a charcoal fire—or lay the tubes on a rack and grill them by the direct method (page xxix) over medium-hot coals. Turn the tubes often and continue cooking until all sides are charred, about 1 to 1½ hours. Remove the tubes from the fire and, when cool enough to handle, scrape off the charred outer portion with a sharp knife until only the thin inner wall remains. Remove the coconut husks (or banana leaves) and serve the rice.

Note:
Taro root, like its cousin the cassava, is a tuber that is starchy like potato and has a potatolike consistency and a nutty flavor. Taro must always be thoroughly cooked; some varieties are toxic when raw. Taro root is sold at most Asian markets and stores well in the refrigerator for several weeks. It must be peeled before you cook it.

Chicken Soup

Seasoning Ingredients

1 stalk lemongrass, thinly sliced
2 to 3 fresh red or green chilies
One 1-inch piece galangal
4 shallots, peeled
1 to 2 teaspoons fish sauce, Laotian
 preferred
1 to 2 cloves garlic, peeled
Salt to taste

2 to 3 tablespoons vegetable oil
1 pound cubed chicken meat
 (include skin)
½ pound green or long beans, cut in
 2-inch lengths
3 Oriental eggplants, unpeeled and
 cubed (or 1 large Western
 eggplant, peeled and cubed)
1 head bok choy, sliced
2 quarts water
1 cup sticky, or glutinous, rice,
 soaked in water to cover
Oriental basil leaves, coriander
 root, or dill leaves for garnish

K*nown as* ao *(or possibly spelled "ork" or "auk"), this stewlike concoction can also be made with beef, pork, or catfish. Thais will add coconut milk to this soup. Since the Lao do not use wheat flour, it is thickened with soaked and crushed sticky rice or with rice flour. (Recipe: Bounsou Sananikone)*

1

Crush the seasoning ingredients with a mortar and pestle or mince them very fine and set aside.

2

Heat the oil in a saucepan and, when bubbly, stir fry the chicken over high heat until browned, about 5 minutes. Lower the heat and add the vegetables, seasonings, and the water. Drain the rice, crush it, and add to the saucepan. Cover the pan and simmer until the vegetables are tender, about 15 or 20 minutes. Serve immediately.

Bamboo Shoot Soup

2 jars (1 pound, 8 ounces each)
 pickled bamboo shoots,
 undrained (see Note)
1 pound ground pork
1 cup toasted sesame seeds
2 shallots, peeled and chopped
3 cloves garlic, peeled
2 to 4 chopped fresh red chilies
30 sprigs coriander, chopped
1 cup chopped fresh mint leaves

This "dry" soup needs the flavoring of the yanang, *the woody stem of a climbing plant known as* Tiliacora trianora. *The Lao cook who taught me this recipe pointed out how much easier it is to use canned bamboo shoots rather than the fresh: With fresh shoots, she would have to peel off the tough outer covering of the bamboo stalks, then proceed with the cooking and shredding of the shoots. (Recipe: Khampain Chanthavisant/Duangrudee Zier, Bangkok West Restaurant)*

1
Pour the liquid from the bamboo shoots into a large saucepan and bring to a boil. Add the pork to the liquid, breaking the meat apart with the tines of a fork so that it does not clump together during cooking. Bring the soup to a boil, then lower the heat and simmer, stirring occasionally, until the pork cooks through, about 10 minutes.

2
While the pork is cooking, shred each piece of bamboo shoot lengthwise into thin strips. Add these to the pan when the pork is cooked and continue simmering.

3
Crush the sesame seeds or pulverize them in the container of a blender.

4
Wrap the shallots, garlic, and chilies in aluminum foil and grill them on a burner for about 10 minutes or until they turn soft. Remove from the heat, unwrap, and mash the mixture with a fork. Add this to the cooked shoots. Use a pair of tongs to stir the mixture well and to serve. Pour the soup into a serving bowl and garnish with the sesame seeds, coriander, and mint. Serve immediately.

Note:
Use the Bai Yanana brand of bamboo shoots which already contains the *yanang* leaf.

Green Papaya Salad

1 large green (unripe) papaya (see
   Note)
½ cup mint leaves
½ cup coriander leaves
One ½-inch piece galangal
3 to 4 lime leaves, finely minced
½ teaspoon crab paste (optional–
   see Note)
2 green chilies
1 clove garlic, peeled and minced
Sugar to taste
½ teaspoon MSG (optional)
2 tablespoons padek (see Note, Beef
   Lap, page 259)
Juice of ½ lime
2 tablespoons fish sauce
½ large tomato, very thinly sliced

Similar to, but more complicated than, the Thai version (see recipe, page 74), this is a slightly labor-intensive dish with a wonderful sharp-sour flavor. The Lao eat this often, but Mrs. Viponsanarath's daughter warns that frequent consumption of papaya could thin the blood. You must shred the papaya with a sharp knife, not with a hand or machine grater and not with a food processor, because you will not get the correct crisp texture. You should pound and grind the ingredients with a mortar and pestle—Mrs. Viponsanarath knelt on the floor to use her large clay mortar and pestle— but, without a mortar and pestle, use your hands to squeeze the ingredients. (Recipe: Nom Viponsanarath)

1

Peel the papaya, then, holding the whole papaya in one hand and a sharpened cleaver or other long kitchen knife in the other, make closely spaced chopping cuts all the way around the fruit. Then slice lengthwise to make shreds. You should have 2 cups of shredded papaya. Wrap the unused portion of the papaya in plastic wrap and refrigerate for another use.

2

Combine all the ingredients in the listed order in a mortar and pound as you add each new one. When everything has been added, serve immediately.

Note:

Use the large green Asian papaya for the salad; these are much larger than the small ripe papayas Westerners are used to eating. They are sold at most Asian markets. Crab paste is available in cans at most Asian markets.

Beef Lap

4 large tomatoes
Salt to taste
2 to 3 teaspoons sugar
1 cup mint leaves
6 scallions, trimmed and cut into
   1-inch pieces
1 Oriental eggplant, skin intact, cut
   into cubes
½ teaspoon MSG (optional)
3 shallots, peeled
3 cloves garlic, peeled
4 to 6 whole green chilies
2 tablespoons dry-roasted ground
   sticky, or glutinous, rice (see Note)
2 teaspoons freshly ground black
   pepper
¼ cup chopped coriander leaves
3 tablespoons fish sauce
1 pound beef roast, trimmed of any
   visible fat
½ pound tripe, boiled for 1 hour
½ cup gourami fish (see Note)
Juice of 1 lime
Garnish
1 cup chopped mint leaves
½ cup chopped coriander leaves
6 scallions, thinly sliced
Platter garnish
Leaf lettuce leaves
Sliced cucumbers
Sprigs coriander

Also spelled larb, *this is a national dish, served often despite its lengthy preparation time, and certainly on special occasions. Mrs. Sananikone explains that* lap *comes from the word* lapha, *which means "good fortune."* Lap *also means to chop, and the cook chops up meat, fish, chicken, or shrimp as well as beef for this dish. Since it is hard to find beef intestines in U.S. markets—Lao typically include the minced stomach, intestines, liver, tripe, and skin with the finely minced beef—they usually use other meats instead. In Laos, cooks would grill the tomatoes to bring out their flavors, and would wrap the shallots and garlic in a banana leaf and grill the packet over charcoal to soften the seasonings. The Lao serve this dish with sticky rice, grilled meat, and Green Papaya Salad (page 257), and use their fingers to scoop up mouthfuls of each. The flavor of* lap *disappears after about 3 hours, so this must be eaten right away. (Recipe: Nom Viponsanarath)*

1

Peel, seed, and quarter the tomatoes. Put them in a heavy skillet with the salt and a pinch of sugar and cook over medium heat until the tomatoes are reduced to a pulpy sauce, about 15 minutes. Stir often. Add the mint leaves, scallions, and eggplant. Continue cooking until all the vegetables are very soft and can be easily mashed. Add the MSG and remaining sugar

2

Meanwhile wrap the shallots and 2 cloves of garlic in foil, place the packet directly on a gas or electric burner, and cook over low to medium heat until the ingredients are browned and softened. Place the chilies in a heavy skillet and cook them over medium heat until the skins darken. When the shallots, garlic, and chilies are soft-

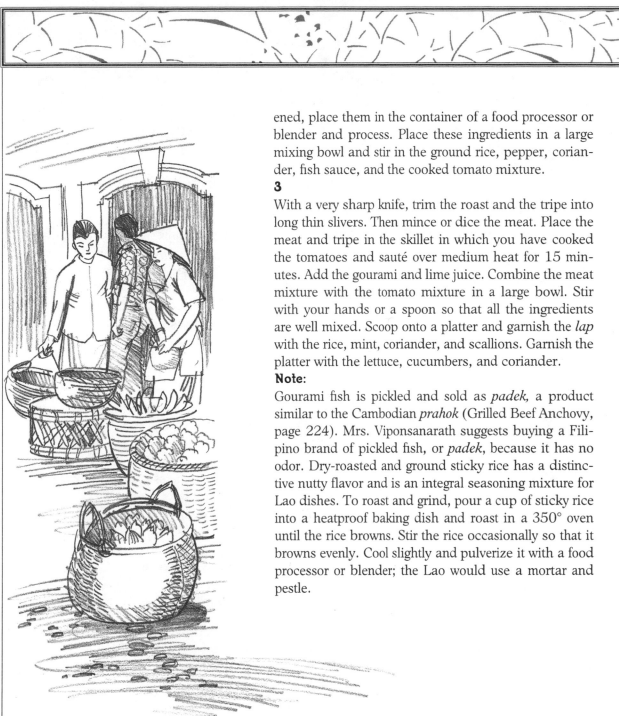

ened, place them in the container of a food processor or blender and process. Place these ingredients in a large mixing bowl and stir in the ground rice, pepper, coriander, fish sauce, and the cooked tomato mixture.

3

With a very sharp knife, trim the roast and the tripe into long thin slivers. Then mince or dice the meat. Place the meat and tripe in the skillet in which you have cooked the tomatoes and sauté over medium heat for 15 minutes. Add the gourami and lime juice. Combine the meat mixture with the tomato mixture in a large bowl. Stir with your hands or a spoon so that all the ingredients are well mixed. Scoop onto a platter and garnish the *lap* with the rice, mint, coriander, and scallions. Garnish the platter with the lettuce, cucumbers, and coriander.

Note:

Gourami fish is pickled and sold as *padek,* a product similar to the Cambodian *prahok* (Grilled Beef Anchovy, page 224). Mrs. Viponsanarath suggests buying a Filipino brand of pickled fish, or *padek*, because it has no odor. Dry-roasted and ground sticky rice has a distinctive nutty flavor and is an integral seasoning mixture for Lao dishes. To roast and grind, pour a cup of sticky rice into a heatproof baking dish and roast in a 350° oven until the rice browns. Stir the rice occasionally so that it browns evenly. Cool slightly and pulverize it with a food processor or blender; the Lao would use a mortar and pestle.

DESSERT

Rice Pudding

4 to 6 cups raw black or white
    sticky, or glutinous, rice
Two 13½-ounce cans coconut milk
5 egg yolks
1½ to 3 cups sugar, or to taste
3 tablespoons tapioca flour
2 cups water
Pinch salt

This is a wonderful rich rice dessert. This recipe serves 8 to 10. (Recipe: Nom Viponsanarath)

1

Soak the rice overnight, in water to cover, or at least for 3 to 4 hours.

2

Combine 1 can of the coconut milk, the egg yolks, sugar, tapioca flour, and salt in a large bowl and mix together well. Pour into a 1-quart baking dish and set on a steamer rack in a large saucepan. Add the 2 cups water to the pan, cover, and steam the custard for about 2 hours. Check that the water does not boil away during cooking.

3

Meanwhile, drain the rice and put it into a steamer. Steam according to the directions on page 253. When the rice is soft, in about 30 to 45 minutes, uncover and spoon the remaining can of coconut milk onto the rice. Or spoon on half the can, reserving the remainder to spoon on just before serving. Replace the cover and steam the rice again for 10 minutes more.

4

When the custard has set, remove from the steamer and let stand for 30 minutes.

5

When ready to serve, mix the remaining coconut milk into the rice, if you have reserved any. Place the rice on a serving dish or individual dishes, top with the custard, and serve.

Chapter
7

NORTHERN
NEIGHBORS

JUST GLANCING AT A MAP OF ASIA TELLS US THAT KOREA AND JAPAN are neighbors, if not particularly good friends. But they are really only neighbors by geography, not by politics, history, or social customs. In fact, much of their recent history has been marked by feuding and bitterness: Japan annexed Korea in the early twentieth century and ruled it, not very benignly, until after World War II.

Some historians conjecture that the Japanese and Koreans may be descended from the same ethnic stock—that is, from the Siberians and Manchurians. But if so, their early ancestors took rather different paths on the way to developing their respective cuisines. There are certain similarities in the kitchen, of course: Both grill many of their foods. Both rely on the new products of the sea, the plains, and the mountains. In fact, a traditional Japanese meal must, traditionally, consist of something from each location. Both are essentially healthful cuisines, depending on fresh foods and calling for only limited fats and oils. And both use rice as a staple. But there most similarities end.

Whereas the Japanese are famous for their lean and elegant foods and their studied presentations, the Koreans are known for their hearty, country-ish stews as well as grilled and fried meats, lightly seasoned vegetables, and colorful arrangements. Korean food is also replete with hot, often complex flavors—at least, with flavors more complex than the Japanese like. Another look at the map tells us why. The Japanese in their remote island nation were virtually untouched until the mid-nineteenth century by outside influences, even those of their Asian neighbors. Korean cooks, on the other hand, picked up ideas and ingredients from Chinese kin across the borders. Such is the heat of some of their food that I sometimes wonder if a Vietnamese, Thai, or Burmese cook with a sackful of chilies strayed into a Korean kitchen some centuries back. If so, that person never made it across the sea to Japan.

Korea

EXCEPT FOR BRIEF STOPOVERS IN SEOUL EN ROUTE TO HONG KONG, I have spent no time in Korea and still find it an inscrutable country peopled by gentle and quiet folk. I do know that my son got lost on a Hong Kong Boy Scout camping expedition in the Korean countryside and was greeted by cordial townspeople. I do know that the country has been split in two geographically and politically. I do know that many foreign governments view the militaristic North with some alarm.

And I do know, from the two Korean ladies who talked to me about their cuisine, that it is primarily a pretty one, with an emphasis on precision cutting—for eye appeal and for ease of chopstick use—and on health benefits. For example, June Lee describes the popularity with new mothers of a particular seaweed soup (see recipe, page 272) because of its high iodine content. This is an important soup, she says: Whales feed on this kelp after giving birth and this particular seaweed apparently promotes milk production as well as cleansing of the afterbirth. "So the first thing a woman must do after giving birth is to eat this soup. And later, eat it three times a day," she says. She adds, however, that all Koreans, regardless of age and sex, enjoy the soup for its light and delicate flavors.

Young Ja Yun (Jamie Faeh) talks about the regionality of Korean cooking: Northern foods are lighter, less spicy, and less salty. Southern foods, on the other hand, are heavier, spicier, and saltier. She also talks about how often Koreans grill. To outsiders, the very popular Korean Barbecue (also known as *bulgogi,* see recipe, page 265) almost summarizes Korean cooking. At Korean restaurants, patrons do their own grilling on an at-the-table charcoal stove with a "Genghis Khan" domed cover on which strips of meat are barbecued. Actually, beef is rarely grilled at a traditional Korean home table, since meats (but not fish) are grilled in the kitchen, a separate room attached to the main house. Cooking there keeps the smoke and fumes out. But Koreans use a traditional brass table-top grill known as a *wharo,* which comes with tongs and a mesh rack for grilling fish at the table.

Despite regional differences, no Korean meal—breakfast, lunch, or dinner—is com-

plete without a bowl of rice and a side dish of *kimchee,* a fermented vegetable pickle that may be about as close to a national dish as anything the Koreans serve (see recipe, page 270). In fact, the traditional Korean family sets aside a *kimchee*-making day in the fall, which assures a winter's worth of this often fiery dish. As June Lee remembers it, making *kimchee* was a big family affair, which started with soaking hundreds of cabbage heads overnight in salty water. On the actual *kimchee* day, the neighbors came in to help out by mixing together as seasonings, the julienned radishes, hot pepper powder, chopped green onions, minced garlic, salt, fresh oysters, chopped chestnuts, and chopped fresh ginger. This is just one popular and traditional winter *kimchee* recipe, explains Ms. Lee. The mixture could as well have featured daikon and cucumbers and cabbage at another season. After four to five weeks of storage in a large underground earthenware crock, the fermented *kimchee* was ready for eating—although the mixture could have been eaten right away.

Few Korean cooks would construct their meals without a generous portion of fresh seafood, beef, or pork, or of fresh whole grains and seasonal vegetables—all seasoned with soy sauce, ginger, garlic, and sesame oil, spiked with chilies or chili powders, and accompanied by rice and *kimchee.* And few Koreans would eat in solitary splendor—a Korean meal is a communal, family-and-friend affair with multiple dishes, and its partakers linger over the table enjoying conversation and the efforts of the cook.

THE GRILLS

Bulgogi

2 pounds flank steak
Marinade
3 to 4 cloves garlic, peeled and
   minced
5 tablespoons Japanese soy sauce
   mixed with 1 tablespoon water
1 teaspoon sugar
2 tablespoons sesame oil
3 to 4 scallions, chopped
1 teaspoon freshly ground black
   pepper
1 tablespoon crushed roasted
   sesame seeds

The name means "fire meat" and the standard recipe usually calls for charbroiled thinly sliced beef—the best is flank steak. The meat strips must not be too thin or too small or they become too difficult to grill. The sesame oil acts as a meat tenderizer. Serve with hot rice. (Recipe: June Lee)

1

Wrap the steak in foil and place it in the freezer until it is half frozen—this makes slicing the meat much easier. Slice it against the grain into 1½-inch-wide x 3-inch-long strips.

2

Combine the marinade ingredients in a bowl, stirring to blend them well. Add the strips of meat and toss to coat them well with the marinade. Cover the dish with foil or plastic wrap and refrigerate for about 1½ hours. To prevent toughness, remove the meat from the refrigerator 30 minutes before grilling.

3

Grill by the direct method (page xxix) over hot coals for about 10 minutes, or until done, turning once. Remove from the fire and serve immediately.

Bulkalbi

2 to 3 pounds short ribs

Marinade

3 to 4 cloves garlic, peeled and
  minced
6 tablespoons Japanese soy sauce
  mixed with 1 tablespoon water
1 tablespoon sugar
3 tablespoons sesame oil
3 to 4 scallions, chopped
1 teaspoon freshly ground black
  pepper
1 tablespoon crushed roasted
  sesame seeds (optional)

The name means "fire ribs." June Lee recommends buying the short ribs at a Korean grocery because the butchers there will cut the meat into the "L. A." cut— that is, the ribs are cut on the parallel and not straight-cut by rib sections. However, you can use standard short or top ribs. Korean men like to eat these ribs with their cocktails. This recipe serves 3 to 4. (Recipe: June Lee)

1

Trim all fat from the ribs and make small intermittent slashes on the surface with a sharp knife so the marinade can penetrate. Place the ribs in a large bowl.

2

Combine the marinade ingredients in a mixing bowl, stirring to blend them well. Pour the mixture over the ribs and coat the meat well with the marinade. Cover the dish with foil or plastic wrap and set it aside for 1 to 2 hours. Turn the meat once or twice.

3

Grill the meat by the direct method (page xxix) over medium-hot coals for a total of 10 minutes, turning the ribs once to brown evenly. Remove from the fire and serve immediately.

Grilled Pork

6 to 8 pork chops, or 1½ pounds
   pork spareribs
Marinade
1 cup hot bean paste (see Note)
1 quart soy sauce
½ cup sugar
2 cloves garlic, peeled and minced
2 scallions, thinly sliced
1 teaspoon chopped or grated fresh
   ginger
¼ cup water
1 tablespoon sesame oil

This recipe is suitable for either spareribs or pork chops —a bland meat for this peppery mixture. You can adjust the amount of pepper paste to suit your palate. You must start this recipe a day in advance to give the meat enough time to marinate. (Recipe: Young Ja Yun [Jamie Faehl])

1

Put the pork chops or ribs in a shallow baking dish and set aside. Combine the ingredients for the marinade and pour over the meat. Cover the dish with foil or plastic wrap and refrigerate overnight.

2

Thirty minutes before cooking time, remove the meat from the refrigerator. Grill by the direct method (page xxix) over medium-hot coals for about 10 minutes, turning once. Remove from the fire and serve immediately.

Note:

The hot bean paste is known as *ko chu jang*. You can buy it in jars at most Asian markets; it can be very strong, so you may want to taste it before you add the entire amount recommended.

Chicken Bulgogi

48 ounces boneless and skinless
    chicken breast meat

Marinade

2 tablespoons Ground Red Pepper
    Sauce (see page 270)
2 tablespoons sugar
2 tablespoons soy sauce
½ tablespoon sesame oil
2 teaspoons chopped scallions

*You can use pork instead of chicken for this recipe.
(Recipe: Chef Kyung Yul Kim, Yokohama Restaurant)*

1

Put the chicken in a shallow baking dish. Combine the marinade ingredients and pour over the chicken. Cover with foil or plastic wrap and set aside for about 1 hour.

2

Grill the chicken by the direct method (page xxix) over medium-hot coals for about 10 minutes, turning once. Remove from the fire and serve immediately.

Grilled Skewered Beef

24 ounces boneless top round
4 large onions, peeled and sliced
  into 4 sections
4 large green bell peppers, each cut
  into 4 thin strips
4 carrots, each cut into 4 uniform
  circles
24 large mushrooms, each cut into
  4 sections

Marinade
2 tablespoons Ground Red Pepper
  Sauce (see page 270)
2 teaspoons sugar
2 teaspoons soy sauce
1 teaspoon sesame oil
2 teaspoons chopped scallions

Known to Koreans as sanjok, *this simple beef-and-vegetable dish resembles a shish kebab offering. (Recipe: Chef Kyung Yul Kim, Yokohama Restaurant).*

1
Trim the beef of all fat. Cut it into 4 strips about ¼ inch thick, 1 inch wide, and 3 inches long. Put the meat in a shallow baking dish and set aside. Combine the marinade ingredients, mixing well. Pour them over the meat. Cover with foil or plastic wrap, and marinate in the refrigerator overnight.

2
An hour before grilling, put the sliced vegetables into the baking dish to marinate with the meat.

3
Thread the meat and vegetables on 2 long metal skewers so that each skewer has 2 strips of beef alternating with 4 pieces of vegetable: 4 vegetables, 1 strip beef, 4 vegetables, 1 strip beef.

4
Grill by the direct method (page xxix) over medium-hot coals for 8 to 10 minutes, turning once. Remove from the fire and serve immediately.

ACCOMPANIMENTS

Ground Red Pepper Sauce

1 cup soy sauce
1 teaspoon ground dried red chilies
¼ teaspoon garlic powder
½ teaspoon sesame oil
1 teaspoon sugar
½ teaspoon grated fresh ginger

This is almost like an all-purpose seasoning used to heighten or intensify many different flavors. This makes about 1 cup. (Recipe: Chef Kyung Yul Kim, Yokohama Restaurant)

Mix all the ingredients together. This stores well in a tightly closed container in the refrigerator for up to 2 weeks.

Kimchee

1 head bok choy, rinsed and
   chopped into bite-sized pieces
3 tablespoons salt
1 bunch scallions, chopped
2 to 3 cloves garlic, peeled and
   minced
2 to 3 tablespoons hot chili powder
2 teaspoons minced fresh ginger

The Koreans eat kimchee 3 times a day—rice and kimchee are a must, says Ms. Lee. This modern version is much simpler and faster—and you do not have to store it in the ground. You can eat it right after you make it or wait 2 days until it has begun to ferment. (Recipe: June Lee)

1
Sprinkle the bok choy with the salt and mix well. After 2 or 3 hours, the cabbage wilts. At this point, add the chopped scallions, garlic, chili powder, and ginger. Mix together well and put this mixture into a sterile 1-gallon glass jar. Add a little salted water. Pack the mixture down before closing the jar.

2
Leave at room temperature for 1 or 2 days so that the cabbage begins to ferment, then refrigerate it. If you leave it out too long, it will get very sour and start to bubble.

Beef Stock Soup

3 pounds oxtail
1 pound chuck roast
Garnish
*Salt and freshly ground black
    pepper to taste*
Chopped scallions

This is a typical winter soup—very concentrated and bracing—and is good accompanied by rice, other vegetable side dishes, and kimchee. The meal is even more filling if you serve a grilled-meat course, too. As a variation, you can dilute the soup and add 1 cup chopped Chinese cabbage or 1 cup slivered daikon. (Recipe: June Lee)

1

Put the meat in a large stockpot, add water to cover, and turn the heat to low. When a scum forms on the surface, pour off all the water, rinse off the bones and meat, and refill the pot with fresh water, about 2½ quarts. This assures that you will have a very clear broth. Return the pot to the stove and simmer for about 4 hours, or until the meat falls off the bones. You may add more water at this point if the soup is too thick for your preference.

2

Cool the meat and remove it from the bone. Put the meat back in the soup and refrigerate it until the fat congeals on the surface. Scoop off the layer of fat. Add the salt, pepper, and scallions and heat the soup almost to boiling. Serve immediately.

Seaweed Soup

1 foot x 3-inch strip of dried seaweed
2 quarts beef stock
Soy sauce and freshly ground black
    pepper to taste

This is a nourishing winter soup. Mee yuk, *the particular type of kelp needed for this soup, is readily available at Korean grocers. You may also use the Japanese* kombu, *but it is not quite the same. When you rinse the seaweed, it has a fragrant smell rather like the ocean. (Recipe: June Lee)*

1

Cut the seaweed into pieces about the size of your hand. Soak in a bowl of water for about 1 hour. The seaweed will swell up and look like its original self.

2

Rinse the seaweed well and chop into bite-sized pieces. Put the beef stock in a large saucepan and add the seaweed. Bring to a boil, lower the heat, and simmer for 30 to 40 minutes. Season the soup to taste with soy sauce and black pepper and serve it hot.

Fried Bean Curd

2 or 3 soft-style tofu cubes (sold
    loose at most Asian markets)
Vegetable oil for frying
Salt
3 scallions, sliced into 1- to 2-inch
    lengths
Soy sauce

This is a simple and nutritious accompaniment for vegetables and grilled meat. You can add stir-fried snow peas, broccoli, or strips of red bell peppers for a more colorful dish. (Recipe: June Lee)

Cut the tofu into thick pieces and drain off the water on a cutting board. Pour about 3 tablespoons vegetable oil into a 10-inch skillet and heat. When sizzling, add the tofu and sprinkle on some salt. Fry till hard and slightly golden on both sides. Remove the tofu to a serving dish and set aside. Add the scallions and when they are softened, scoop them on top of the tofu. Sprinkle with soy sauce and serve immediately.

Mung Bean Pancake

1 pound dried mung beans, split and
   peeled
1 bunch scallions, sliced in half
   lengthwise and cut into 1½-inch
   lengths
1 medium onion, peeled and thinly
   sliced
1 small carrot, cut into julienne strips
Salt to taste
Vegetable oil for frying
Soy sauce to taste
Sugar to taste
Vinegar to taste

This is a popular pancakelike dish that can be served as an appetizer or with the main course. Some people add thinly sliced cooked pork to the pancake "batter." You can cook the pancakes ahead and freeze them for later use. This recipe makes about 20 or 30 pancakes about 4 inches in diameter. (Recipe: June Lee)

1

Rinse the mung beans in cold water and soak them overnight in a bowl in the refrigerator.

2

Drain and put in the container of a food processor or blender and puree. You may need to add some water to help process. This should have the consistency of a pancake batter.

3

Ladle the bean puree into a mixing bowl and add the sliced scallions, onion, and carrot. Sprinkle in some salt and stir well.

4

Heat 3 tablespoons of oil in a 10-inch skillet. When the oil sizzles, spoon in the puree mixture to make 3 or 4 small, round pancakes at a time. Keep the heat at a constant temperature so that it does not burn the pancakes. Turn the pancakes when the underside is brown. Cook the other side until golden. Repeat the process until all the batter is used up. Serve hot, with soy sauce, a sprinkle of sugar, and a few drops of vinegar.

Mandu

1 package 3- x-3-inch won ton skins
Filling
1 pound lean ground beef,
    preferably ground sirloin
3 or 4 soft-style tofu cubes (sold
    loose at Oriental groceries)
4 cloves garlic, peeled and mashed
1 cup finely chopped onions
2 cups finely shredded, lightly salted
    cabbage; or 2 cups steamed and
    squeezed mung bean sprouts
Freshly ground black pepper to
    taste
1 tablespoon sesame oil
1 teaspoon garlic powder
Salt to taste
1 egg yolk, lightly beaten

These are little dumplings that look like ravioli and can be served in soup. You can buy square won ton skins from any Oriental grocer and in many Western supermarkets. For the filling, use the inside portion of a round cabbage, not the tough outer leaves nor the fibrous core section. You can make these part of a more substantial first course soup by boiling them in beef stock then adding thin egg noodles, sliced scallions, or rice cakes—served this way, mandu *becomes a holiday food for the Korean community. Rice cakes are sliced from a rice product sold at Korean markets. (Recipe: June Lee)*

1

In a large mixing bowl, break up the beef with your fingers or a fork. Crumble the tofu and combine it with the meat.

2

Mix in the garlic and chopped onions. Squeeze the excess moisture out of the cabbage and add it to the mixing bowl. Season the mixture with pepper, sesame oil, garlic powder, and salt.

3

Place a sheet of aluminum foil on a flat surface. Then, lay a won ton skin on the foil. Moisten 2 adjacent edges of the skin with a dab of egg yolk—too much yolk will make the edges hard when cooked. Place 1 tablespoon of the filling into the center of the square. Fold over to form a triangle and crimp the edges shut.

4

There are several ways to cook the *mandu:* 1) Cook them in a pot of boiling water, removing them with a slotted spoon when they float to the surface. Serve them with soy sauce mixed with a few drops of vinegar and some sugar. 2) Heat 1 tablespoon oil in a skillet and fry them,

a few at a time, until golden. Turn once and fry till the other side is golden. Put all the cooked *mandu* into the skillet. Raise the heat, splash 3 tablespoons cold water into the pan, and put a cover on immediately. This steaming cooks the filling. After about 30 seconds or 1 minute, or when the water sizzles and heavy steam pours out, turn the heat down to medium, remove the lid, and let the mixture simmer until all the water evaporates and the dumplings are dry and brown. Serve hot with the same soy sauce mixture as above. 3) Cook the *mandu* in boiling beef stock, season with salt and pepper and chopped green onions, add noodles if you wish, and serve hot.

Fresh Vegetable and Meat Platter

½ seedless hothouse cucumber, julienned

2 large carrots, scraped and julienned

1 large can (20 ounces) bamboo shoots, julienned

1 Japanese pear, peeled and julienned (see Note)

One 4-ounce package brown dried Oriental mushrooms, soaked

4 large eggs, separated

1 tablespoon vegetable oil, or more if needed

½ pound flank steak or London broil, cut into strips

½ pound small shrimp, peeled, deveined, and cooked

One 8-ounce package Japanese jellyfish, rinsed

This cook serves this platter to her family on Christmas Eve but says that it is a popular dish all year long. You should use your creative skills to arrange the components in a pleasing way. Be sure that when you are cutting the vegetables into julienne strips, you make them uniform in size, preferably 2 inches or 2½ inches in length. (Recipe: Young Ja Yun [Jamie Faeh])

1

Put the cucumber, carrots, bamboo shoots, and Japanese pear in separate piles in a large baking dish and set aside. Squeeze the water out of the mushrooms and julienne them. Put them in the baking dish.

2

Beat each egg separately and make 4 separate omelets by pouring one beaten egg at a time into a skillet heated with a little vegetable oil. Make a sheet, as thin as paper, of the egg. Try to make the egg as square as possible in the pan and cook it quickly over moderately high heat, 30 to 45 seconds. Carefully remove it with a spatula and place it on a flat baking sheet. Cut it into a square and julienne into pieces about ¼ inch x 2 or 2½ inches. Stack the pieces in the baking dish. Repeat the procedure with the remaining eggs.

3

Boil the steak for about half an hour, squeezing out as much of the juice as possible from the cooked meat. When cool enough to handle, julienne the meat and stack it in the baking dish. Cool the shrimp and stack them in the dish. Wash and drain the jellyfish, squeezing out all excess moisture. Stack it in the baking dish.

Seasoning Sauce

2 tablespoons dry mustard

2 tablespoons boiling water

½ cup cold water

2 tablespoons sugar

2 tablespoons Japanese rice vinegar

1 tablespoon salt

1 teaspoon sesame oil

1 tablespoon soy sauce

Dash of MSG

4

Put the dry mustard into a small mixing bowl and whisk in the boiling water. You must use boiling water—warm or cold water will not bring out the intense flavor of the mustard. Whisk in the remaining sauce ingredients and pour the sauce into a small serving bowl.

5

On a round serving dish, make a symmetrical arrangement of the ingredients, with half the portions on one side of the platter and half on the other. Leave an open space in the center for the jellyfish and the bowl of seasoning sauce. After presenting the dish, pour the sauce over all the ingredients and mix them together. Serve immediately.

Note:

Japanese or Asian pears, known as *nashi,* come in several varieties but generally are crisp, apple-shaped fruits that are sold fresh at many Japanese markets.

Chap Chae

Marinade
¼ teaspoon ground black pepper
3 to 4 tablespoons soy sauce
2 tablespoons sesame oil
4 to 5 cloves garlic, peeled and
    crushed
2 to 3 chopped green onions
1 teaspoon sugar

1 to 1½ pounds flank steak, cut into
    thin strips
5 or 6 shiitake mushrooms
1 bunch spinach (about 1 pound) or
    pickling cucumbers, sliced into
    circles
½ pound mushrooms
1 large onion, peeled and thinly
    sliced
1 bunch scallions, cut into 2-inch
    lengths
1 red bell pepper, seeded and thinly
    sliced
2 carrots, peeled and shredded
Vegetable oil for frying
2 egg yolks, beaten

Seasonings
Soy sauce or salt
Sesame oil
Sugar
Garlic powder
Freshly ground black pepper
Roasted sesame seeds

Known as "multiple vegetables," this dish makes a perfect accompaniment for any Korean grilled meat meal. You can combine any fresh vegetables in any quantity you need. You can also enrich this with left-over beef. Use about the same amount of each vegetable —the result is a colorful dish of greens, reds, yellows, and oranges. The following is a suggested list of ingredients to serve 4 to 6. (Recipe: June Lee)

1
Combine the marinade ingredients. Put the steak in a baking dish and pour the marinade over it. Cover and set aside while you prepare the vegetables.

2
Soak the shiitake mushrooms in cold water, then cut them into thin strips. Blanch, rinse, and squeeze out the spinach and cut it in small pieces—set aside and season with soy sauce, sesame oil, garlic powder, and roasted sesame seeds. Or if you use the cucumbers, sprinkle the slices with salt and after an hour, squeeze out the water and sauté the slices quickly in 2 to 3 tablespoons vegetable oil. Clean, slice, and sauté the mushrooms. Sauté the onions. Sauté the scallions. Stir-fry the red pepper. Sauté the carrots. Cook and rinse the noodles in cold water. Set all the prepared vegetables aside.

3
Cook the egg yolks in a thin omelet and, when cooked, cut it into shreds. Set aside.

4
Put 3 tablespoons oil in a wok or skillet and heat. When sizzling, stir-fry the steak and transfer it to a large salad bowl. Add the cooked and cooled vegetables and garnish with the shredded egg. Season with soy sauce or salt and sesame oil, sugar, garlic powder, pepper, and roasted sesame seeds to taste. Serve immediately.

DESSERTS

Sweet Rice Flour Cake

3 cups sticky, or glutinous, rice flour
½ teaspoon salt
2 teaspoons baking powder
1 egg
½ cup sugar
½ cup vegetable oil
2 cups milk
1 cup raisins
1 cup Western-style black beans,
  cooked
1 cup chopped walnuts or pecans

This makes a very easy-to-assemble dessert. (Recipe: June Lee)

1
Preheat the oven to 350°. Grease a 9- x 10- or 12-inch baking pan and set it aside.

2
Combine the rice flour, salt, and baking powder. Combine the egg and sugar in a separate mixing bowl and beat until frothy. Gradually add the oil and beat well. Stir the rice flour mixture into the egg mixture and add the milk. If the batter is too stiff to beat easily, you can add a little more milk. Stir the raisins, black beans, and nuts into the batter and transfer to the baking pan.

3
Bake in the preheated oven for about 45 minutes. A few minutes before the cake is ready to take out, brush the surface with milk to give it a golden glaze. When a skewer inserted in the center comes out clean, remove the cake from the heat and cool thoroughly before slicing. The texture will be slightly sticky, but that is normal. Serve with hot tea for dessert.

Sweet Red Bean Paste with Cinnamon

2 cups water
⅓ cup raw medium-grain white rice
One 18-ounce can prepared
   Japanese red bean paste (see
   Note)
Sprinkle of ground cinnamon

This is a simple and nutritious dessert. You can vary the recipe by omitting the rice. (Recipe: Young Ja Yun [Jamie Faeh])

Pour the water into a large saucepan and bring to a boil. Add the rice and cook uncovered until the rice grains are enlarged by half their size, about 20 minutes. Add the red bean paste, lower the heat, and simmer until the mixture reaches the desired consistency. Some people like their dessert to be very liquid. The cook prefers hers much thicker, with a custardlike consistency. When ready, spoon the mixture into individual serving bowls and sprinkle with cinnamon.

Note:
The cook suggests buying already prepared red bean paste. At a Korean or Japanese grocer ask for the Morinaga brand of *ogura an*.

Japan

THE FIRST TRULY AUTHENTIC JAPANESE MEAL I EVER ATE WAS NOT IN Tokyo, but 10,000 miles away in a Washington, D.C., restaurant. I say authentic because the ingredients, the chef, and the staff had quite literally just gotten off the jet from Japan. They served a meal that was an aesthetic experience, memorable not so much for its flavors as for its breathtaking beauty. Each dainty, exquisite morsel and each plate arrangement looked like a still life constructed of very expensive modeling clay—a case of art and life getting all mixed up. One dish in particular was meant to fool the eye: delicacies of textured and tinted fried noodles wrapped around chestnuts to resemble fancy green sea urchins or spiny golf balls. Served on a ceramic plate, these were accompanied by jellied vegetables with okra and fish roe.

I wondered then if that obsession with detail and presentation was part of the Japanese character. The answer is yes, and so is their obsession with food in general. I listened while a journalist friend recounted her days in Tokyo, when she was bombarded daily by television shows featuring cooking demonstrations, recipes, and eating tours through one or another kitchen. On these shows and in those kitchens, a happy participant always beamed that the food was "delicious." The Japanese will go to any expense, to any trouble, to eat well, she said. She suggested watching the Japanese movie *Tampopo*—a silly romp through a Tokyo noodle kitchen restaurant—to begin to appreciate the Japanese obsession with food.

Later, I sat mesmerized over tea one morning while Mrs. Hidiaki Ueda showed me cookbook after cookbook and magazine after magazine filled with beautiful glossy photos of beautiful glossy Japanese food. Each presentation was more astonishing in its intricate and fanciful construction than the one before. Could it be, I asked, that this is food meant to be eaten? She smiled. I gathered that to the Japanese—from the housewife, who spends her off hours learning how to cook, to the professional chef, who must spend all of his hours cooking—food and beauty are almost synonymous.

One chef said that as part of his training he had studied *ikebana,* the art of Japanese

flower arranging, so he would know how to present food creatively and beautifully. Another friend, who had once owned and managed a Japanese country inn, explained that the precision of Japanese cooking is a natural spin-off of the rigid social rules that dictate Japanese life. As an example, the Japanese chef must learn to slice raw fish in a certain and very precise way so that he follows the grain of the flesh and the cut is pretty and clean. Rules, common sense, and tradition dictate which sauces go with which dish, how rice is arranged in the bowl, and even the most serene arrangement of food on a plate. Seasonality prevails, of course, in a land that was once self-sufficient. And, of course, foods were once completely different in winter and in summer. Now, technology has created more than the obvious changes in the Japanese kitchen: If someone wants to eat a heating winter stew in midsummer, for example, all he or she must do is enjoy it in air-conditioned comfort.

The outside world has definitely intruded into the kitchens of this tiny nation. As a result, in some ways, traditional Japanese cooking has taken a battering, with workers opting for foods-on-the run rather than the slower, more contemplative traditional meals —although many Japanese still eat their customary breakfast of rice with a bracing bowl of *miso* soup. Historically nondessert eaters, the Japanese have also discovered the poetry of creamy, buttery Western pastries and cakes. But in other ways, what is truly Japanese exists right below the surface of the American steak houses, pizza parlors, and curry-rice outlets. And one of the most enduring of these traditions is that of grilling, or *yakimono* (literally, "grilled things"). That the Japanese have perfected grilling is not very surprising, considering that theirs is a cuisine of small food morsels eaten raw or just-cooked. Open-fire, quick-cooking with intense heat preserves the integrity of the delicate foods, such as fresh fish, the Japanese revere. They also skewer every edible part of an animal. One young friend talks about his adventures at a Tokyo *yakitori* (strictly speaking, *yakitori* means "grilled chicken" but the Japanese have expanded the term to mean grilled bits of meat) restaurant where his host was testing my friend's mettle: "The restaurants specialize in a particular animal, and at a chicken place you get every part—liver, chicken tails, brains, tongue, the works. We went to a pork place. I told my host I could eat anything and he ordered pig's ears for me. They were sliced very thin, but they are very fatty and look like jellyfish," says Ted Gauld.

Japanese grilled foods are usually skewered—they do not cook a whole side of any animal—and seasoned with salt, a seasoned dressing, or *miso* (a soybean paste). Even in

skewering the Japanese are artists: Instead of just sliding food onto a skewer any which way, they have developed many fancy and dramatic techniques—such as stitch skewering or fan skewering—that ultimately produce beautiful cooked food.

Probably every non-Japanese who has ever barbecued knows about the *hibachi*— that mini cast-iron portable grill that fits into a car and suits the cooking of delicate portions of food, such as the Japanese would eat. The Japanese also grill foods on very hot rocks, on shiny metal table-top griddles (the *teppan*), on regular grills, and occasionally in the cumbersome old *kamodo,* a wood- or coal-burning oven that is almost never used in urban centers. "Too dirty," said one chef, who prefers the simpler barbecue grills. My journalist friend also tells of the popular Tokyo barbecue restaurants—the *robata-yaki* —that borrow their format from the olden days of open-hearth cooking.

In keeping with the beauty of their cuisine, the Japanese select a hard coal *(bincho-tan)* that burns consistently hot and clean—they do not want their foods sullied by the look or taste of smoke. In fact, this charcoal is so hard that it clinks when dropped and was once used as the noisemakers in wind chimes. Skilled cooks also learn how to monitor cooking times so that the outside is crispy, the interior warmed to perfection—just another facet of creating beautiful foods.

Japanese food is for those who eat with their eyes. But it will not suit people after dramatic flavors. Using ultra-fresh ingredients cooked as little as possible and often eaten raw, Japanese dishes are appreciated for their natural and simple tastes. Rather than smothering their ingredients with chilies, Japanese cooks turn to a gentle application of soy sauce, sesame oil, *mirin,* and *sake* to heighten the flavors of the rice, fish, meats, seaweed, tofu, and fresh produce that make up their streamlined national diet.

THE GRILLS

Grilled Duck Breast with Eggplant

1 Oriental eggplant
2 boneless and skinless duck breasts
2 whole carrots, peeled and trimmed into 4-inch pieces
Poultry Seasoning Sauce (see page 296)
1 bunch scallions for grilling (optional)

This recipes makes 2 servings. (Recipe: Chef Hiroyuki Ohashi)

1
Peel strips of skin from the eggplant so that some skin remains to give the cooked eggplant body. Cut the eggplant into strips 4 inches long x 2 inches wide and put the strips into lightly salted water.

2
Cut the duck breast into strips the same dimensions as the eggplant. Remove the eggplant from the water. Lay 2 thin metal skewers 3 inches apart and parallel on a flat surface. First, slide a piece of carrot down onto both skewers—this provides the bottom layer of the "sandwich" for the duck and eggplant strips. Slide a strip of duck, then a strip of eggplant, another strip of duck, and another strip of eggplant down the skewers. Top with another piece of carrot; this is the top of the "sandwich." Brush the skewered meat and vegetables with the poultry seasoning sauce.

3
Grill by the direct method (page xxix) over hot coals for 3 to 5 minutes, turning often and brushing the duck and eggplant with the seasoning sauce. Remove from the fire and serve immediately, garnished with grilled scallions, if desired.

Beef Negamaki

½ cup mirin

½ cup soy sauce

5 scallions, trimmed into
2-inch pieces

2 carrots, peeled and julienned

12 fresh orange sections, or about
2 oranges

12 thin slices of tomato, or about
1 tomato

7 ounces New York strip steak,
trimmed of all fat

Vegetable Garnish

½ cup sake or sherry

2 tablespoons butter

1 tablespoon soy sauce

Pinch salt

½ baking potato, peeled and
cut into thin strips

1 carrot, julienned

½ cup cauliflower flowerettes

½ cup broccoli flowerettes

One old-school chef said that this dish is a very Americanized preparation; traditionally, the Japanese would use thin sheets of fresh tuna fish wrapped around trimmed scallions. That sounds like a worthy option. However, another friend says she ate this often in Tokyo. The trick is to be sure the meat is very thin —to achieve this, roll it out with a rolling pin. Also, handling the meat and grilling are easier if you do not cut the meat into sections until after the whole roll has been grilled. This recipe makes 1 serving of about 12 pieces. (Recipe: Kenji Akiho, Cafe Japone)

1

Heat the mirin and ½ cup of soy sauce in a saucepan. Add the scallions, carrots, orange, and tomato pieces and simmer for 2 to 3 minutes. Remove from the heat, drain off and save the liquid to use as a dipping sauce, and set the vegetables aside.

2

Cut the steak in half through the middle so that you have 2 large thin pieces, about ¼ inch thick. Take a rolling pin or mallet to flatten the meat to ⅛ inch thick. Cut uniform pieces of beef about 1½ inches wide and 6 inches long. Place 2 pieces of scallion and 2 pieces of cooked carrot at one end of each slice of beef, and roll it up tightly, enclosing the vegetables in a roll. These will look like *sushi* rolls. Repeat this process until all the vegetables and beef are used up. Set the meat aside. Alternatively, fill the whole flattened pieces of steak, roll the pieces up, grill them, then slice them into uniform pieces before serving.

3

Meanwhile, to make the vegetable garnish, put the *sake,* butter, soy sauce, and salt in a saucepan. Add the vegetable pieces and cook them over high heat until they are

just crisp-tender, about 5 to 7 minutes. Remove from the heat and set aside.

4

Grill the beef rolls by the direct method (page xxix) over medium-hot coals for 3 to 4 minutes, turning them often to brown evenly. Transfer to a serving dish, top with the cooked vegetables, and serve with the dipping sauce.

Grilled Eel

1 whole eel, bone removed
  (see Note)
Fish Seasoning Sauce (see
  page 296) mixed with a sprinkle
  of brown rock sugar and
  sweet wine

(Recipe: Chef Hiroyuki Ohashi)

Grill the eel by the direct method (page xxix) over medium-hot coals for 8 to 10 minutes, turning it once and brushing it with the fish seasoning sauce. Remove it from the fire and serve immediately with additional fish seasoning sauce.

Note:

Freshwater eel, or *unagi,* may be used fresh or frozen. Japanese markets usually carry the frozen eel and some might even be able to special-order the fresh. To use, steam the eel first before grilling.

Salt-Grilled Whole Boston Mackerel

One 1-pound whole mackerel or
   red snapper
Salt

When cooked, the fish curves in a graceful splash, held in mid-swim by the skewers. This method is called uneri-gushi, *or "wave skewering." This is done by inserting 1 or 2 long metal skewers through the fish from tail to head, or head to tail. The two would run nearly parallel, going from slightly above and slightly below the mouth to the tail end. If the cook uses 2 skewers for larger whole fish, the skewers are threaded into the fish on the same side of the body, starting behind the head. The salt not only prevents the fish skin from burning, it enhances the appearance of the grilled fish. (Recipe: Chef Hiroyuki Ohashi)*

1

About 2 hours before cooking, lightly salt the fish—this brings out the excess juices. Before grilling, rinse off and dry the fish. Salt it again very lightly, but more heavily on the tail so that it doesn't burn during grilling.

2

Thread the fish on 2 metal skewers head to tail: Place the fish in front of you with its head at your left. Insert the first skewer beneath the eye, bend the fish slightly in a gentle U shape (this gives it the "wave" effect) and have the skewer emerge from the fish at the tail. Repeat this with the second skewer, leaving a ½-inch gap between the 2 skewers.

3

Grill the fish for 8 to 10 minutes by the direct method (page xxix) over hot coals, turning it often to brown and crisp evenly. Remove from the fire and serve immediately.

Yakitori

1 pound chicken breast, boned
   and skinned
1 bunch scallions, trimmed and cut
   into 1-inch lengths
Bamboo skewers
Marinade and Seasoning Sauce
3 cups mirin
2 cups soy sauce

Yakitori *may be the best-known grill dish in Japan. In some ways it is a kind of chicken kebab or* satay. *Chef Iwai gave me the basic seasoning sauce recipe, which he says can be varied by adding ginger juice, scallions,* sake, *and garlic, according to taste. This recipe serves 2. (Recipe: Chef Tokuji Iwai, Mikado Restaurant)*

1
Cut the breast meat into 1-inch cubes and set aside. Combine the marinade ingredients and soak the chicken in the marinade for about 20 minutes.
2
Thread the chicken cubes on the bamboo skewers alternately with the scallion pieces. Grill the chicken by the direct method (page xxix) over hot coals, basting it occasionally with the marinade, until browned, 10 to 12 minutes. Remove from the fire and serve immediately.

Miso-Grilled Beef

3 pounds sirloin steak.
One 1-pound packet miso paste
  (see Note)
Lemon juice for sprinkling

Simple, delicious, and flavorful—though maybe the fermented taste of miso is not to everyone's liking. The steak would be good with the Grilled Whole Potato (see page 298) or the Grilled Rice Balls (page 299). (Recipe: Mary Lord)

1

Spread the miso paste over both sides of the steak. Put the steak in a shallow baking dish, cover with foil or plastic wrap, and refrigerate overnight, or at least for 6 to 8 hours.

2

Scrape or rinse off the excess paste. Grill the steak by the direct method (page xxix) over medium-hot coals for 8 to 10 minutes, or until done. Remove from the fire, sprinkle with lemon juice, and serve immediately.

Note:

Miso paste is available at Japanese markets, some general Asian markets, and many health-food stores.

Grilled Marinated Beef

1½ pounds flank steak, trimmed

⅓ cup soy sauce, or more as
desired

2 tablespoons sake, or more as
desired

¼ cup sugar, or more as desired

1½ tablespoons grated fresh ginger,
or more as desired

2 tablespoons vegetable oil, or more
as desired

3 cloves garlic, peeled and crushed,
or more as desired

Teriyaki (literally, "shining broil") foods are glazed by the marinade brushed on during the last seconds of grilling. Steak teriyaki has become a backyard barbecue staple for Americans. The teriyaki taste is so popular that merchants have bottled the sauce, but it's simple to prepare at home. This is an Americanized version of a Japanese dish. The cook uses a minimal amount of soy sauce because she prefers less salty food, but you may increase the ingredient to suit your taste. (Recipe: Judy Watanabe, adapted)

1

Cut the steak into thin strips and place in a flat baking pan. Combine the remaining ingredients and pour over the meat. Cover with foil or plastic wrap and refrigerate for at least 4 hours.

2

Before grilling the meat, pour the marinade into a saucepan and cook it over medium heat until it reduces and becomes shiny. Grill the beef by the direct method (page xxix) over medium-hot coals, turning it once when the first side browns, for about 10 minutes or according to desired doneness. Brush the meat with the reduced marinade during cooking and immediately after removing it from the grill.

Grilled Shrimp

4 jumbo shrimp, shelled and
    deveined
Salt and lemon juice for seasoning

The chef advises using short metal skewers for grilling these large shrimp, which are threaded with the skewer inserted at the tail and then straight through to the head end. Plan to fit 2 shrimp on a skewer and offer 2 skewers per serving. This recipe serves 1. (Recipe: Chef Akira Watanabe, Tako Grill)

Thread the shrimp on the skewers and grill them by the direct method (page xxix) over medium-hot coals, turning to brown the shrimp evenly. These should cook quickly if your fire is hot enough, so watch them closely. Remove from the fire and sprinkle them with salt and lemon juice. Serve immediately.

Mochi

Strips of mochi squares, or
    individual mochi squares, as many
    as desired

Mochi is a rice product made from pounded cooked glutinous rice that is formed into cakes. The Japanese use it as a celebratory dish for New Years and usually grill pieces of mochi seasoned with mirin or soy sauce. (Recipe: Chef Hiroyuki Ohashi)

Grill *mochi* by the direct method (page xxix) over medium-hot coals for 3 to 4 minutes, turning often. Be careful not to burn the *mochi*. Remove from the fire and serve immediately.

Note:
Squares, round pieces, or sheets of *mochi* cakes wrapped airtight are sold at Japanese markets.

Teppanyaki

2 large shrimp, shelled and
  deveined
6 sea scallops
4 ounces squid
1 chicken cutlet, cut into thin strips
  and then cubed
7½ ounces sirloin or tenderloin
  steak, cubed and sprinkled with
  salt and pepper
Corn oil for grilling
2 cups vegetable mixture: for
  example, mushrooms, green and
  red bell peppers, Oriental
  eggplant (skin on), bean sprouts,
  and shredded carrots

Seasonings

Lemon juice, white wine, butter, soy
  sauce, rice wine vinegar, fresh
  lemon juice, salt, and pepper
Brandy for the steak

Dipping Sauces

For the seafood: rice wine vinegar
  and soy sauce, combined, to taste
For the chicken: sesame seeds and
  peanut sauce mixed in a blender,
  to taste
For the steak: soy sauce

Teppanyaki, or foods grilled on a griddle, are very popular in the United States. At the Unkai Restaurant in Washington, D.C., the teppanyaki *grill—which resembles the cast-iron grills Americans use—is mirror bright, polished during and after each use. Keeping the grill clean, the chef explains, keeps the food clean. Americans are used to a flamboyant show at a* teppanyaki *meal, but in Japan, the* teppanyaki *chef is a silent server who does not toss sharp knives into the air or entertain patrons with a stream of conversation. Instead, he concentrates on cooking, and presents his cooked treasures in a formal, even mannered way. He cooks one course at a time and does not jumble everything together at once on the grill. Presentation is also important—for example, when the chef prepares a steak, the meat is diced for cooking and stir-frying and reassembled when it is served. The chef trims the food as he goes along, but you may find that it is easier to have all the ingredients ready in advance. A* teppanyaki *meal usually consists of seafood, meat, chicken, and vegetables, delicately seasoned. But you can use anything you want, depending on what's freshest in the market. The meal below is presented in the order that the chef from Unkai prepares it, but you may rearrange this to suit your convenience. You can use a cast-iron griddle or a marble griddle top for cooking. This recipe serves 1 or 2 people. (Recipe: Chef Carlos Elespura, Unkai Restaurant)*

1

Cook each seafood, chicken, and steak portion separately, adding oil to the grill as necessary. As each portion cooks, use a spatula to turn and stir the ingredients. Allow about 3 minutes cooking time for each one. As the food cooks, sprinkle the grill with teaspoonfuls of the lemon juice, white wine, butter, soy sauce, and rice wine vinegar, and add the salt and pepper in dashes. Add a splash or two of brandy for the steak. Blend the seasoning mixture well on the grill and stir it into the food. Serve the portion as it is cooked.

2

Trim the mushrooms, peppers, and eggplant into finger-sized pieces. Combine all the vegetables on the grill and stir-fry them together with the seasonings for about 1 minute, sprinkling extra soy sauce over the top just before serving. The vegetables should be crisp-tender, not soggy or limp.

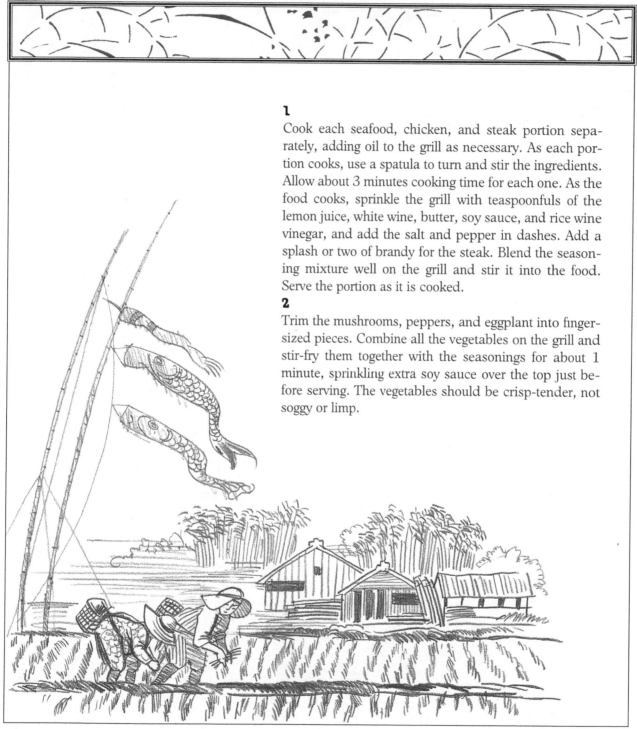

ACCOMPANIMENTS

Fish Seasoning Sauce

1 cup soy sauce
¾ cup mirin
2 tablespoons sake

For marinating/brushing on grilled fish. (Recipe: Chef Hiroyuki Ohashi)

Combine all the ingredients in a small saucepan and cook very slowly for about 45 minutes to reduce by about one half.

Poultry Seasoning Sauce

1 cup mirin
¾ cup soy sauce
2 tablespoons sake

For marinating/brushing on grilled chicken or other poultry. (Recipe: Chef Hiroyuki Ohashi)

Combine all the ingredients in a small saucepan and cook very slowly for about 45 minutes to reduce by about one half.

Teriyaki Sauce

1 cup soy sauce
¾ cup mirin
2 teaspoons grated fresh ginger

For marinating/brushing on grilled beef. (Recipe: Chef Hiroyuki Ohashi)

Combine all the ingredients in a small saucepan and cook very slowly for about 45 minutes to reduce by about one half.

Soba Noodle Sauce

Use this sauce for seasoning hot or cold soba noodles. (Recipe: Chef Hiroyuki Ohashi)

Combine the ingredients and put in a serving container.

1 cup soy sauce
¼ cup mirin
¼ cup fish stock (see Note,
    Soba Soup, below)

Soba Soup

You can vary this soup by using spinach leaves instead of the scallions or by adding strips of chicken or duck meat, or pieces of crispy tempura. (Recipe: Chef Hiro-yuki Ohashi)

Combine the soup stock ingredients in a large saucepan and bring to a gentle boil. Add the noodles and serve immediately, garnished with the eggs and scallions.

Note:

Fish stock, or *dashi,* is to the Japanese kitchen what salt and pepper are to the Western one, but it is even more important as an essential ingredient, since it is used as the basis for soups and for simmering. Traditional Japanese chefs and purists would make the fish stock from scratch with scraped hardened bonito and seaweed. But modern cooks can use an instant *dashi* that comes packaged in a liquid form, or can be bought in a powder or granule form known as *hon-dashi.* To use, dissolve 1 teaspoon *hon-dashi* in 1 quart hot water.

Soup Stock:
6 cups fish stock (see Note), 1 cup
    soy sauce, 1 cup mirin

One 8-ounce package soba noodles,
    cooked
Garnish
2 eggs, hard-boiled, quartered
4 scallions, thinly sliced

Cucumber Soup

2 quarts chicken stock
½ pound chicken breast meat,
    thinly sliced
Salt to taste
5 to 6 thin slices fresh ginger
3 scallions, trimmed and cut into
    1-inch lengths
1 cucumber, peeled and thinly sliced
Several drops of sesame oil
¼ cup sake

(Recipe: Peter and Diana Semon, Minka Japanese Country Inn)

1
Put the chicken stock in a large saucepan and bring to a simmer. Drop the chicken slices one by one into the stock to prevent their sticking together.

2
Add the salt, ginger, and scallions. Add the cucumber slices, sesame oil, and *sake* just before serving.

Grilled Whole Potato

1 large potato, peeled
Butter and salt for seasoning

Simplicity itself, this grilled whole potato is crusty and flavorful with a wonderful smokiness. The recipe serves 1. (Recipe: Chef Akira Watanabe, Tako Grill)

Boil the potato until it is fork tender. Cool slightly, then grill the potato by the direct method (page xxix) over medium-hot coals, turning it until the outside is brown and crispy. Slice the potato in half and grill the inside halves. Quarter the potato and once again grill the inside surfaces. The total cooking time should be 8 to 12 minutes. When all exposed parts of the potato are browned, remove from the fire and serve with butter and salt.

Grilled Rice Balls

1 cup cooked Japanese short-grain
  rice, still warm and sticky (see
  Introduction, page xxiv)
Soy sauce for seasoning
Ginger sauce for seasoning
  (see Note)
Garnish
Japanese pickles (see Note)
Chopped scallions

These crusty and flavorful rounded triangles of rice make an unusual accompaniment to other main-course dishes. This recipe serves 1. (Recipe: Chef Akira Watanabe, Tako Grill)

1

Divide the rice into 2 equal portions. Moisten your hands and compress each ball firmly into a rounded triangle. Fry the triangles very quickly in a lightly greased skillet—the light frying helps the rice balls hold their shape.

2

Grill the rice cakes about 5 to 8 minutes by the direct method (page xxix) over medium-hot coals, turning them often to brown and crisp evenly. Remove from the fire, sprinkle both sides with soy sauce, and grill again, about 1 minute per side. Remove from the fire, garnish with the pickles and scallions, and serve immediately.

Note:

To make the ginger sauce, combine 1 cup soy sauce, 1 cup rice wine, and 1 to 2 tablespoons grated fresh ginger, or to taste. Boil the mixture and add a 1-inch-square piece of *kombu* seaweed.

Japanese pickles are sold at Japanese markets.

Pork and String Beans

2 pounds lean pork loin
1 pound string beans, trimmed
    and cut diagonally
Seasoning Sauce
Salt to taste
4 tablespoons soy sauce
1 tablespoon vinegar
2 tablespoons sesame oil
2 tablespoons sake
Garnish
2 scallions, finely chopped
One 3-inch piece fresh ginger,
    thinly sliced
Sprinkle of sansho (see Note)

Serve this meat-and-vegetable dish with other entrée courses, such as grilled fish or grilled chicken. (Recipe: Peter and Diana Semon, Minka Japanese Country Inn)

1
Combine the ingredients for the seasoning sauce and set aside.

2
Put the pork roast in a stockpot with just enough water to cover. Boil the pork until tender, about 1 hour. Remove the pork from the broth and put it into a pot of cold water to stop the cooking.

3
Meanwhile, blanch the beans and dunk them in cold water to stop the cooking. Place the beans in a serving bowl and sprinkle with the seasoning sauce.

4
Thinly slice the pork and place the meat strips in the bowl with the beans, stirring to mix well. Refrigerate until chilled.

5
To serve, transfer to individual serving bowls and garnish with the scallions, ginger, and *sansho*.

Note:
Sansho is Japanese pepper and is sold at Japanese markets.

Egg Custard

6 large shrimp, peeled and
    deveined
Sake *for soaking the shrimp*
¼ cup diced chicken breast meat
Soy sauce *for soaking the chicken*
2 teaspoons soy sauce
1 teaspoon mirin
1 teaspoon salt
1 quart dashi *(see Note, Soba Soup,*
    page 297)
3 to 4 large eggs, lightly beaten
18 ginkgo nuts *(see Note)*
Scallions, thinly sliced, and
    watercress sprigs, flattened, for
    green color on top of custard

Chawan mushi is the classic Japanese egg custard dish that everyone considers a year-round favorite— although a Japanese chef might alter some of its ingredients to suit the season. It is always eaten very hot and can be served as a very light first course. (Recipe: Peter and Diana Semon, Minka Japanese Country Inn)

1

Soak the shrimp in *sake* for 15 minutes. Soak the diced chicken in soy sauce for about 15 minutes.

2

Meanwhile, combine the soy sauce, *mirin,* and salt with the *dashi* in a large stockpot. Gently stir in the eggs. Strain this mixture through a cheesecloth or strainer.

3

Divide the shrimp, chicken, and ginkgo nuts equally among 4 to 6 individual custard cups and pour the egg *dashi* over the top. Cover each cup with foil or plastic wrap or its own lid. Place the cups on the rack of a large steamer pot, fill the bottom section with water, and cover the steamer with the lid. Steam the custards for 20 to 25 minutes over moderate heat.

4

Remove from the heat and serve in individual cups, garnished with the scallions and watercress.

Note:

Ginkgo nuts are the slightly bitter nuts from the maidenhair tree. These nuts are favorites with the Chinese, and also with the Japanese and Koreans, who eat them as snacks, or grill them, or mix them with other ingredients in more complicated dishes. The nuts are sold in cans at Japanese groceries.

Cold Soba Noodles

8 ounces soba noodles, cooked and
  chilled in a bowl with ice water
  and ice cubes

Seasoning Sauce

One 1½-inch x 3-inch sheet of kombu
  (see Note)

1¼ cups water

⅓ cup mirin

½ cup katsuobushi (see Note)

⅓ cup soy sauce

2 tablespoons sake

These noodles can be an accompaniment or served as a meal by themselves. (Recipe: Peter and Diana Semon, Minka Japanese Country Inn)

1

Soak the *kombu* in the water for 10 minutes.

2

Pour the *mirin* into a saucepan and bring to a boil. Add the *kombu* with its soaking water and bring the mixture back to a boil.

3

Remove the *kombu* with a slotted spoon and discard it. Add the *katsuobushi* to the *mirin*. Add the soy sauce, and continue to simmer 10 to 20 minutes longer. Add the *sake,* and remove from the fire. To serve, place the noodles in a bowl with ice cubes and pass the sauce separately. Using chopsticks, each person puts his portion of noodles into an individual bowl. Each mouthful is then dunked in the dipping sauce before eating. (A simpler version calls for combining 1 cup water, ⅓ cup soy sauce, ⅓ cup *mirin,* and ⅔ teaspoon *hon dashi,* [an instant granular form of *dashi* that dissolves in liquid] and heating, then cooling the mixture.)

Note:

Kombu, a type of seaweed, is sold as sheets or shreds. *Katsuobushi* is dried bonito (from the mackerel family) that comes in flakes or in a chunk that can be shaved into the flakes that are used for making the fish stock *dashi.* Both chunks and flakes are available at Japanese markets.

DESSERT

Lima Bean Pastries (Shiro-an Kurimanju)

Poppy seeds for sprinkling
Filling
1 pound dried lima beans
1½ cups water
2½ cups sugar
1 teaspoon salt
Wrappers
1 stick butter or margarine
2 cups sugar
4 large eggs, separated
One 5-ounce can evaporated
   milk, plus extra
6 cups all-purpose flour
1 teaspoon baking powder
1 teaspoon baking soda
⅛ teaspoon salt

These little pastries make an unusual finale to a Japanese meal. They would also be good served with an afternoon tea. The lima-bean filling should have an easy-to-mold consistency. The size ball you shape will determine the overall size of the dumpling. The cook says, "Practice makes perfect." This recipe makes about 24 balls. The dough is easier to work with if it has been chilled. (Recipe: Anonymous)

1
Soak the beans overnight in water to cover. Rinse them and remove the skins and the germ sprouts—if the latter are not removed, they will turn the filling dark and bitter-tasting. Put the beans in a saucepan and add water to cover, plus 1 inch. Cook the beans until soft, between 30 and 60 minutes.

2
Strain the beans into a cotton bag, such as a pillow case, and hold the open end of the bag under the faucet. Fill the bag with water then squeeze out the water. Repeat this process several times—this "bleaches" the beans.

3
Put the crushed beans into a saucepan and add the 1½ cups water, the sugar, and salt. Bring the mixture to a boil, lower the heat, and simmer for 1 to 2 hours, or until the mixture is shiny and has turned pale ivory in color. Watch this carefully because it could scorch. The consistency should be firm—you should be able to mold the filling into an almond- or walnut-sized ball. Set aside.

4
Preheat the oven to 375°.

5
To make the wrappers, cream the butter and sugar together in a mixing bowl. Add the egg yolks and the milk.

Stir in the flour, baking powder, baking soda, and salt. In a separate bowl, beat the egg whites until stiff and stir them slowly into the batter.

6

Take a tablespoon of dough and flatten it with the palm of your hand. Take a tablespoon of filling and wrap it with the dough. Brush the top of the ball with milk and sprinkle it with the poppy seeds. Place the balls on an ungreased cookie sheet and bake in the preheated oven for 20 minutes. Do not overbake or the *manju* will crack.

Glossary

THE INGREDIENTS IN MANY ASIAN DISHES ARE AS FOREIGN AND EX-
otic to most Westerners as are the countries that grow and use them. Some ingredients,
like pandan (a long, thin, green leaf that imparts a mysterious, earthy flavor to many
Malaysian and Singaporean dishes), are easy to find in a freezer case or bottled as an
extract. Others become a challenge to track down, and this search will quickly familiarize
you with the marvels of Asian markets—if you are lucky enough to have one or several
nearby.

Note the plural: Years ago when Chinese food was so popular, all the shopping any
home cook needed was a quick trip to a Chinatown grocery for ingredients. But today is a
different story. The shrimp pastes and chili sauces used in Chinese cooking can't be
readily substituted for the Malaysian versions, for example. Nor may small Chinese groceries stock some of the more esoteric foodstuffs—Malaysian palm sugar, fresh sugarcane,
and sticky, or glutinous, rice, for example—that a Thai or Lao cook would use. Unless
your local Oriental grocer stocks most of Asia under one roof, you may need an Indian
spice shop, a Vietnamese greengrocer, a Japanese grocer, and a Thai or Cambodian deli/
shop/market to complete your shopping list. On the other hand, most basics—such as
lemongrass, several chili varieties, galangal, and coconut milk—are so universal that most
Asian markets stock them. And many Western supermarkets, catering to the growing
numbers of Asian immigrants, now offer such standards as canned coconut milk and
tamarind juice. Browse and experiment with what you find. Your search for Asian grill
ingredients, and for the other items you need, will lure you into a new and exciting world
of food and eating.

Agar-Agar: Also known as agar, this is a seaweed product that works like gelatin by firming
liquids into solids. It is sold as dried wands or dried sticks that look like long, crinkly pods, or as
powder in packets. All forms are readily available; the powdered is easiest to use and can be
softened in small amounts of cold or hot water. As a rule of thumb, about 1 ounce of agar-agar, or

the contents of the small packet (0.9 ounces) of powdered agar-agar, should thicken about 6 to 8 cups of liquid. Stored tightly wrapped, agar-agar lasts indefinitely.

Ajwain (Carom Ajowan): A popular and commonly used Indian spice, *ajwain* has no English translation or Western equivalent, but the seed belongs to the same family as cumin, resembles lovage, and tastes a little like a composite of licorice, thyme, and oregano. It is often used medicinally to settle upset stomachs, but its real value comes in the cookpot where it imparts a subtle but distinct flavor to curries, seafood, and *tandoori* dishes. Look for this at Indian spice stores or Indian markets.

Amchor: Also known as *amchoor* or *amchur,* this product comes from grinding dried unripe mangoes to a fine powder. *Amchor* adds an astringent sourness to many Indian dishes. Because it loses its punch quickly, buy *amchor* in small amounts and store it in the freezer.

Bamboo: Many Asians use the hollowed stems of mature bamboo as a cooking utensil—that is, cooks stuff the bamboo with ingredients, seal the open end, and then steam or grill the bamboo with its food. Bamboo is readily available as shoots, and many Asian grocers may think that is what you are looking for. One of the recipes testers found only one Asian market out of the dozens she visited that sold any mature bamboo, and that was not exactly what she needed. It worked in a pinch, but unless you grow your own bamboo or can find it at the right season, you may have to make do with what your grocer supplies. You need a tube that has been cut just below two external nodes—each node is separated (or sealed) with an internal "wall"—so that you have a closed end and an open end of the tube. BANANA LEAVES make an almost acceptable substitute for wrapping, but the effect is not the same.

Bamboo Shoots: There are dozens of bamboo varieties but only a few produce edible sprouts. These tender shoots come from the bamboo plant and are favorite additions to many dishes in most Asian countries. Canned or freshly cooked bamboo shoots are readily available at most Asian groceries and are simple to use. They will keep for about a week if refrigerated in a container of fresh water.

Bamboo Skewers: Used widely throughout Asia for skewering meats and vegetables for *satays* and other grilled dishes, these are slim sticks made from bamboo that come in different lengths and thicknesses. Most supermarkets and all Asian grocers carry these skewers. To prevent burning, bamboo skewers must be soaked from fifteen to thirty minutes before use.

GLOSSARY

Banana Leaves: Instead of foil, many Asians wrap their foods prior to cooking in the large, pliable, and aromatic leaves of the banana plant. To the inexperienced, wrapping food up in a banana leaf or leaves can be tricky, especially since many types of packets require complex folds. To complicate matters, the banana leaves available in this country are usually frozen, and even after thawing and warming, they may be brittle and tear or shred easily. As a precaution against running out of usable leaf, recipes in this book call for "leaves," although under ideal circumstances for most recipes using one fresh leaf would be ample. To ready the leaf for use, cut away the spine and trim the leaf with scissors into usable sections. Wipe off any white spots on the leaf and rinse it in warm water; to soften it, hold the leaf for a few seconds over a lit gas burner or brush it across the top of heated electric burner coils. Or you can dip it quickly into a pot of very hot water. You may use several layers of leaves, if you wish. One of the chefs suggested brushing the outside of the leaf with oil, to prevent its sticking to the grill rack, but others recommend instead brushing the inside of the packet so that the food does not stick to the banana leaf; still others say not to use any oil at all because that would make the food too greasy. This seems to be a matter of personal preference with no hard-and-fast rules to follow. To make folding simple, you can use the easiest method: Lay the piece of banana leaf out flat and place the food in the center of the leaf. Fold one side of the leaf to the center and fold the other side over the first fold. Use toothpicks or short bamboo skewers to "stitch" the ends shut. You can use aluminum foil instead of banana leaves, but you will lose the subtle flavor and delicate green color the leaves impart as they cook. If the leaves seem particularly brittle, you can overwrap the packet with foil to prevent leaking. Frozen banana leaves packed in sealed plastic bags keep indefinitely in the freezer.

Basil, Thai: Also known as sweet basil (or *bai horapa* in Thailand), this variety has a more distinctive and minty taste and aroma than the more familiar, garden-variety basil of the West. Actually the Thais, Lao, Cambodians, and Vietnamese—and less commonly, Indonesians—use several varieties of basil in cooking, including the purplish "holy" basil and another variety sold as "Oriental" basil. Asian basils are often available fresh at Asian markets but, if not, you can substitute fresh Western basil, although the flavor will not be the same.

Bay Leaves, Indonesian or Oriental: The Indonesian bay, or *salam,* leaf is an aromatic leaf that grows on a tree native to Indonesia. Dried *salam* leaves are available at some Asian markets, particularly those that specialize in Southeast Asian foods. If you cannot find it, substitute the Western bay leaf.

Black Beans: These are soybeans that have been cooked, salted, and fermented until they turn

307

black. These are readily available packed in cans at most Asian markets. The beans should be rinsed before use.

Black Cumin: Sweeter than regular cumin, these black seeds are popular in Indian, Indonesian, and Malaysian dishes. The seeds are readily available at any Indian market.

Candlenuts: Even to this day in remote parts of Indonesia, the creamy-white flesh of these nuts is used as a component for making candles—the source of the name. But in all Indonesian kitchens these are intrinsic to many dishes. They are also used in some Malaysian dishes. When ground to a paste, the candlenut helps thicken and enrich sauces, *sambals,* and curries. Macadamia nuts make a fine substitute and are readily available—except, according to one Indonesian, you should use three or four more macadamia nuts than the amount of candlenuts required.

Cardamom: Green and black cardamom seeds are very popular seasonings in the Indian kitchen. Whole green cardamom pods, the seeds, and powdered cardamom are widely available at Indian markets and supermarkets. Look for the black cardamom at Indian markets.

Chapati: see Flours.

Chili Pastes and Sauces: Universal Asian seasonings, chili pastes and sauces are made from ground chilies and other ingredients that vary according to the country and the cuisine. Because each country has its own version—for example, one common Indonesian paste is called *sambal ulek*—your best bet for the most authentic flavor is to select a chili paste or sauce that comes from the same country as your recipe. Pastes and sauces keep almost indefinitely if stored in the refrigerator in a container with a tight-fitting lid.

Curry Pastes, Thai: You can buy small cans of Thai curry pastes in several different varieties in many Asian markets. Recipes in this book call for Masaman curry paste and "red" curry paste.

Dal: This is the general Indian name for all dried legumes that are cooked up to make the ubiquitous protein/vegetable accompaniment for Indian meals. These dishes may be thick or soupy, mild or spiced. A common legume is the *urad dal,* or black gram or horse gram in English. This protein-rich gray-black bean is available whole or split and is very commonly used in both Northern and Southern Indian dishes. It is readily available at any Indian market and less com-

monly at Middle Eastern and Asian markets. The beans last almost indefinitely when stored in a tightly sealed glass or plastic container. Other commonly used *dals* include red or green lentils, mung beans, and yellow split peas.

Fish Paste: As with many commonly used Asian seasonings, fish paste has many different local versions. This salty ingredient is usually made of the thick residue from the manufacture of fish sauce combined with thickening agents. Fish paste is readily available in Asian markets and lasts almost indefinitely if stored in the refrigerator in an airtight container.

Fish Sauce: Almost as universal as soy sauce, this fermented fish product varies slightly from country to country. Made by layering fish (often anchovies) and salt into large jars or barrels, the sauce that is siphoned off after several months can range from pale brown to almost black. An Asian market may provide a bewildering array of fish sauces—sometimes the sauces are interchangeable in a recipe, but for a Thai dish, buy the Thai *nam pla* and for a Vietnamese dish, buy the Vietnamese *nuoc mam.* When asked which sauce Cambodians used, my local Cambodian grocer said that his family makes its own at home. Fish sauce lasts almost indefinitely if stored in the refrigerator in an airtight bottle or container.

Five-Spice Powder: An aromatic Chinese seasoning, this powder is a blend of star anise, cassia bark (or cinnamon), Szechuan peppercorns, cloves, and fennel seeds. It is readily available both in Asian markets and in most supermarkets.

Flours:
   Rice flour—This is used throughout Southeast Asia for making pastries and sweets and as a thickener. Plastic packets of rice flour are readily available at most Asian markets. Do not use this flour as a substitute for glutinous (sticky) rice flour because the two are not at all alike and produce very different results.
   Glutinous rice flour—Made from ground glutinous rice, this flour produces a gooey, almost gelatinous product when cooked. This is sold at most Asian markets.
   Tapioca flour—Tapioca flour, or tapioca starch, is used as a thickener with other rice flours and with liquid. This is sold at most Asian markets.
   Gram flour—Also known as *besan* flour, this is made from pulverized dried chick-peas and is a common ingredient in the Indian kitchen. This is sold at Indian and Middle Eastern markets.
   Chapati flour—This is a finely milled whole-wheat flour from India, finer than Western flours,

that produces a smooth bread dough. You can buy *chapati* flour at many Indian markets, or you can make a reasonable substitute for this fine flour by mixing together equal quantities of whole-wheat and white flours.

Fried Shallots: These are popular garnishings for many Southeast Asian dishes. They are available already fried and packaged in small plastic containers at many Asian markets. But they are also very easy to prepare at home, and surely taste better freshly made. Chef Mok Tai Heng from the Palm Beach Hotel in Penang, Malaysia, suggests cooking the shallots this way: Take ½ cup peeled shallot slices and wash and drain them. Heat some oil in a skillet and deep-fry the slices until golden brown. Scoop out and drain on paper towels. The shallots will be crispy and fragrant.

Galangal: Also spelled *galanga* or *galangale,* this fragrant rhizome looks something like ginger and is from the ginger family, but it has a totally different, almost citruslike taste. It is a primary seasoning ingredient in many Southeast Asian dishes and it imparts a wonderful aroma to foods as they cook. Fortunately, it is readily available frozen and occasionally fresh in Asian markets. If it is not available in either of these forms, you may find it as a powder labeled *"laos* powder" or as the dried and sliced rhizome, wrapped in cellophane packets. Some authorities say to use double the amount of ginger as a substitute, but that really does not provide the same taste at all.

Garlic Paste: This is an easy form in which to use garlic and is a critical ingredient in many Indian sauces and marinades. According to Delhi food authority J. Inder Singh Kalra, garlic paste can be made by pureeing 1 cup peeled and chopped garlic with 3 tablespoons water. This paste can be stored in a tightly sealed container in the refrigerator for up to three days. Commercially prepared garlic paste is also readily available at most supermarkets. Follow the manufacturer's directions for use and storage.

Ghee: This clarified butter is essential to proper Indian cooking and is used for frying or for seasoning. You can make *ghee* at home by slowly heating sweet butter without letting it brown and draining off the yellow top layer. Do not include any of the under layer of milk solids. Ghee is also sold at every Indian market. It may be stored at room temperature for several weeks and in the refrigerator for several months.

Ginger Paste: This is an easy form in which to use ginger and, like garlic paste, is a critical ingredient in many Indian sauces and marinades. According to Delhi food authority J. Inder Singh

GLOSSARY

Kalra, ginger paste can be made by pureeing 1 cup peeled and chopped ginger with 3 tablespoons water. This paste can be stored in a tightly sealed container in the refrigerator for up to three days.

Gram Flour: See FLOURS.

Hoisin Sauce: Made from fermented soybean paste, this reddish-brown sauce is used as a condiment and for basting grilled meats. It is sold at Asian markets and many supermarkets and keeps indefinitely in its jar in the refrigerator.

Indonesian Sweet Soy Sauce: See Introduction, "On Other Common Ingredients," page xxvii.

Jellyfish: To the uninitiated, shredded jellyfish may look and feel more like strips of rubber than food. But jellyfish has its place in many Asian pantries. Sold whole, or as dried, salted, or damp-packed shreds, jellyfish needs brief soaking in very hot or boiling water to "cook" it. According to my Cambodian grocer, jellyfish also needs soaking to get rid of its "fishy" aroma.

Lemongrass: An almost ubiquitous seasoning in many Southeast Asian dishes, this ingredient has a wonderful and assertive lemon flavor that seems to both intensify and complement other flavors—in fact, lemongrass seems almost crucial as a seasoning and many dishes would fall flat without it. The grass actually comes as clumps of tall stalks that look like leeks but are tough and need a sharp knife for cutting. How you use lemongrass depends on the recipe: Sometimes chunks of it are put into a dish and removed before serving; other times, it is crushed to release its aroma and flavor or ground with other ingredients and left in the dish to be eaten. Before using it, you must peel off the outer leaves and trim the ends. One stalk yields about 2 to 3 tablespoons of sliced or crushed lemongrass, depending on the thickness and freshness of the stalk. You can find dried lemongrass either shredded or powdered, but its flavor does not resemble that of the fresh. Fortunately, fresh and frozen lemongrass are almost always available at Asian markets. Lemongrass freezes well without losing its flavor and fresh lemongrass stores in the refrigerator for up to one week.

Limes: Asian limes include the kaffir and kalamansi limes and some Indonesian recipes call for a variety known in Indonesia as the *limo* lime, which may be a garbled translation of the Malaysian word, *limau* for *limo*, or lime. Nobody seems to know for sure. The juice of the knobby-skinned kaffir lime is sometimes used in cooking, but the glossy leaves of this lime are a particular favorite

in many Asian dishes and provide a subtle but distinct citrus flavor. The leaves are sometimes available fresh, but more often they are frozen or dried. If they are not available at all, substitute a curry leaf. Tiny kalamansi limes are indigenous to the Philippines and are actually lemons that have a tart limey flavor. In season, these are often available fresh in Asian markets and the juice is available in cans. If *limo* limes are a distinct variety, they are not sold in the United States as such, and you can substitute the standard Western lime.

Mirin: This sweetened Japanese rice wine is intended for cooking, not for drinking. Japanese chefs use *mirin* as a glaze for grilled foods and in basting sauces. Although it is readily available in many supermarkets, you can substitute sweet sherry or dry sherry mixed with some granulated sugar for sweetening.

Mung Beans: Vegetarians may well be acquainted with mung beans, but the general American public probably is not. These are small green beans that are popular protein sources from India all the way to Korea. Sold as sprouts in health-food stores, they are also available dried either whole with skins, or split and skinned. Before use, mung beans need soaking to soften them.

Noodles: Besides rice, noodles—in several different varieties—are another popular starch staple in many Asian countries.
   Soba: Japanese soba noodles are buckwheat noodles sold dried at many Asian markets, health-food stores, and all Japanese markets.
   Vermicelli: A typical Italian egg pasta sold at all supermarkets. Indian vermicellis are made from either wheat or rice flour and are sold at Indian markets.
   Rice vermicelli: Made from rice paste and water, these white, dried noodles look translucent. They can be easily rehydrated, or softened, by soaking in hot water for a few minutes, then rinsing them, before further boiling. These are sold dried in bundles and packages and are available at most Asian markets.
   Bean thread: Known as "cellophane," "glass," or "transparent" (in Japanese, *harusame*) noodles, these thin, clear strands are made from mung-bean flour and water. The noodles are popular for soups, salads, and curries, and Malaysians and Singaporeans even use them in drinks and desserts. The noodles are very brittle and hard and may fly around the kitchen when you cut them with scissors. To soften them, soak the thinner noodles in hot water for fifteen minutes; the thicker noodles may need up to thirty minutes of soaking. The softened noodles will be translucent and gelatinous. Drain them briefly before use, unless you are putting them into a soup or other liquid. These are readily available at most Asian markets.

Chinese egg noodles: Sold fresh or dried at most Asian markets; you can substitute a Western spaghetti-type noodle if you wish.

Rice stick: Rice sticks and rice vermicelli are virtually the same except that the rice-stick noodle is flatter. These are sold dried in bundles and packages and are available at most Asian markets.

Rice noodles: Fresh rice noodles are readily available at most Asian markets and are a delicious pasta with a wonderful slippery, chewy texture. You can store these in the refrigerator until needed.

Nuoc Mam: See FISH SAUCE.

Oyster Sauce: This dark salty-sweet sauce will be familiar to anyone who has cooked Chinese food. Used for its pungent flavor and dark color, oyster sauce is made from dried oysters. It is available in bottles in Asian markets and most well-stocked supermarkets and should be refrigerated after opening.

Palm Sugar: This sweet substance from the juice of either the palmyra or the sugar palm has different names and different forms depending on its country of origin. For example, in Malaysia, it is known as *gula melaka* and comes in a solid dark-brown brick or cone that must be scraped, cut, or chopped apart before use. The Thai and Vietnamese versions look like a sticky, thick goo and may be caramel-colored or off-white. The Malaysian product is not readily available but the other forms of palm sugar are. If not available, substitute dark brown sugar. The Thai and Vietnamese versions last well if kept tightly sealed.

Pandan: Also known as pandanus leaf or screw pine, the long thin leaves of this plant provide an unusual fragrance and flavor for many Indonesian, Thai, Malaysian, and Singaporean dishes. The juice extracted from the leaves is often used for green coloring. Pandan leaves are sometimes available fresh but most often are sold frozen in Asian markets. The extract—and an artificial chemical product—is also available but its flavor is very intense and the product must be used sparingly. The artificial extract, I was told, does not have a pleasing taste. If you cannot find pandan in any form, use vanilla flavoring instead in desserts. Otherwise, simply omit it because there is no other substitute.

Paneer: Also known as *panir,* this fresh-cheese product is an Indian staple and a major source of protein in the Indian diet. Most housewives make *paneer* and yogurt daily. It resembles a cross between the Western cottage cheese and ricotta, but is more versatile because *paneer* can be used

in its soft form or drained of excess liquid to become a firmer cheese that can be shaped into balls or blocks. Once you get the knack of it, *paneer* is extremely easy to make if it is not overheated during cooking and if the milk you use is very fresh (see recipe, page 36). Cottage cheese and ricotta are not substitutes. *Paneer* is sometimes available at Indian markets. In her wonderful volume on Indian cooking, *Lord Krishna's Cuisine, The Art of Indian Vegetarian Cooking,* Yamuna Devi explores the world of *paneer* and the best ways to make it.

Red Chili Powder: This powder is made from finely ground red chilies, and it was, I am told, the original red coloring for *tandoori* dishes. Unlike other chili powders, the Indian red chili powder is mild and subtle. The red Kashmiri chili powder should be used only in curries, I'm told. Both are available at all Indian groceries.

Rice Flour: See FLOURS.

Rice Papers or Rice Paper Wrappers: These are the rice flour-and-water wrappers that Vietnamese and other Asians use for wrapping so many of their foods. These papers come as brittle, almost-translucent discs or triangles with a cross-hatch, or "waffle," design on one side that results from the surface of the material on which these wrappers are dried. They must be soaked briefly in warm water to soften them for use. The wrappers are available at most Asian markets and keep indefinitely in a cupboard.

Rice Vinegar: Many Asian vinegars are made from fermented rice, and of these, the mild Japanese rice vinegar is probably the most familiar. It is available at most well-stocked supermarkets.

Rice Wine: The most well-known Asian rice wine is the sweetish and potent Japanese *sake,* which is used both for drinking and for cooking.

Rose Essence, Rose Water: Rose essence is a concentrated distillation of fragrant rose petals that perfumes dishes with a delicate rose flavor. Rose essence is also known as rose-water concentrate. Rose water, sometimes mistakenly called rose essence, is a diluted, and therefore, weaker form of the essence. Both are sold at Middle Eastern and Indian markets.

Sago: These tapiocalike pellets come from the starch of the sago palm and, when rehydrated, make a popular addition to many Asian desserts or become the desserts themselves. The pearls are available both large and small; although no recipe book tells you so, you should use the smaller

GLOSSARY

size—apparently these are more refined—and you must soak the pearls for at least fifteen minutes —better half an hour—before trying to cook with them. If you use large, unsoaked pearls you will be stirring and boiling them for hours before they soften and become totally translucent. Flavorless on their own, the pearls must be sweetened or otherwise flavored to be palatable. These are readily available in cellophane packets at most Asian markets. The pearls last indefinitely stored on a cool, dry shelf.

Sake: See RICE WINE.

Sambals: *Sambals* are the Indonesian chili relishes that are used liberally as a condiment or a cooking ingredient to increase the heat of many Indonesian and Malaysian dishes. Basic *sambal* ingredients are usually chilies, dried fish, shrimp paste, and a sour agent such as vinegar or tamarind, but there are numerous *sambal* variations, and flavors can be sweet, hot, or mild. Although they are easy to make at home and are delicious fresh, some *sambal* preparations are sold at Asian markets.

Sesame Paste: The Asian sesame paste is made from toasted sesame seeds and has a nutty taste. The Middle Eastern sesame paste *tahini,* or a quality peanut butter may be used as substitutes. Sesame paste lasts indefinitely when stored in the refrigerator.

Shrimp Crackers: Shrimp crackers, shrimp chips, or *krupuk udang,* are Indonesian specialties usually made from shrimp and tapioca starch. They come as flattened discs but when they are deep-fried, they puff up magically. They are then used as garnishes and as snacks. These are available at Asian markets and some specialty food stores.

Shrimp Dried: These tiny, dried shrimp could startle Westerners who may find their salty, fishy taste a bit overwhelming. Used whole, chopped, or pulverized, the dried shrimp are a common seasoning in many Southeast Asian recipes. If you find the flavor too strong, you may reduce the quantity in future use or omit them altogether, although the resultant taste will lack a certain something. These shrimp are readily available in Asian markets and usually come wrapped in plastic bags. Select shrimp that are pink; gray or white shrimp are old and may be getting too old to use. Dried shrimp last for several months at room temperature if kept tightly wrapped.

Shrimp Paste: This pungent product of dried, salted shrimp or shrimp heads crushed together with other ingredients has an unmistakable aroma that can be very unsettling to Westerners,

315

especially in inexpensive brands. It is an acquired aroma and taste for many Westerners, but it is an absolutely vital ingredient in Malaysian, Singaporean, and Indonesian cooking and is also used in many Thai and Vietnamese dishes. Compressed into easy-to-slice cubes or scooped as a softer product into plastic or other containers, shrimp paste comes in a range of colors, from the cocoa-colored shrimp paste from Malaysia (where it is known as *belacan, blachan,* or *blacam*) to the pale gray-pink paste from China. For best results, fry or roast the paste before using. Shrimp paste seems to keep indefinitely at room temperature when stored tightly sealed or wrapped.

Soybean Paste: An assertive seasoning used in Cantonese cooking, this thick, dark paste is made from salted and fermented soybeans. You can find it at most Chinese and some Asian markets.

Suckling Pigs: Roasted suckling, or baby, pigs are often the focal point of celebratory meals in several Asian countries. The pigs are usually quite small, from 10 to 20 pounds. If you live in an urban area, you may have trouble locating these pigs. They may be sold only at specialty butchers, and even then you may not find one as small as 15 pounds. Suckling pigs are also very expensive, because, as one butcher explained, they are so small that they must be dressed by hand, not by machine. Another caution: Even if you can locate pigs at the 10- to 12-pound weight that several recipes call for, they may be too long for standard ovens or covered barbecues. A fresh ham leg or shank portion, bone-in or deboned, can be substituted in some cases with similar results, but will not present with the same grandeur or flair as the suckling pig. If you can locate a suckling pig and have access to a large or commercial-sized barbecue or oven, you will find these suckling pig recipes wonderful.

Sugarcane: The use of sugarcane in cooking is not a common practice, but it is certainly an enjoyable one. You may find long stalks of the fresh cane in Asian and Latin markets, but sugarcane is also sold water-packed in at least two different sized cans. For the Shrimp on Sugarcane recipe (page 234), if you use the canned cane, select the large size and cut the long stalks into quarters. If you use the fresh cane, peel off the tough outer skin with a sharp paring knife and trim the cane into 4- or 5-inch lengths. The best part of using the cane—canned or fresh—is sucking on and chewing it after enjoying the meal. One of the Lao recipes calls for using sugarcane leaves —I have never seen these sold either fresh or frozen, but if you have access to sugarcane in the field, you will be able to acquire this ingredient.

Sweet Bean Paste: For Japanese and Korean cooks, this means the product made from the mashed and sweetened adzuki bean. The Chinese sweet bean paste is made from mashed and

sweetened soybeans. Both are available at many Asian markets or at Korean, Japanese, and Chinese markets.

Sweet Red Beans: These are whole adzuki *(azuki)* beans popular in Chinese, Japanese, and Korean desserts and sweets. Look for them at Asian markets.

Tamarind: The large brown pods of the tamarind tree contain seeds and a sour pulp prized in many Asian kitchens for its tartness. Sometimes it is available fresh, but pulp is more readily available in a compressed block form—seeds, pith, and all—or in pastes. The pastes are very convenient to use and you can make tamarind water by dissolving the pulp in water. If you cannot find tamarind in any form, substitute twice the amount of lemon juice as the tamarind juice called for in a recipe. Tamarind paste keeps well when stored in the refrigerator in a tightly sealed container. Tamarind leaves are often used for seasoning and are also available in the freezer case at many Asian markets.

Tangerine Peel, Dried: Dried whole tangerine peel is a popular seasoning in many Chinese and some other Asian dishes. According to Chef Joyce Piotrowski, you can make your own by using tangerine peels soaked in water, put on a sunny windowsill, and left there until bubbly, then rinsed off and dried on a sheet pan in a 150° oven until they turn black and leathery. You can also use a dehydrater. Stored in a jar, this product lasts indefinitely. You can also buy this at Chinese and most Asian markets.

Tapioca Flour: See FLOURS.

Turmeric: Fresh turmeric, a member of the ginger family, is a rhizome with bright orange meat and a somewhat astringent flavor. Turmeric is an essential in curries and currylike dishes, imparting its distinctive golden color and bright acidic taste. Whole turmeric is not readily available fresh but is often sold frozen; you can use ground turmeric as a satisfactory substitute. Most recipes in this book specify ground turmeric; in those that specify fresh, use half the amount called for of the ground dried turmeric.

Yam Bean: This sweet tuber is served both raw and cooked in Malaysian and Indonesian dishes. Some sources call it a turnip; others say it is like jicama. The only grocer who recognized this name handed me a dark, round, slightly hairy root shaped like a beet. If you cannot find yam bean, use jicama instead.

Bibliography

Anderson, E. N. *The Food of China.* New Haven and London: Yale University Press, 1988.

Armawa, Sarita, ed. *Paon Bali: A Guide to the Balinese Kitchen.* Bali, Indonesia: Bali Hyatt Hotel, n.d.

Bhatia, Savitri. *Shahi Tukre.* Allahabad, India: A. H. Wheeler & Co., Pvt. Limited, 1975.

Brennan, G., and C. Glenn. *Peppers Hot & Chile: A Cook's Guide to Chile Peppers from California, the Southwest, Mexico, and Beyond.* Berkeley: Aris Books, 1988.

Brennan, Jennifer. *The Cuisines of Asia.* New York: St. Martin's Press, 1984.

Brent, Carol D., ed. *Barbecue: The Fine Art of Charcoal, Gas and Hibachi Cooking.* Chicago: Tested Recipe Publishers, Inc., 1971.

Brissenden, Rosemary. *South East Asian Food (Indonesia, Malaysia, and Thailand).* Middlesex, England: Penguin Books, 1969.

Burum, Linda. *Asian Pasta: A Cook's Guide to the Noodles, Wrappers and Pasta Creations of the East.* Berkeley: Aris Books, 1985.

Callahan, Ed. *Charcoal Cookbook.* San Francisco: Pacific Productions, 1970.

Center for Applied Linguistics. *The Peoples and Cultures of Cambodia, Laos, and Vietnam.* Washington, D.C., 1981.

Chow, Dolly. *Chow!* Shanghai: Kin Ma Publishing Co., 1963.

Coedes, G. *The Making of South East Asia.* Translated by H. H. Wright. Berkeley: University of California Press, 1966.

Cohen, Barbara. *The Vietnam Guidebook.* 2d ed. Boston: Houghton Mifflin Co., 1991.

Conway, Linda Glick, ed. *The New Professional Chef.* The Culinary Institute of America. New York: Van Nostrand Reinhold, 1991.

Davidson, Alan. *Fish and Fish Dishes of Laos.* Vientiane, Laos: Imprimerie Nationale Vientiane, 1975.

de Berval, Rene. *Kingdom of Laos.* Limoges, France: A. Bontemps Co., Ltd., 1959.

Devi, Yamuna. *Lord Krishna's Cuisine: The Art of Indian Vegetarian Cooking.* New York: Bala Books, Inc., 1987.

DeWitt, Dave, and Nancy Gerlach. *The Whole Chile Pepper Book.* Boston: Little, Brown and Co., 1990.

Eckhardt, Linda West. *Barbecue: Indoors and Out.* Los Angeles: Jeremy P. Tarcher, Inc., 1987.

Eve, Paul. *Cooking With Rice.* London: Elm Tree Books, 1973.

Famularo, Joe. *The Joy of Grilling.* New York: Barron's, 1988.

Fitzgerald, Don. *Easy to Barbecue Cookbook.* Toluca Lake, California: Pacifica House, Inc., 1969.

Greeley, Alexandra. "Rice," *The Peninsula Group Magazine,* April 1979.

Handy, Ellice. *My Favorite Recipes.* 2nd ed. Singapore: MPH Publications SDN.BHD., 1968.

Hansen, Barbara. *Barbara Hansen's Taste of Southeast Asia: Brunei, Indonesia, Malaysia, the Philippines, Singapore, Thailand & Vietnam.* Tucson: H. P. Books, 1987.

Jatada, Takashi. *A History of Korea.* Santa Barbara: ABC-CLIO, Inc., 1969.

Jaffrey, Madhur. *An Invitation to Indian Cooking.* New York: Vintage Book Editions, 1988.

Jaffrey, Madhur. *Far Eastern Cookery.* New York: Harper & Row, 1989.

Kalra, J. Inder Singh. *Prashad, Cooking with Indian Masters.* 4th Printing. New Delhi: Allied Publishers Limited, 1990.

Khaing, Mi Mi. *Cook and Entertain the Burmese Way.* Rangoon: Daw Ma Ma Khin, 1975.

Khin, Yvonne M. and U. *Adventures in Burmese Cooking.* Unpublished manuscript, 1973.

Kohno, Sadako. *Home Style Japanese Cooking in Pictures.* Tokyo: Shufunotomo Co., Ltd., 1977.

Lew, Linda, Agnes Less, and Elizabeth Brotherton. *Peking Table Top Cooking.* North Hollywood, California: Gale Books, 1972.

Lo, Kenneth H. C. *A Guide to Chinese Eating.* Oxford, England: Phaidon Press Limited, 1976.

———. *Chinese Food.* Middlesex, England: Penguin Books, 1972.

———. *Peking Cooking.* New York: Pantheon Books, 1971.

Marahimin, Hiang, and Roos Djalil. *Indonesian Dishes and Desserts.* Femina Cookbook Series. Jakarta: Gaya Favorit Press, 1990.

Natividad, Bella Flor. *Lao Foods.* Vientiane, Laos: Imprimerie Nationale Vientiane, 1973.

Ngo, Bach, and Gloria Zimmerman. *The Classic Cuisine of Vietnam.* New York: Barron's Educational Series, 1979.

Owen, Sri. *Indonesian Food and Cookery.* London: Prospect Books, 1990 (1976, 1980).

Parkes, Carl. *Southeast Asia Handbook.* Chico, California: Moon Publications, Inc., 1990.

Passmore, Jacki. *The Encyclopedia of Asian Food and Cooking.* New York: Hearst Books, 1991.

Perkins, David W., ed. *Hong Kong & China Gas Chinese Cookbook.* Hong Kong: Pat Printer Associates Limited, 1978.

Rai, Ranjit. *Curry, Curry, Curry: The Heart of Indian Cooking.* London: Penguin Books, 1990.

Rai, Ranjit. *Tandoor—The Great Indian Bar-Be-Cue.* (To Be Published)

Rau, Santha Rama. *The Cooking of India.* New York: Time-Life Books, 1969.

Ross, Russel R., ed. *Cambodia: A Country Study.* Washington, D.C.: Federal Research Division, Library of Congress, 1990.

Roth, Shirley Janairo. *Cooking the Filipino Way.* (Compilation of Filipino recipes) 1981.

Schlesinger, Chris, and John Willoughby. *The Thrill of the Grill: Techniques, Recipes & Down-Home Barbecue.* New York: William Morrow and Company, Inc., 1990.

Simmons, Marie. *Rice: The Amazing Grain.* New York: Henry Holt and Company, 1991.

Sing, Phia. Alan Davidson, ed. *Traditional Recipes of Laos.* London: Prospect Books, 1981.

Singh, Mrs. Balbir. *Indian Cooking.* London: Mills & Boon Limited, 1961.

Skrobanek, Detlef, Suzanne Charle, and Gerald Gay. *The New Art of Indonesian Cooking.* Singapore: Times Edition, 1988.

BIBLIOGRAPHY

Steinberg, Rafael. *Pacific and Southeast Asian Cooking.* New York: Time-Life Books, 1972.

Steinberg, Rafael. *The Cooking of Japan.* New York: Time-Life Books, 1976.

Tanaka, Heihachi. *The Pleasures of Japanese Cooking.* Englewood Cliffs, New Jersey: Prentice-Hall, Inc., 1963.

Tannahill, Reay. *Food in History.* New York: Stein and Day, 1973.

Trent, May Wong. *Oriental Barbecues.* New York: Macmillan Publishing Co., Inc., 1974.

Tsuji, Shizuo. *Japanese Cooking: A Simple Art.* Tokyo: Kodansha International, 1980.

Von Welanetz, Diana and Paul. *The Van Welanetz Guide to Ethnic Ingredients.* Los Angeles: J. P. Tarcher, Inc., 1982.

Waldron, Maggie. *Fire & Smoke.* San Francisco: 101 Productions, 1978.

Woman's Society of Christian Service. *Rangoon International Cook Book.* Rangoon, Burma: Methodist English Church, 1956.

Index

Accompaniments
  Burmese, 215–18
  Cambodian, 226–29
  Filipino, 198–200
  Hong Kong, 172, 179–86
  Indian, 27–43
  Indonesian, 143–50
  Japanese, 296–302
  Korean, 270–78
  Laotian, 260
  Macanese, 206–7
  Malaysian, 95–100
  Singaporean, 112–17
  Thai, 59, 64–75
  Vietnamese, 240–42
Achiote, 197
Aditi Restaurant (Washington, D.C.), 12
Adobo Chicken, 199
Adzuki beans (azuki beans), 317
African Chicken, 205
Agar-agar, 305–6
  in almond "bean curd" with lychees, 118
  in egg and coconut jelly, 120
Ais kacang, 84, 101
Ajwain, 306
Akiho, Kenji, 286
Almond Bean Curd with Lychees, 118
Amado, Paul, 192
Amchor, 306
Anchovies
  in dipping sauce for beef, 224
  dried, in sambal ikan bilis, 99
Anderson, E. N., xvi
Angkor Wat Restaurant (Virginia), 220, 221, 225, 228, 230

Annatto oil, 197
Ao, 255
Apples
  pickled, 217
  toffee, and bananas, 187
Asian pears, 276–77
Asparagus, pan-fried scallops with, and pine nuts, 183
Atibodhi, Sarayuth, 56, 64, 67, 70
Ayam rica-rica, 134
Azuki beans (adzuki beans), 317

Bacalao cakes, fried, 206–7
Baked Sesame Seed Buns, 174
Bakmie Ayam, 143–44
Bali Hyatt, 122, 125, 130, 141, 142, 149, 153
Balinese cooking, 122–23, 125, 130–31, 133, 141, 142, 149, 153
Balinese Pancakes, 153
Bamboo, 306
  chicken in, 136
  fish in, 221
  shoots, 306
    in Korean vegetable and meat platter, 276–77
  soup, 256
  skewers, 306
  sticky rice in, 254
Bamboo Shoot Soup, 256
Banana and Coconut Dessert, 243
Banana and Coconut Milk Pudding, 230
Banana leaves, xxii, 307
  for Balinese duck, 130–31
  for chicken in bamboo, 136

compressed rice in, 147
fish in, 89
  curried, 60
  grilled pomfret, 88
  spicy, 141
  stuffed with tomato and onion, 196–97
  with turmeric marinade, 108
prawns in
  with glutinous rice, 94
  Singaporean style, 110–11
tofu in, 137
Banana Porridge, 105
Bananas
  with coconut milk
    in glutinous rice, 243
    pudding, 230
  hot sugary, 77
  toffee, and apples, 187
Banana shoots, 216–17
Bangkok Garden Restaurant (Thailand), 59, 62, 71, 73, 76, 77
Bangkok West Restaurant (Thailand), 54, 256
Banik, Sambhu, xviii
Barbecued Peking Duck, 166–67
Barbecued Pork Cutlets, 194
Barbecued Pork Filet, 168
Barbecued Pork Loin, 197
Barbecued Shrimp, 213
Barbecued Whole Suckling Pig, 164–65
Basil, Thai (sweet basil), 307
Basting sauces
  for beef, 128, 129
  for suckling pig, 249

Basto, Lenor, 195, 201
Bay leaves, Indonesian or Oriental,
      307
Bean curd. *See* Tofu
Beans
   green, with coconut, 39
   lima, pastries, 303–4
   string
      with ground pork, 200
      with pork loin, 300
   sweet red, in ais kacang, 101
   See also Adzuki beans: Black
         beans: Mung beans
Bean thread noodles. *See* Vermicelli
Beard, James, xix
Beef
   with basil leaves and chilies, 73
   Cambodian style, 223
   ginger-flavored sirloin cubes, 184
   ground
      with grape leaves, 236–37
      in mandu dumpling filling, 274
   jerky, Laotian version of, 248–49
   in Korean "multiple vegetables"
         dish, 278
   in Korean vegetable and meat
         platter, 276–77
   Laotian national dish of, 258–59
   lemongrass, 237
   miso-grilled, 291
   in Mongolian barbecue, 172–73
   in nasi goreng, 149
   with red chili, 62
   in rendang, 146–47
   rolls, Japanese style, 286–87
   salad, 57
   satay
      Malaysian style, 90–91
      Thai style, 56
   sate
      clipped, 135
      ground beef, 129
      sweet steak, 128
      with tongue and heart, 126–27
   short ribs, Korean style, 266
   skewered Korean style, 269

soup
   Laotian style, 255
   spicy, 228
sour vegetables with, 148
stock, soup, 271
in teppanyaki, 294–95
teriyaki, 292
thinly sliced, Korean style
      (bulgogi), 263, 265
tripe, in Laotian beef dish, 258–59
Beef Lap (Beef Larb), 258–59
Beef Negamaki, 286–87
Beef Satay
   Malaysian style, 90–91
   Thai style, 56
Beef Stock Soup, 271
Beggar's Chicken, xvi, 160–62
Belacan, 316
Besan flour, 309
Bhandoola, Janky, 28, 45
Bhatia, Savitri, xiv, xvii
Bibingka Royal, 203
Blacan (blacam), 316
Black beans, 307–8
   hot bean paste from, 173, 267
   sauce, 71
Black cumin, 308
Black Dal, 32
Black gram, 308
Black Rice Pudding, 123, 151
Bogambal, Joey, 194, 202
Bok choy
   in chicken soup, 255
   in kimchee, 270
Bonito, dried, 302
Bora Chu, 226, 231
Borax, in rice flour pudding, 231
Breads
   fried stuffing, 226
   See also Murtabagh; Naan; Paratha
Brillat-Savarin, J. Anthleme, xv
Broccoli, in beef rolls, 286
Buckwheat noodles, 312
Bukhara Restaurant (New Delhi),
      xviii, xix–xxx, xxxi, 5, 8, 15,
      18–20, 23, 26, 31

Buko Pie, 190, 201
Bulgogi, 263, 265
Bulkalbi, 266
Burmese food, 210–19
   accompaniments with, 215–18
   dessert in, 219
Burmese Pickles, 217
Burmese Rice Vermicelli, 216–17
Burmese Sweet Cakes, 219

Cabbage
   choi sam, 143–44
   in coconut milk, 97
   fragrant (with shrimp), 186
   in mandu dumplings, 274
   preserved, 143–44
   in Vietnamese spring rolls, 252
   See also Bok choy
Cabbage Braised in Coconut Milk, 97
Cafe Japone, 286
Cakes
   Burmese sweet, 219
   coconut
      Filipino, 203
      pandan, 119
      rice, 78–79
   Empress Dowager, 189
   sweet rice flour, 279
   See also Pancakes
Caldo verde, 207
Cambodian food, 210, 220–31
   accompaniments with, 226–29
   desserts in, 230–31
Cambodian Restaurant, The, 222,
      224, 226–29
Cambodian Special Shrimp, 229
Camphor and tea-smoked duck,
      176–77
Candlenuts, 308
Cantonese cooking, 158
Cantonese Ginger-Flavored Beef
      Cubes, 184
Cantonese Roast Pigeons, 178
Caramel Sauce, 241
Caramel Shrimp, 241
Cardamom, 308

Carom ajowan, 306
"Carrot" cake, 116–17
Carrot Halvah, 45
Carrots
   in beef rolls, 286
   for duck breast with eggplant, 284
   in Korean "multiple vegetables"
      dish, 278
   in Korean vegetable and meat
      platter, 276–77
   pickled, 227
   pudding, 45
   in skewered beef, Korean style, 269
Cashew-raisin filling, 24–25
Cassava, 254
Cassia flowers or blossoms, 189
Catfish
   cakes, fried, 215
   with curry, 60
   soup, Thai style, 255
Cauliflower
   in beef rolls, 286
   pickled, 227
Cellophane noodles. *See* Vermicelli
Chaat masala, 20–21, 24–25
Cha gio, 182, 233
   recipe for, 252
Chan, Alan, 168, 178
Chanthavisant, Khampain, 256
Chapati, recipe for, 41
Chapati flour, 309–10
Chap Chae, 278
Char siu, 168
Chawan Mushi, 301
Cheese
   Cheddar, marinade for chicken
      breasts, 19
   See also Paneer
Chen Yu-ping, 160, 189
Cheo, 251
Cheung Hoi Cheung, 164, 183
Chicken
   African, 205
   breasts
      barbecued Jakarta style, 140
      with basil leaves and chilies, 73

      in Cheddar cheese marinade, 19
      curry, 72
      in egg custard, 301
      with ground red pepper sauce,
         268
      kastoori kebab, 18
      kebab, 22
      lemon barbecued, 195
      with lime marinade, 239
      in Mongolian barbecue, 172–73
      with paneer filling, 12–13
      satay, 53, 55
      satay Kajang style, 92
      soup, with coconut milk, 68
      yakitori, 290
   Cambodian style, 222–23
   casserole, sour and sweet, 199
   clay-covered, 160–62
   curry, green, 72–73
   drumsticks
      Laotian style, 250
      for nasi goreng, 149
   gingered, 228
   legs, seasoned, 222
   Malaysian style grilled, 86
   in nasi goreng, 149
   soup
      Laotian style, 255
      lemongrass, 227
   spiced, 58
   spicy, 134
   tandoori, 15
   in teppanyaki, 294–95
   wings, honeyed, 181
Chicken Adobo, 199
Chicken Breasts with Paneer Filling,
   12–13
Chicken Bulgogi, 268
Chicken Ginger, 228
Chicken in Bamboo, 136
Chicken in Coconut Milk Soup, 68
Chicken Satay, 55
Chicken Satay Panang, 53
Chicken Soup, 255
Chicken with Basil Leaves and Hot
   Chilies, 73

Chickpeas, fried, 38
Chili Crabs, 115
Chilies, xxiv–xxv, xxxi–xxxii, 50,
      84, 124
   Cambodian, 220
   in chicken
      curry, 72
      Manado style, 134
      with basil leaves, 73
   fried potatoes with, 37
   in glass noodle salad, 69
   green
      in chutney, 35
      in green papaya salad, 74
      in recipes for chicken breasts, 12,
         19
      in soup, 66
      in whole potatoes, 24
   jam, 64
   in Korean all-purpose seasoning,
      270
   steak with, 62
   in Thai curry paste, 60
Chili Jam, 64
Chili-Lime Dipping Sauce, 108
Chili pastes and sauces, 308
   Thai recommendation for, 59
   Vietnamese, 147
Chili powder
   in kimchee, 270
   red, 314
Chili Sambal, 145
Chili sauce, for fish, 89
Chinese Barbecued Pork Spareribs,
   163
Chinese egg noodles, 313
   soup, with pork, 198–99
Chinese parsley, xxvii
Choi sam, 143–44
Chor Bizarre (Delhi), 5, 22
Chutney, coriander, 35
Cilantro, xxvii
Cinnamon, sweet red bean paste with,
   280
Claiborne, Craig, xx
Clipped Beef Sate, 135

INDEX

Coconut leaves, prawns in, 110–11
Coconut milk, xxi, xxv–xxvi, 84
  in beef sate, 135
  cabbage braised in, 97
  cakes with, Filipino, 203
  with chicken
    curry, 72
    Malaysian style, 86
    satay Penang style, 53
  in desserts
    in banana porridge, 105
    with bananas, 243
    egg jelly, 120
    grilled rice cakes, 78–79
    pandan cake, 119
    parfait with mung beans, 243
    pudding, 152
    sago pudding, 104
    sticky rice and mango, 76
    sweet cakes, 219
  in dipping sauce for beef, 127
  with duck, 61
  in laksa soup, 114
  pudding, with bananas, 230
  in rice dish, 98
  in rice vermicelli, 216
  soup, chicken in, 68
Coconut Milk Pudding, 152
Coconut Pandan Cake, 119
Coconut Rice, 98
Coconuts, 84
  custard, 76–77
  green beans with, 39
  macapuno, 202
  pie, 190, 201
Coconut vinegar, 194
Codfish cakes, fried, 206–7
Cold Soba Noodles, 302
Compressed Rice, 147
Congee, 233
Conpoy, 162
Coriander, xxvii
Coriander Chutney, 35
Corn and Crab Meat Soup, 179
Cornish game hens, 132
Crab paste, 257

Crabs
  chili, 115
  in fried bread stuffing, 226
  soup, with corn, 179
Crying Tiger, 62
Cucumbers
  in beef with anchovies, 224
  in Korean "multiple vegetables"
    dish, 278
  pickled, 227
  soup, 298
Cucumber Salad, 100
Culinary Institute of America, xv
Cumin, black, 308
Curry
  beef meatball, 30
  in Burmese pickles, 217
  chicken, green, 72–73
  duck, 61
  fish, freshwater, 60
  in satay dishes, 54, 55
Curry pastes, Thai, 308
  recipe for, 60
Custard
  coconut, 76–77
  egg, Japanese style, 301
  with saffron and rose essence, 44

Daikon
  fried, 116–17
  in shrimp and pork salad, 242
Dal, 31–32, 308–9
Dal Bukhara, 31
Dan bing, 185
Dashi, 297, 301, 302
Date-Paste Pancake, 188
Davidson, Alan, 245, 253
Desserts
  Burmese, 219
  Cambodian, 230–31
  Filipino, 201–3
  Hong Kong, 187–89
  Indian, 44–47
  Indonesian, 151–53
  Japanese, 303–4
  Korean, 279–80

  Laotian, 260
  Macanese, 208
  Malaysian, 101–5
  Singaporean, 104, 118–20
  Thai, 76–79
  Vietnamese, 243
Devi, Yamuna, xxv, 46, 314
DeWitt, Dave, xxv
Dipping sauces
  for barbecued pork filet, 168
  for beef, 127, 224
  for camphor and tea-smoked duck,
    176–77
  chili-lime, 108
  for lamb, 125
  Laotian, 251
  for suckling pig, 164–65
  sweet and sour, 112
  for teppanyaki, 294
  for Vietnamese spring rolls, 252
Direct cooking method, xxix–xxx
Dosai, 5
Duck
  Balinese, 130–31
  breast, rolled with eggplant, 284
  camphor and tea-smoked, 176–77
  minced, wrapped with waffle
    papers, 182
  Peking, 166–67
  in red curry, 61
  roasted on sugarcane, 214
Dugal, Kitty, 32–36
Dumplings, Korean mandu, 274–75
Dusit Inn (Thailand), 63, 68

Eel, Japanese style, 287
Egg and Coconut Jelly, 120
Egg batter, kastoori, 18
Egg Custard, 301
Egg noodles. *See* Chinese egg noodles
Eggplant
  in chicken soup, 255
  with onions and tomatoes, 33
  rolled duck breast with, 284
Eggplant Bhartha, 33
Elespura, Carlos, 294

Embassy of Malaysia (Washington, D.C.), 96, 104
Embassy of the People's Republic of China (Washington, D.C.), 189
Embassy of the Republic of Indonesia (Washington, D.C.), 136, 153
Empress Dowager Cakes, 189
Epicurean Events (Hong Kong), 65, 163, 169, 173, 176, 185
Everyday Dipping Sauce, 251

Faeh, Jamie (Young Ja Yun), 263, 267, 276, 280
Fiery Fried Potatoes, 37
Filipino food, 190–203
    accompaniments for, 198–200
    desserts in, 201–3
Firni (Phirni), 44
Fish
    Cambodian style grilled, 221
    freshwater, with curry, 60
    garlicked, 194
    Malaysian style grilled, 89
    in rice vermicelli, 216–17
    salt-grilled wave-skewered, 288
    soup, sour, 241
    spicy, 139
        in banana leaf, 141
        fried, 71
    stock, Japanese style (dashi), 297, 301, 302
    tandoori, 11, 23
    See also Anchovies; Catfish; Codfish; Pomfret; Sea bass; Tuna; other types of fish
Fish paste, 309
    prahok, 224, 259
Fish sauce, 309
    Vietnamese (nuoc cham), 232–35, 309
    recipe for, 240
Fish Seasoning Sauce, 296
Fish Sour Soup, 241
Fish Stuffed with Tomatoes and Onions, 196–97

Five-spice powder, 309
Flounder
    fried spicy, 71
    in rice vermicelli, 216
    tandoori, 23
Flours, 309–10
Foreign Correspondents' Club (Hong Kong), 168, 178
Fragrant Cabbage, 186
Fresh Vegetable and Meat Platter, 276–77
Fried Bean Curd, 272
Fried Bread Stuffing, 226
Fried Burmese Fish Cakes, 215
Fried Carrot Cake, 116–17
Fried Chickpeas, 38
Fried Codfish Cakes, 206–7
Fried shallots, 241, 310
Fried Spicy Fish, 71
Fried Spicy Okra, 117

Gado-gado, 150
Galangal, 310
    in Cambodian grills and soup, 222, 223, 225, 228
    in Indonesian grills, 126, 128, 133, 148
        Balinese duck, 130
    in Malaysian grills, 86, 87, 91–93
    in soup, 66, 68, 228
    in Thai grills, 53, 60, 72
Game hens, 132
Gandhi, Indira, 4
Garam Masala, 27
Garewal, Prakbeen, 40
Garlic, xxvii
Garlic paste, 310
Gauld, Ted, 282
Gaya Favorit Press, 128, 135, 148
Generic Sate Sauce, 145
Gerlach, Nancy, xxv
Ghee, xxi, 310
Gill, Manjit S., xxxi, 8, 10
Ginger
    beef cubes flavored with, 184
    in beef teriyaki, 292, 296

chicken with, 58, 228
    in cucumber soup, 298
    juice, 186, 229
    paste, 310–11
    for pork and string beans, 300
    sauce, 299
    in shrimp marinade, 229
    whether substitute for galangal, 310
Gingerroot, xxvi–xxvii
Gingko nuts, 301
Gladson, Muttika Setatayak, 74, 77
Glass noodles. See Vermicelli
Glutinous rice (sticky rice), 244–45, 309
    in bamboo, 254
    banana and coconut dessert with, 243
    for banana and coconut milk pudding, 230
    in black rice pudding, 151
    in chicken soup, 255
    dry-roasted and ground, 258–59
    mango and, 76
    mochi from, 293
    with prawn filling, 94
    steamed, 253
    in sugar-filled pastry balls, 102
Goat, leg of, 14
Goose, roast, 170–71
Gourami
    fermented, 224
    in Laotian beef dish, 258–59
Gram flour, 309
Grape leaf, ground beef with, 236–37
Grass jelly, 101
Green Beans with Coconut, 39
Green Chicken Curry, 72–73
Green Mango Salad, 75
Green Papaya Salad
    Laotian style, 257
    Thai style, 74
Greiert, Detlef, xiii, 131, 138, 144, 147
Grilled Balinese Duck, 130–31
Grilled Bananas, 77

Grilled Beef, 223
Grilled Beef Anchovy, 224
Grilled Beef Salad, 57
Grilled Chicken
  Cambodian, 222–23
  Malaysian, 86
Grilled Chicken Legs, 250
Grilled Coconut Rice Cakes, 78–79
Grilled Duck in Red Curry, 61
Grilled Eel, 287
Grilled Fish
  Cambodian, 221
  Malaysian, 89
Grilled Freshwater Fish with Curry,
  60
Grilled Game Hens, 132
Grilled Garlicked Fish, 194
Grilled Glutinous Rice with Prawn
  Filling, 94
Grilled Ground Beef with Grape Leaf,
  236–37
Grilled Lao Sausages, 246–47
Grilled Leg of Goat, 14
Grilled Lemongrass Beef, 237
Grilled Lime Chicken, 239
Grilled Lobster, 63
Grilled Marinated Beef, 292
Grilled Meatballs, 235
Grilled Pomfret, 87
Grilled Pomfret in Banana Leaf, 88
Grilled Pork, 267
Grilled Pork Strips on Rice Vermicelli,
  238–39
Grilled Prawns, 142
Grilled Rack of Lamb, 131
Grilled Rice Balls, 299
Grilled Shrimp, 293
Grilled Skewered Beef, 269
Grilled Spiced Chicken, 58
Grilled Spicy Fish Wrapped in
  Banana Leaf, 141
Grilled Squid, 59
Grilled Suckling Pig, 133
Grilled Tofu in Banana Leaf, 137
Grilled Tuna, 138
Grilled Whole Potato, 298

Grilled Whole Sea Bass in Turmeric
  Marinade, 108
Grilling
  Asian, general remarks on, xvi–
    xx
  definition of, xv
  equipment for, xxviii, xxx
  methods of, xxviii–xxx
Ground Meat Sate, 129
Ground Red Pepper Sauce, 270
Grouper
  spicy, in banana leaf, 141
  in turmeric marinade, 108
Gula melaka, 313
Gurkhas, Brigade of, 39

Halal butchers, 14
Halibut, tandoori, 11
Hall, Trish, xi
Halliday, Bob, 50, 52, 69, 78
Halo Halo, 202
Halvah, carrot, 45
Handi (cookpot), 31
Harusame, 312
Herbed Soup, 67
Hinshaw, Devyani Singh, 16
Hoisin sauce, 311
Honeyed Chicken Wings, 181
Hong Kong food, xi–xii, 157–89
  accompaniments for, 172, 179–86
  desserts in, 187–89
  Vietnamese, 232
Horse gram, 308
Hot and Sour Glass Noodle Salad, 69
Hot bean paste, 173, 267
Hotel Imperial (Delhi), 5
Hyatt Regency Singapore, 108–10,
  112–14, 118

Ice beans, 101
Ice cream
  in Halo Halo, 202
  saffron mango, 46
Iddhi, 5
Indian food, xvii–xviii, xxii, xxiii, 4–
  48

accompaniments with, 27–43
desserts in, 44–47
Indirect cooking method, xxix
Indonesian food, xiii, xxiii, xxiv,
  122–53
  accompaniments for, 143–50
  desserts in, 151–53
Indonesian Fried Rice (nasi goreng),
  xxi, 123, 149
Indonesian sweet soy sauce, xxvii
Inversin, Bounheng, 248
Iwai, Tokuji, 290

Jabar, Mrs. Abdul, 84, 86, 89, 92,
  97, 98, 100–103
Jackfruit, 202
Jaffrey, Madhur, xx
Jaiswal, Madan Lal, xviii, xix–xx,
  xxxi, 5, 8, 31
Jakarta Barbecued Chicken, 140
Jakarta Hilton International, 131,
  138, 144, 147
Jalea ube, 202
Jalebi, 5
Japanese food, xix, xxiii, xxiv, 262,
  281–304
  accompaniments with, 296–302
  dessert in, 303–4
Japanese pears, 276–77
Jasmine flowers, dried, 161, 162
Javanese cooking, 136
Jaya Hotel and Tower (Jakarta), xxxi
Jellyfish, 311
  in Korean vegetable and meat
    platter, 276–77
  salad, 242
Jicama, 317
  in rojak, 96
  in Vietnamese spring rolls, 252
Jujubes, in pancakes, 188

Kaffir limes, 311–12
Kai Yang, 58
Kajang style satay, 92
Kalamansi limes, 311–12
Kale (kailaam), stir-fried, 186

Kalra, J. Inder Singh (Jiggs), xvi, xx, xxii, xxv, xxxi, 5–6, 8, 10, 15, 18–20, 22–24, 26, 31, 44, 310–11
Karim's Hotel (Delhi), 5, 14
Kastoori Kebab, 18
Katsuobushi, 302
Kebabs
  chicken, 22
    kastoori, 18
  vegetarian, 20–21
Kecap mantis, xxvii
Kencur galangal, 130
Khaing, Mi Mi, 211
Khanom Krok, 78–79
Khin, U, 211, 213, 215–19
Khin, Yvonne, 211–13, 215–19
Kim, Kyung Yul, 268–70
Kimchee, 264, 270
Koch, Alma, 35
Ko chu jang, 267
Kofta Curry, 30
Kombu, 302
Korean Barbecue (bulgogi), 263, 265
Korean food, 262–80
  accompaniments with, 270–78
  desserts in, 279–80
Kowloon Shangri-La (Hong Kong), 164, 183
Krupuk udang, 315
Kulfi, saffron mango, 46
Kumoro, Mrs., 148
Kunchai, Darunee, 78

Laksa, Singaporean, 114
Lamb
  as goat substitute, 14
  leg of
    barbecue, 16–17
    with Indian seasoning, 8–9
    sate, 125
  Mongolian, 169
  in Mongolian barbecue, 172–73
  rack of, 131
Lamb Sate, 125
Lanif, Aminah, 146, 147, 152

Lan's Vietnamese Restaurant, 236, 238, 240
Laohapant, Visith, 59, 62, 71, 73, 76, 77
Laos galangal, 130
Laos powder, 310
Laotian food, xviii, xxiii, xxiv, 210, 244–60
  accompaniments with, 251–59
  dessert in, 260
Lap (larb), 258–59
Lassi, mango, 47
Lauw, Douglas, 137, 140, 143, 145
Lechon Liver Sauce, 192–93
Lee, June, 263–66, 270–74, 278, 279
Lee Gardens Hotel (Hong Kong), 166, 182
Lemon Barbecued Chicken, 195
Lemongrass, 311
  in Burmese rice vermicelli, 216
  in Cambodian grills and soup, 221, 222, 225, 227, 228
  in Indonesian grills, 126, 128, 131–34, 136, 139
  in Laotian grills and soup, 246, 250, 255
  in Malaysian grills, 88–92
  in Singaporean grills and soup, 108–10, 113, 114
  in soup, 66, 68, 113, 114, 227, 228
  in Thai grills, 53, 57, 60
  in Vietnamese beef marinade, 237
Lemongrass Soup, 227
Lentils, 309
Leow, Anna, 116, 117, 119
Leung Kit, 166, 182
Li Jian, 189
Lim, Jimmy, 108–10, 112–14, 118
Lima Bean Pastries, 303–4
Lime marinade, 239
Limes, 311–12
Linguiça, 207
Lo, Kenneth H. C., xvi, 166, 180
Lo, Lucy, 180

Lobster, 63
Lontong Daun, 147
Lord, Mary, xix, 291
Lorenz, Hubert, 122, 125, 130, 141, 142, 149, 153
Lotus leaves, 160–62
Luk Yu Tea House (Hong Kong), 158
Lychees, almond "bean curd" with, 118

Macanese food, 204–8
  accompaniments with, 206–7
  dessert in, 208
Macapuno, 202
Macau. See Macanese food
Macau Tourist Information Board, 205, 207, 208
McDonald, Katie, 179
Mackerel, 87
  in banana leaves, 88
    with prawns, 110–11
  salt-grilled wave-skewered, 288
Malaysian food, xiii, xix, 82–105
  accompaniments for, 95–100
  desserts in, 101–5
Maltose, 164–65
Manado cooking, 134
Mandarin Oriental Hotel (Macau), 206
Mandu, 274–75
Mangda, 52
Mangoes
  green, salad, 75
  ice cream, saffron, 46
  pulp, 46
  sticky rice and, 76
Mango Lassi, 47
Manila Restaurant, The, 192
Maphungphong, Sanee, 51, 53
Marinades, xix
  for beef, 56, 90, 223
    ginger-flavored cubes, 184
    Korean bulgogi, 265
    Korean short ribs, 266
    Laotian jerky, 248
    lemongrass, 137

Marinades, for beef (*cont.*)
    for skewered beef, Korean style, 269
    teriyaki, 292
  for chicken, 15, 53, 55, 58, 86, 92
    African Chicken, 205
    Beggar's Chicken, 160
    Cheddar cheese, 19
    with ground red pepper sauce, 268
    legs, 222
    lemon, 195
    lemongrass, 250
    lime, 239
    yakitori, 290
  for Cornish game hens, 132
  for fish, 11, 87
    garlicked fish, 194
    pomfret, 23
    tuna, 138
    turmeric marinade, 108
  for goat, 14
  for lamb, 125
    Mongolian Lamb, 169
  for pork, 54, 194, 197, 225
    barbecued filet, 168
    hot bean paste, 267
    sliced, on rice vermicelli, 238–39
  for prawns, 10, 142
  for shrimp, 109, 213
  for spareribs, 163
Mark, William, x, xi–xii, 158–59, 184, 186–88
Masala dosai, 85
Masalas, xxii, 6–7. *See also* Chaat masala; Garam Masala; Masala dosai
Mateh khamang, 220
Meatballs, pork, 235
"Meat from Heaven," 248–49
Mee yuk (Seaweed Soup), 263, 272
Meridien, The (Delhi), 5
Mikado Restaurant, 290
Minka Japanese Country Inn, 298, 300–302

Mirin, 312
Miso-Grilled Beef, 291
Mochi, 293
Mohamad, Mahani, 120
Mok Tai Heng, 88, 90, 93–95, 105
Mongolian Barbecue, xvi, 172–73
Mongolian grilling, xvi
Mongolian Lamb, 169
Mon hinga, 216–17
Monkfish, tandoori, 11
Moo shu wrappers or pancakes, 185
Mrs. Tatie Wawo-Runtu's Gado-Gado, 150
MSG, xxvii
Mudfish, fermented, 224
Mung Bean and Coconut Milk Parfait, 243
Mung Bean Pancake, 273
Mung beans, 309, 312
  in Halo Halo, 202
Murgh Malai, 19
Murtabagh, 107
Musa, Rachmi, 126
Musa, Rasuna, 126
Mushrooms
  black
    in soup, 179
    in Vietnamese spring rolls, 252
  dried brown, in Korean vegetable and meat platter, 276–77
  in Korean "multiple vegetables" dish, 278
  in skewered beef, Korean style, 269
  straw, 71
Myanmar. *See* Burmese food

Naan, 43
Nair, Suku, 30, 36, 47, 48
Nair brothers, 12
Nam pia, 309
Nashi, 276–77
Nasi goreng (Indonesian Fried Rice), xxi, 123,149
Nasi lemak, 98
Natividad, Bella Flor, 254
Nepali dish, 39

Noodles, 312–13
  soba
    cold, 302
    sauce for, 297
    soup, 297
  soup
    with pork, 198–99
    vegetable, 179
  stir-fried, Thai style, 70
  See also Rice vermicelli; Vermicelli
Nuoc cham (Vietnamese fish sauce), 232–35, 309
  recipe for, 240
Nuoc mam, 235, 237, 239, 241, 242
  definition of, 240
Nyonya cooking, 84, 106
  Fried Spicy Okra, 117

Oberoi (New Delhi), 5
Ogura an, 280
Ohashi, Hiroyuki, 284, 287, 288, 293, 296, 297
Okra, fried spicy, 117
Onde-onde, 102
Onions
  in eggplant-tomato dish, 33
  in Korean "multiple vegetables" dish, 278
  in skewered beef, Korean style, 269
Oon, Violet, 107
Oranges, in beef rolls, 286
Oriental Bangkok Hotel. *See* Thai Cooking School
Owen, Sri, 123
Oysters, dried, 161, 162
Oyster sauce, 313

Paad Thai (Pad Thai; Pud Thai), 70
Pabros, Ildefonsa, 199
Padek, 257, 259
Palm Beach Hotel (Malaysia), 88, 90, 93–95, 105
Palm nut, 202
Palm Pudding, 104

Palm sugar, 313
  in banana porridge, 105
  in black rice pudding, 151
  for pancakes, 153
  in rice flour pudding, 231
  in sago pudding, 104–5
  sweet potatoes with, 152
Palmyra fruit, 202
Pancakes
  Balinese, 153
  date-paste, 188
  mung bean, 273
  Peking (moo shu), 185
Pandan, 313
  in coconut cake, 119
  in rice flour pudding, 231
Paneer, 313–14
  filling, chicken breasts with, 12–13
  recipe for, 36
  in vegetarian kebabs, 26
Paneer Ka Tikka, 26
Pan-fried Scallops with Pine Nuts and
    Greens, 183
Papaya, green, salad
  Laotian style, 257
  Thai style, 74
Paratha, 5
  potato, 42–43
Parkes, Carl, 210
Pasanda Lamb Barbecue, 16–17
Pastry
  balls, sugar-filled, 102
  samosas, 28–29
  See also Cakes
Peanut sauce
  for gado-gado, 150
  for satay dishes
    beef, 90–91
    chicken, 55, 92
    pork, 54
    shrimp, 109
  for sate dishes, 145
Pea Pulao, 34
Pears, Japanese, 276–77
Pecans, in sweet rice flour cake, 279
Peking Pancakes, 185

Penang cooking, 85
  Beef Satay, 90–91
  po piah, 95
Pepper, Japanese, 300
Peppercorns, Szechuan, 176–77
Peppers
  in Korean "multiple vegetables"
    dish, 278
  in skewered beef, Korean style, 269
Peranakan cooking, 143
Pheng Chu, xxv
Philippines. See Filipino food
Phirni, 44
Phở, xxi
Phulek, Somboon, 69
Pickled Vegetables, 227
Pickles
  Burmese, 217
  Japanese, 299
Pie, coconut (buko), 190, 201
Pigeons, roast, 178
Pilaf, pea, 34
Pine nuts, pan-fried scallops with,
    183
Piotrowski, Joyce, xxiv, 65, 163,
    166, 169, 172–73, 176, 184,
    185, 317
Plums, mashed sour (salted dried),
    170–71
Pomfret
  baked, 87
  Malaysian style grilled, 87
    in banana leaf, 88
  tandoori, 23
Pompano, tandoori, 23
Po piah, Penang, 95
Pork
  with basil leaves and chilies, 73
  with Cambodian marinade, 225
  chops
    with hot bean paste, 267
    lemon barbecued, 195
  cutlets, barbecued, 194
  filet, barbecued, 168
  ground
    in fried bread stuffing, 226

    Lao sausages, 246–47
    meatballs, 235
    string beans with, 200
    in Vietnamese spring rolls, 252
  with ground red pepper sauce, 268
  loin
    barbecued, 197
    string beans with, 300
  in Mongolian barbecue, 172–73
  in nasi goreng, 149
  salad, with shrimp and jellyfish,
    242
  satay, 54
  sliced, on rice vermicelli, 238–39
  soup
    with bamboo shoots, 256
    Laotian style, 255
  spareribs
    barbecued, 163
    caramel, 241
    with hot bean paste, 267
  in won ton soup, 180
  See also Suckling pigs
Pork and String Beans, 300
Pork Brochette, 225
Pork Noodle Soup, 198–99
Portuguese Green Vegetable Soup,
    207
Portuguese sausage, 207
Potatoes
  in codfish cakes, 206
  fiery fried, 37
  Japanese style, 298
  paratha, 42–43
  in vegetarian dish, filled, 24–25
  in vegetarian kebab, 20–21
  in yogurt dish, 35
Potato Paratha, 42–43
Potato starch, 238–39
Poultry Seasoning Sauce, 296
Prahok, 224, 259
Prawn Mee Soup, 113
Prawn Otak Otak in Banana Leaf,
    110–11
Prawns
  Balinese style, 142

INDEX

Prawns (*cont.*)
  in banana leaves, 110–11
  with cabbage, braised in coconut
    milk, 97
  glutinous rice filled with, 94
  in sanbal seasoning, 99
  soup, 113
  spicy, in banana leaf, 93
  tandoori, 10
Prig khee fa, 72
Prig khee nu, 72
Puddings
  banana and coconut milk, 230
  carrot, 45
  coconut milk, 152
  phirni (firni), 44
  rice
    black rice, 123, 151
    Laotian style, 260
    Macanese style, 208
    steamed, 103
  rice flour, 231
  sago, 104–5
  vermicelli, 48

Quang, David, 181, 232–33, 243

Radishes, Japanese. *See* Daikon
Rai, Ranjit, xvii, 11, 43
Raita, 35
Reagan, Ronald, 4
Red bean curd, 164–65
Red chili powder, 314
Red dates, in pancakes, 188
Red sea bream, tandoori, 23
Red snapper. *See* Snapper
Rendang, xxi
  West Sumatran, 146–47
Reshmi Purdeh Mein, 22
Rhizome, 310
Rice, xxiii–xxiv, 51, 123, 212, 220,
    233
  balls, grilled, 299
  compressed, 147
  fried Indonesian style. *See* Nasi
    goreng

pea pilaf, 34
pudding
  black, 123, 151
  Laotian style, 260
  Macanese style, 208
  steamed, 103
  See also Glutinous rice (sticky rice)
Rice cakes, coconut, 78–79
Rice flour, 309
  pudding, 231
  sweet cake, 279
Rice Flour Pudding, 231
Rice noodles, 313
  stir-fried, Thai style, 70
Rice papers (rice paper wrappers),
    234, 252, 314
Rice stick, 313
Rice vermicelli, 312
  Burmese, 216–17
  pork strips on, 238–39
Rice vinegar, 314
Rice wine, 314
Roasted Duck on Sugarcane,
    214
Roasted Pig, 249
Roast Goose, 170–71
Roast Suckling Pig, 192–93
Rojak, 84, 96
Rolled Duck Breast with Eggplant,
    284
Rolls. *See* Po piah; Spring rolls
Rolnick, Harry, 205, 207, 208
Rose essence (rose water), 314
  in Indian desserts, 44, 46–48
Roth, Shirley Janairo, 191, 192, 194,
    196, 198, 200, 201, 203
Routh, Rungnapa, 60, 62, 68, 75,
    76
Royal Orchid Sheraton Hotel &
    Towers (Thailand), 55, 57,
    61
Rume, 51

Sabang Restaurant (Indonesia), 132,
    139
Saffron Mango Kulfi, 46

Saffron threads, 44, 46, 97
Sago, 314–15
  in banana and coconut milk
    pudding, 230
Sago Pudding, 104–5
Sahid Jaya Hotel & Tower
    (Indonesia), 129, 134
Sake, 314
Salads
  beef, 57
  cucumber, 100
  glass noodle, hot and sour, 69
  green mango, 75
  green papaya
    Laotian style, 257
    Thai style, 74
  with pork brochette, 225
  rojak, 85, 96
  sauces and dressings for, 57, 75,
    96, 100, 218
  shrimp and pork, 242
  watercress, 218
"Salt and Pepper," 226
Salt-Grilled Whole Boston Mackerel,
    288
Sambal Ikan Bilis, 99
Sambals, 124, 315
  kecap, 144
  ulek (chili), 145, 308
Samosas, 28–29
Sananikone, Bounsou, xviii, xxiv,
    244–45, 249, 251, 252, 253,
    255, 258
Sananikone, Vasouthep, 179
Sanjok, 269
Sansho, 300
Sareth Kim, 222, 224, 227–29
Satay
  beef, 56
  chicken, 53
  definition of, 84
  Indonesian. *See* Sate
  pork, 54
  shrimp, 109
  Singapore's fame for, 107
Satay Kajang, 92

Sate, 123, 124
  beef
    clipped, 135
    ground beef, 129
    sweet steak, 128
    West Sumatran, 126–27
  lamb, 125
Sate gapit, 135
Sate sauce, generic, 145
Satit, Khun, 63, 68
Sausage casings, 246–47
Sausages
  Lao, 246–47
  Portuguese, 207
Sautéed Minced Duck Meat Wrapped
    with Waffle Papers, 182
Sautéed Mixed Vegetables, 40
Saw Ying Thai Restaurant (Bangkok),
  69
Say Oua Lao, 146–47
Scallion oil, 238
Scallions
  in cucumber soup, 298
  in soba soup, 297
Scallops
  dried, 161, 162
  pan-fried, with pine nuts and
    greens, 183
  in teppanyaki, 294–95
Screw pine, 313
Sea bass
  spicy, in banana leaf, 141
  stuffed with tomatoes and onions,
    196–97
  in turmeric marinade, 108
Seafood
  soup, spicy, 66
  See also Crabs; Fish; Lobster;
    Prawns; Scallops; Shrimp
Seasoned Chicken Legs, 222
Seasoning
  for beef, 126–27, 128, 135, 236
    chili steak, 62
    ginger-flavored sirloin cubes, 184
  for beef soup, 228
  Cambodian "salt and pepper," 226

for chicken, 86, 136
  honeyed wings, 181
  Laotian soup, 255
  sauce, 296
chili, 64
for cold soba noodles, 302
for Cornish game hens, 132
for duck, 130, 176
for fish, 88, 89
  sauce, 296
  spicy, 139, 141
Korean all-purpose, 270
for Korean vegetable and meat
  platter, 277
for lamb, 8, 131, 169
for lobster, 63
for prawns, 93
for rice vermicelli, 216
sambal ikan bilis, 99
for shrimp in ginger-juice marinade,
  229
for suckling pig, 164–65, 249
for teppanyaki, 294
Sea trout, fried spicy, 71
Seaweed, kombu type of, 302
Seaweed Soup, 263, 272
Semon, Diana, 298, 300–302
Semon, Peter, 298, 300–302
Sesame paste, 315
Sesame seed buns, baked, 174
Shafie, Noorhayati, 87
Shallots
  fried, 241, 310
  in Laotian dipping sauce, 251
  in Vietnamese spring rolls, 252
Shang Palace Restaurant (Hong
  Kong), 164
Shangri-La Hotel (Malaysia), 87
Shao ping, 174
Shikoras (cups), 44
Shiro-an Kurimanju, 303–4
Shrimp
  barbecued, 213
  cabbage with, 186
  caramel, 241
  crackers, 315

dried, 315
in egg custard, 301
in ginger marinade, 229
Japanese style, 293
in Korean vegetable and meat
  platter, 276–77
in laksa soup, 114
paste, 315–16
salad, with pork and jellyfish, 242
satay, 109
soup
  herbed, 67
  with squid, 66
on sugarcane, 234–35
in teppanyaki, 294–95
Shrimp and Pork Salad, 242
Shrimp on Sugarcane, 234–35
Sikandari Raan, 8–9
Sing, Phia, 245, 253
Singaporean food, xiii, 82–83, 106–
  20
  accompaniments with, 112–17
  desserts in, 104, 118–20
Singaporean Laksa, 114
Singaporean Shrimp Satay, 109
Singaporean Spring Rolls, 112
Singh, Mrs. Balbir, 7
Singh, Sohan, 12
Singh, Surinder, 16, 37, 38
Sinha, Mrs. Narain, 41
Sivong Chea, 222, 223, 227
Skrobanek, Detlef, xiii, 124
Snapper
  salt-grilled wave-skewered, 288
  spicy, 139
    in banana leaf, 141
  stuffed with tomatoes and onions,
    196–97
  tandoori, 11
  in turmeric marinade, 108
Soba noodles, 312
  cold, 302
Soba Noodle Sauce, 297
Soba Soup, 297
Soetjepto, Mrs., 132, 139
Soft Thai Spring Rolls, 65

INDEX

Souay khao, 253
Soups
  beef
    Laotian style, 255
    spicy, 228
    stock, 271
  chicken
    in coconut milk, 68
    Laotian style, 255
    lemongrass, 227
  Chinese-Indonesian, 143–44
  corn and crab meat, 179
  cucumber, 298
  fish, sour, 241
  herbed, with shrimp, 67
  pork
    Laotian style, 255
    noodle, 198–99
  prawn, 113
  seafood, spicy, 66
  seaweed, 263, 272
  soba, 297
  vegetable
    noodle, 179
    Portuguese green, 207
  won ton, 180
Sour Vegetables with Beef, 148
Souvanna-Phouma, Princess Moun, 246
Soybean paste, 316
Soy sauce, xxvii
Spareribs
  barbecued, 163
  caramel, 241
  with hot bean paste, 267
Spicy Beef Soup, 228
Spicy Grilled Chicken, 134
Spicy Grilled Prawns in Banana Leaf, 93
Spicy-Hot Fish, 139
Spicy Seafood Soup, 66
Spinach
  in Korean "multiple vegetables" dish, 278
  in soba soup, 297
Spring rolls
  Singaporean, 112

soft Thai, 65
  Vietnamese, 182, 233
    recipe for, 252
Squab, roast, 178
Squid
  with chili sauce for dipping, 59
  cleaning of, 66
  in sanbal seasoning, 99
  soup, with shrimp, 66
  in teppanyaki, 294–95
  in turmeric marinade, 108
Star fruit, 148
Steamed Rice Pudding, 103
Steamed Sticky Rice, 253
Sticky rice. See Glutinous rice
Sticky Rice and Mango, 76
Sticky Rice in Bamboo, 254
Stir-fried Chinese Kale, 186
Stir-fried Noodles, Thai Style, 70
Straw mushrooms, 71
String Beans with Ground Pork, 200
Striped bass, 89
Stuffing
  for Beggar's Chicken, 161
  for fish, tomato and onion, 196–97
  fried bread, 226
  for roast goose, 170–71
  for roast pigeons, 178
  for suckling pig, 133
Subz Seekh Kebab, 20–21
Suckling pigs, xvi, 316
  Balinese style, 133
  Chinese style, 164–65
  Filipino style, 192–93
  Laotian style, 249
Sugar. See Palm sugar
Sugarcane, 316
  duck roasted on, 214
  shrimp on, 234–35
Sugar-filled Pastry Balls, 102
Sujartha, Nenjah, 125, 130, 141, 149, 153
Sumatran cooking, 126–27, 136, 146, 152
Sweet and Sour Dipping Sauce, 112
Sweet bean paste, 316–17

Sweet Beef Sate, 128
Sweet Potatoes with Brown Sugar, 152
Sweet Red Bean Paste with Cinnamon, 280
Sweet red beans, 317
Sweet Rice Flour Cake, 279
Swordfish, tandoori, 11
Sykhammountry, Tanh, 252
Syrup, for sago pudding, 104–5
Szechuan Camphor and Tea-Smoked Duck, 176–77
Szechuan peppercorns, 176–77

Tahini, 315
Taj Mahal Hotel (New Delhi), 12
Tako Grill, 293, 298, 299
Tamarind, 317
  for grilled fish, 221
  juice, 109
Tanaka, Heihachi, xiv
Tandjung Sari Hotel (Bali), 133, 150, 151
Tandoori Aloo, 24–25
Tandoori Chicken, 15
Tandoori cooking, xvii–xviii
Tandoori Fish Tukra, 11
Tandoori Pomfret, 23
Tandoori Prawns, 10
Tangerine peel, dried, 317
Tang Hin Wa, xviii, 170
Tannahill, Reay, xvi
Tapioca flour, 309
  in rice flour pudding, 231
Taro root, 254
Tea-smoked duck, 176–77
Teixiera, Manuel, 204
Tempeh, 150
Teng Kim Soeun, 220, 221, 225, 228, 230
Teppan, 283
Teppanyaki, 294–95
Teriyaki, 292
Teriyaki Sauce, 296
Thai Coconut Custard, 76–77
Thai Cooking School (Bangkok), 52, 56, 64, 67, 70

Thai food, xii–xiii, 50–79
    accompaniments with, 59, 64–75
    desserts in, 76–79
Thai Luang Restaurant (Thailand),
    74, 77
Tiger Cry, 62
Toffee Apple and Banana, 187
Tofu (bean curd), xxvi, xxvii
    in banana leaf, 137
    fried, 272
    red, 164–65
    in rojak, 96
Tô-Ly, 234, 235, 237, 239, 241–43
Tomatoes
    beef and
        with anchovies, 224
        in Laotian dish, 258–59
        rolls, 286
    in eggplant-onion dish, 33
    fish stuffed with onions and, 196–
        97
Tom yam kung, 66
Transparent noodles. See Vermicelli
Trent, May Wong, xvi
Tum Nak Thai (Bangkok), 52
Tuna, with lime marinade, 138
Turmeric, 317
    in grilled tuna, 138
    leaves, 126, 138, 146
    marinade, 108

Ueda, Mrs. Hidiaki, 281
Unagi, 287
Uneri-gushi, 288
Unkai Restaurant (Washington,
    D.C.), 294
Urad dal, 32, 308

Vaish, Coco, 37, 38
Varaq, 5, 45
Varma, Vicky, 4, 42
Vegetable Garnish, 286
Vegetable Noodle Soup, 179
Vegetables
    in gado-gado, 150
    garnish, 286
    pickled, 227

soup
    noodle, 179
    Portuguese green, 207
sour, with beef, 148
in teppanyaki, 294–95
See also Vegetarian dishes; specific
    kinds of vegetables
Vegetarian dishes
    Coconut Rice, 98
    Cold Soba Noodles, 302
    Eggplant Bhartha, 33
    Fiery Fried Potatoes, 37
    Fried Carrot Cake, 116
    Fried Chickpeas, 38
    Green Beans with Coconut, 39
    Grilled Tofu in Banana Leaf, 137
    Grilled Whole Potato, 298
    Kimchee, 270
    Mochi, 293
    Paneer Ka Tikka, 26
    Pea Pulao, 34
    Potato Paratha, 42–43
    Raita, 35
    Sautéed Mixed Vegetables, 40
    Stir-fried Noodles, Thai Style, 70
    Subz Seekh Kebab, 20–21
    Tandoori Aloo, 24–25
    See also Dal
Vermicelli, 312
    in laksa soup, 114
    pudding, 48
    salad, hot and sour, 69
    in vegetable noodle soup, 179
    See also Rice vermicelli
Vermicelli Pudding, 48
Vietnamese food, 210, 232–43
    accompaniments with, 240–42
    desserts in, 243
    garlic chili paste, 147
    waffle papers for, 182
Viet Royale Restaurant, 234, 235,
    237, 239, 241–43
Vinegar
    coconut, 194
    rice, 314
    white, 242
Viponsanarath, Nom, 257–60

Waffle papers, 182
Walnut cakes
    with cassia flowers or blossoms,
        189
    sweet rice flour, 279
Watanabe, Akira, 293, 298, 299
Watanabe, Judy, 292
Watercress Salad, 218
Wave skewering, 288
Wawo-Runtu, Mrs. Tatie, 133, 150,
    151
West Sumatran Rendang, 146–47
West Sumatran Sate, 126–27
Wharo, 263
Wilding-White, Mrs. Charles, 76
Win, Mrs. Kyi, 214
Won ton skins (wrappers), 180, 274
Won Ton Soup, 180
Wrappers
    for lima bean pastries, 303–4
    moo shu, 185
    rice paper, 234, 252, 314
    waffle paper, 182
    won ton, 180, 274
    See also Banana leaves

Yakitori, 282, 290, xix
Yam bean, 317. See also Jicama
Yams, 202
Yanang, 256
Yann Ker, 220, 226
Yazmin Restaurant (Kuala Lumpur),
    85
Yellow cassia flowers or blossoms,
    189
Yellow split peas, 309
Yogurt
    in barbecue lamb, 16–17
    in raita, 35
Yokohama Restaurant, 268–70
Yone, Eleanor Law, 212
Yun, Young Ja (Jamie Faeh), 263,
    267, 276, 280
Yung Kee Restaurant (Hong Kong),
    xviii, 170

Zier, Duangrudee, 54, 58, 256